You or
Someone
You Love

You or Someone You Love

*Reflections from an
Abortion Doula*

Hannah
Matthews

ATRIA PAPERBACK

New York   London   Toronto   Sydney   New Delhi

ATRIA
PAPERBACK

An Imprint of Simon & Schuster, Inc.
1230 Avenue of the Americas
New York, NY 10020

First Atria Paperback edition May 2023

ATRIA PAPERBACK and colophon are trademarks
of Simon & Schuster, Inc.

For information about special discounts for bulk
purchases, please contact Simon & Schuster Special Sales at
1-866-506-1949 or business@simonandschuster.com.

The Simon & Schuster Speakers Bureau can bring authors
to your live event. For more information or to book an event,
contact the Simon & Schuster Speakers Bureau at 1-866-248-3049 or
visit our website at www.simonspeakers.com.

Interior design by Lexy East

Manufactured in the United States of America

1   3   5   7   9   10   8   6   4   2

Library of Congress Cataloging-in-Publication Data

Names: Matthews, Hannah (Abortion doula), author.
Title: You or someone you love: reflections from an abortion doula / Hannah Matthews.
Description: First Atria Paperback edition. | New York: Atria Books, 2023. |
Includes bibliographical references and index.
Identifiers: LCCN 2022054541 (print) | LCCN 2022054542 (ebook) |
ISBN 9781668005255 (paperback) | ISBN 9781668005262 (ebook)
Subjects: LCSH: Abortion—United States.
Classification: LCC HQ767.5.U5 M367 2023 (print) | LCC HQ767.5.U5 (ebook) |
DDC 362.1988/800973—dc23/eng/20221116
LC record available at https://lccn.loc.gov/2022054541
LC ebook record available at https://lccn.loc.gov/2022054542

ISBN 978-1-6680-0525-5
ISBN 978-1-6680-0526-2 (ebook)

For my mother,
and for you

The jasmine drops its branches.
Sitting by my friend, I will be healed.

—*Ancient songs of the Women of Fez*

Contents

You or
Someone
You Love

Preface

The stories in this book belong to their tellers. Any stories in these pages that are not my own have been shared with me by doulas, midwives, nurses, physicians, clinic staff, abortion care and support workers, friends and partners and companions, and by people who have had abortions. Pieces of those stories are retold here only insofar as these community members' full and informed consent has been extended to me. And I have tried, as best I can, to tell the stories of my own care work such that they are sewn up tightly along the edges of *my* experiences of them—my squares in this quilt self-contained and not intruding upon or spilling over into the squares made by other people's hands, other people's truths of what happened and how. I have tried to keep those borders clear and straight. I do not speak for anyone but me.

Many names, pronouns, locations, and other identifying details have been changed or omitted, many interview subjects and friends have been made anonymous or unrecognizable in these pages to protect their safety and their privacy. Some of these stories have also been told on stages and social media and in newspapers, and some have been whispered secretly between friends or written in private journals. Some are leaving the bodies of their tellers for the first time here.

You do not owe your story to anyone, ever, in any context. I am honored to hold it, see it, protect it, should you ever decide to share it with me. And I am happy to help you create new spaces in which you can best tell that story—even if just to yourself. But telling is never required. Telling is not what makes your stories real, or important, or yours.

And if no one has ever given you *their* abortion story to hold, I'll go first.

Here. Hold out your hands.

Introduction

Olivia[1] is on the procedure bed, her sock feet in the stirrups, bare thighs falling open, flanked by women on three sides. She grips the middle and index fingers of my left hand, white-knuckled and squeezing arrhythmically, while my right hand passes an instrument to the midwife, bent in focus on her stool between Olivia's spread-apart legs. The assisting nurse stands across from me, smoothing Olivia's hair away from her forehead. The three of us, midwife, nurse, and doula, fall seamlessly into deep grooves of braided movement. Our workflows cross over and under and through one another, our motions polished smooth by months and years of collaboration. Months and years of holding one another's babies, drawing one another's blood, providing and supporting one another's abortions. Of giving each other rides and hand-me-downs and breast milk, of passing the same $20 back and forth between us for coffee, doughnuts, flowers, birthday cakes. Lifetimes of community are in this room.

Our tools are basic, ordinary. A tissue to press against the corner of Olivia's eye, when it releases a silent tear. A cool wash-cloth for her face, a heating pad to hold across her abdomen, a different speculum. A joke to make her laugh. A mellow playlist, humming softly along over the hidden speakers of the clinic's sound system. A question; a soothing sound; a murmur of affirmation; a bright *You're doing great*; a gentle and clear *You'll feel my fingers now. There will be some pressure in a minute.* Olivia is the center of this darkened procedure room, and also of this moment in each of our lives. Our worlds have narrowed to her: what she needs, what she wants, what she feels. Together, we keep moving. Together, we weave and weave and weave a net of support beneath her. Together, we love her through her abortion.

* * *

This book is for Olivia, but it's not for her alone.

It's for anyone who's had, or will someday have, an abortion.

And it's also for anyone who loves or even just *knows* someone who has had, or will someday have, an abortion. Someone who will hold their partner's hand, or help their friend pay for their flight and hotel room, or stay on the phone with their sister for hours as her body releases a pregnancy. It's for anyone who wants to understand the differences between a self-managed medication abortion at eight weeks of pregnancy and an in-clinic aspiration at twenty weeks, anyone who is curious about what the pregnant people in their lives might need from them. This book is for anyone who wants pregnancy, birth, and parenting to be consensual. For anyone who wants to create and expand their own communities of mutual aid and care and tenderness, anyone feeling a pull toward liberation and joy and pleasure and the work of protecting one another from reproductive violence and criminalization. All that to say: this book is for everyone.

What will community abortion care and support work look like for you? Where will you carve out some space for its presence in your own life? Forget the abortion care we *need*. What is the abortion care we dream of? How can we, together, imagine, and invest in, and create, and sustain that dream care, in our own communities? There are as many answers to that question as there are abortions. Answers that are changing, expanding, and evolving all the time.

Should you need someone to ask you this question, to phrase and rephrase it in some new and different ways, to offer (and offer and offer) you permission and encouragement and a bedrock of belief in your innate abilities to find and make and hold space for abortion care and support work in your life: Hey. It's me.

* * *

I am a collection of small and ordinary things: a clinic worker, in coffee-stained scrubs and a name tag, helping the patients of a small-town health center access the abortion care, contraception, and any other forms of sexual and reproductive care they need or want. I am, also: a writer, a lapsed musician, a retired party girl, a mother, a community care worker, a sometimes–board member, a dynamite pen pal, and an abortion doula.

I only know what I know, and that is a life spent using my (often clumsy) hands and my (deeply imperfect and very tired) heart in order to help people get the abortion care they need. I've arrived at doula work on a winding path, a foggy, nonlinear journey of struggle and mess: through the hallways and exam rooms of two reproductive health care clinics; on city sidewalks packed with antiabortion protesters; at the kitchen tables and on the front porches of my communities; into the bedrooms and bathrooms and hospital rooms of people who have trusted me with their abortions—their bodies, their questions, their lives, and their stories.

I wrote this book in the months leading up to, and over the weeks immediately following, the Supreme Court's release of their catastrophic *Dobbs v. Jackson Women's Health Organization* decision.[2] This is the darkest season I've ever known, soaked in grief and fear and rage and uncertainty. It's a destabilizing moment for US abortion providers, for reproductive health care workers, and for anyone who could become pregnant (and anyone who *loves* someone who could become pregnant). Many of the stories in this book may soon read like relics of the past: access to abortion clinics in or near our own communities, the methods of communication and the information we share with each other on social media and in unencrypted emails and text messages, and the relative safety and freedom that make it possible for me to tell my own abortion stories here: all these are born of privileges that very few of us held to begin with, and fewer of us do now. There are vast constellations of practical support organizations and resources in this country. There are doula collectives and trainings organized locally and remotely, held in physical and online spaces. There is the National Network of Abortion Funds, and its tessellation of independent, grassroots state and local member funds. There are legal helplines and bail funds; extensively researched histories and how-to guides; abundant online care directories like INeedAnA.com, and heavily trafficked (but expertly moderated) forums such as the Online Abortion Resource Squad (OARS). There are telemedicine and mail-order abortion-pill services. These, among all the other bright and steadfast and undimmable stars, are fixed points in our sky. They guide us home. They orient and reorient us, over and over, toward justice and compassion and liberation and community, as the earth beneath our feet continues to shift and move.

Abortion clinics (and the practitioners who pass through them, often traveling back and forth across state lines and working long hours to provide as much care as they possibly can) are stars in these constellations. The others who move through these sacred physical spaces—midwives, nurses, medical assistants, schedulers, custodians, security and IT teams; the clinic staff who schedule appointments, wash speculums, measure blood pressure, organize medical information, who record the histories of our bodies, who find money and shelter and resources for us, who squeeze our hands and bring us tissues and menstrual pads and cups of water and disposable underwear, who counsel us and answer all our questions and tell us *It's okay* and *We're almost done* and *You're doing great*—more stars, unwavering clusters of light, scattered all across that same sky.

The activists who speak truth to power every day, in public *and* in private, at enormous personal and professional risk? The storytellers who share their own abortion experiences on platforms large and small—with their neighbors in their local papers, and with the family members and faith communities who may communicate their displeasure, disapproval, or discomfort in a million passive-aggressive (or simply *aggressive*-aggressive) ways? Those who openly and honestly discuss their abortions on Twitter and

Instagram and TikTok and sites viewed by millions? The advocates and public figures who work against stigma and shame by saying the word *abortion* with no equivocation or apology, in their full-hearted, clear, unwavering voices—no matter who tries to silence or shame them? Glowing, twinkling, damn beautiful stars, visible at twilight and dawn and in all kinds of weather. Dodging clouds and defying black holes, resisting those forces who seek to extinguish their light.

And you, who have found your way here to this book, enduring all your private and personal griefs against the backdrop of our big collective grief, of mass trauma, our culture of violence and neglect and isolation and decay and disaster, all the struggle and loneliness of this moment. You, who are ready to reclaim these pieces of yourself from the world that's stolen them—starting with the piece that knows how to practice direct care work in pursuit of liberation. A glowing little piece of you that's always ready to come home. An indestructible star.

We can capture some of this stardust for ourselves, dragging our own little nets through the sky in search of those self-pieces, any time we choose. When we're able to give money, or supplies, or lend our bodies and our time to the movement, as volunteer clinic escorts or drivers or hand-holders or data collectors or canvassers. When we train to become abortion doulas and companions, when we get curious enough to follow one of the infinite threads connecting abortion to birth justice, climate justice, racial justice, trans justice, Earth, God, ourselves. When we explore (and read and ask questions) beyond what we've been taught abortion is and is not. When we begin to peel off all the layers of abortion stigma and the shame we've accumulated through years of church sermons and network teen dramas and *New York Times* headlines and the off-hand comments made by parents and peers alike. When we relax into the understanding that we actually don't know anything about anyone else's abortion, except for what *they* may choose to tell us. When someone makes a shitty joke in our presence, or spreads misinformation, or uses inaccurate or antiquated language, and we empower ourselves to say: *Hey. No. Here's why not. Here's something else, something better, instead.* When we refuse to speak in euphemisms for abortion, and we refuse to lower our voices to a whisper when we talk about it. Let's start there.

* * *

It's early 2021, and I'm reporting on abortion representation in pop culture and media for a feature in a magazine. I put out a call to my Instagram followers. That silly little block of text, overlaid across a rainbow ombré background: *Have you ever had an abortion?* it reads, and: *Have you ever found an accurate representation of experiences like yours? Have you ever felt seen or understood by an abortion storyline or depiction in any medium?* I expect to receive two, maybe three messages, at most. I'm asking about a deeply private experience, after all. But the question blooms and expands, filling my phone's screen before my eyes. I watch my Instagram in-box flood with responses. Dozens and dozens of them, in fact, by the time the post's twenty-four-hour life span comes to an end. Some of the answers are from close friends and family members, some are from acquaintances I haven't seen in years, or colleagues I've only met once at a conference or party. And some of the messages are from complete strangers.

"People are hungry to talk about their abortions, to be listened to without judgment," my friend and fellow doula Cait tells me one day as she sits across from me in my living room. We have settled on the floor, she and I, by my small cast-iron woodstove, with mugs of hot black coffee. We are deep into one of our long and winding abortion conversations—about the gaps in access and care in our small northeastern city, about who in our communities is doing what, and how, and where we might plug in or support those organizers and carers and their work. How we might better serve people who have abortions. "They're hungry," says Cait, my dog curled in her lap and the reflection of our fire dancing in her eyes, "for somebody to *give a shit*."

As she speaks, I grab a notebook. I scrawl the words *GIVE A SHIT* across a fresh blank page and then I underline them twice. I love the bluntness of the phrase, its simplicity, its brash vulgarity. It's a clear directive, a ringing bell that cuts through all the theory and opinion about abortion as political football, abortion as academic, hypothetical, philosophical. It's a tangible thing to do, for tangible human beings. An active verb, right where I need one.

Whether or not you have had, or will someday have, an abortion yourself, you know someone who has or will—and you probably know them pretty damn well. The oft-cited figure of one in four women (according to the Guttmacher Institute) who have abortions make up plenty of these someones—and when you take into consideration that an as-yet-uncounted number of men and nonbinary people are having abortions, too? Abortion havers (and the countless abortion seekers who are denied the care they need) make up, undeniably, a significant cut of our population. We're everyone, and we're everywhere.

At the table next to yours in your favorite diner, or sitting behind you on the crosstown bus, or passing the collection basket down your church pew, is someone who has driven their sibling or child or college roommate to a clinic, or who has curled into the abundant softness of their best friend's couch with a heating pad to ride out the hormonal ebbs and flows of the cramping and bleeding and nausea. Behind you in line at the post office is someone deeply grieving the long-wanted pregnancy they terminated for medical or financial or logistical reasons; stamping your letters and ringing you up for your postage at the counter is someone who is excited and relieved to no longer be pregnant.

As you and I move through the world, we are frequently and unknowingly encountering strangers, acquaintances, neighbors, and friends who remember their own abortion like it was yesterday (or whose abortion actually was yesterday). Our aunts. Our pastors' wives. Our teachers, our students, our coworkers, the kid crossing the street, the driver of that car with the Make America Great Again bumper sticker. And even more of these people—all those whose paths cross and touch and diverge from and run parallel to our own—have supported someone through an abortion. In any given room, it could be any one of us. Hell, in some rooms, it's all of us.

* * *

Periods, sex, infertility, miscarriage, birth, death, postpartum physiologies—the plain and neutral facts of our bodies have always been declared taboo by those who feel small in the face of their power. This culture of shame and secrecy ensures that those armed with misinformation—those who make outlandish claims about pregnancy and abortion on the Senate floor, and those who shout vile rhetoric and false statistics on the sidewalks outside the clinics—can be difficult for the average person to counter with well-informed arguments grounded in reality. The complex biological and sociological facts of our bodies' reproductive processes are hard to remember, and even harder to articulate in the heat of the moment—by design, as they've been deliberately hidden, distorted, and obscured from us by those who create and control the curriculum, and who uphold the power structures built to enforce their imaginary rules. Because the American education system has been designed to keep us ignorant of basic and vital information about our own sexual lives and reproductive health care needs, even the most passionate "pro-choice" or pro-abortion person is often ill-equipped to describe or explain just how abortion functions, or what it feels like, without resorting to the same old clichés that have helped the mythology, moralization, and politicization of abortion eclipse its actual nuanced realities.

Parents have abortions. Grandparents have abortions. Wealthy thirty-eight-year-old people in loving, stable marriages, with abundant resources and all the traditional markers of capitalist "achievement" and "success" have abortions. People dying of cancer have abortions. Healthy, young, wholesome, purity-ring-wearing Evangelical Christians and devout Catholics have abortions. Lesbians have abortions. Disabled people have abortions. Men have abortions, nonbinary and gender-fluid and gender-nonconforming people have abortions, trans people have abortions. And if you really can't think of anyone you know, if—to your memory—you have met no one who's felt safe enough to entrust you with their abortion story? Well, now you've met me.

In my work, and in speaking with other doulas and care workers, one thing is clear. The patients, clients, community members, strangers, and friends whose hands we've held, whose blood we've drawn, whose tea we've brewed, and whose hair we've braided in their hours of preparation, pain, rest, recovery, and reflection? They—and the circumstances surrounding their pregnancies and their abortions—have not fit neatly within the boundaries of any simple narrative or clear binary. Human bodies and human lives rarely do.

The stories, ideas, and information you will find in these pages are merely access points; they aim to situate you on the intricate map of abortion support work, with all of its sharp peaks and deep valleys and winding roads. They aim to invite you into some forms of radical, compassionate care work that may fit into your busy, stressful, complicated life. I hope that you come to them as you are, with all of your messy, half-formed questions, your preconceptions and moods and biases. We all carry these things, shaking one off here, clinging to another there, gradually unburdening ourselves of them and leaving them behind, in order to keep moving forward, together, into our shared future.

A future in which "I had an abortion" will not be considered a provocation or a brave confession but rather the neutral statement of fact that it often is, like "My eyes are brown" or "I have two children" or "I had a root canal." No public commentary invited or accepted, no press conference or talk show or pressure to offer up one's story for scrutiny and consumption. No shame, blame, or stigma.

Though of course it's all connected, and though every abortion *must* be viewed and considered in the cultural context in which it occurs, this book is *not* the work of an expert on our rapidly shifting landscape of policy, case law, public health data, or statistics—both because I have never found math to be a trustworthy friend of mine but also because abortion is not a monolith, not a single thing in which expertise or authority can be claimed. Every abortion experience is unique. **The only expert on any abortion is the person who has it.**

Every time I support someone as they seek and receive abortion care, and every time I hold space for someone's story, it strikes me anew. We seem to have so little in the way of common and practical understandings of abortion: its mechanisms and processes, how it functions in a body and a life, what it can look and feel like, and its place in our communities and lives. We have such insufficient and inaccurate cultural language with which to describe it. There is no universally accepted term like *postpartum* in our vocabulary to describe the period of time after an abortion—the physical recovery, the hormonal shifts, the tangle of complex emotions, the processing that needs to occur. Abortion, like birth, is a transition, and sometimes a life-altering one. The people I have supported through their abortions, and those who have told me their stories, have described loss, grief, beauty, rage, peace, joy, pain, ambivalence, confusion, and transformation, but they have often struggled to give themselves permission to express these feelings, or to find or create the language to act as a vehicle for them.

The facts of my body and my social location—namely that I am a white, cis, queer, disabled woman with class privilege, living as an uninvited settler on unceded Wabanaki land—guarantee the limitations of my knowledge and my lived experiences. In acknowledgment of those limitations and my complicity in the violence and oppression that has lent me these privileges, I am on a lifelong payment plan, and I will always be making my tiny deposits toward the incalculable debt I owe specifically to the leaders of the reproductive justice movement. Fifty percent of this book's advance, and 100 percent of any royalties I might earn from its sales, will go directly to abortion funds—but, to be clear, those modest payments won't be nearly enough. There is, simply, no amount of money or gratitude that could ever touch the debt of reparations long past due to the abortion care workers and activists of the global majority, from whom I have been lucky enough to learn and with whom I have had the immense privilege of collaborating and cocreating systems and practices of care. But I will always walk the path of trying.

This book—like a doula practice, like all the social movements and writings of its lineage, like any abortion care worker of any kind, in any context—cannot and does not stand alone. It exists because of, and in conversation with, the abundant, essential, beautiful, and borderless bodies of work by my countless teachers and heroes, and the various movements they lead. These doulas, midwives, abortion storytellers, and activists—most of them Black or Indigenous or other people of color, and many of them trans or gender-expansive—are the creators and innovators of this work. It is them to whom we owe everything, and to whom I direct you for further reading.

This book is just a newly sprouting bud on the branch of an ancient, sprawling, deep-rooted tree.

* * *

My deepest hope for you is that, if abortion care or support is something you find yourself in want or need of, at this moment or any other, there is someone who can accompany you through the experience in the way you deserve. A partner, a sibling, a parent, a relative, a friend, a community member, or someone else you trust. If you don't, now you have this book, which is to say: now you have me.

* * *

Our country's current abortion care crises are urgent and compounding: we must contend not only with the violence, authoritarianism, surveillance, and white supremacy of the state but also with the social and cultural crisis of inattention, cowardice, and neglect by those who identify as "pro-choice" but who lack a practical understanding of what abortion-seekers need or a curiosity about abortion's place in our own lives and what we can do to protect and support one another. A crisis of rooms full of people who care, in the abstract, but not enough to act. Of a Democratic Party that promises liberation in exchange for our votes while continuing to champion the idea that abortion is shameful, private, abnormal, a privilege to be granted on a conditional basis; that demands that we suffer rape, violence, illness, or other trauma in order to obtain our abortion care; and that accepts that we must be forced to seek that care within an ever-shrinking window of time and place. A crisis of unlearned histories, of woefully inadequate or actively propagandist educations. Of leaders who lack a clear view of bodily autonomy and reproductive justice as the roots and foundations of *all* things—including the organizations under their leadership. A crisis of silence, of sickness, of isolation, of stigma. A crisis of systemic abandonments.

But we will not abandon each other.

The legal protections of our bodily autonomy are now—as they have always been, in this country—contingent on race, class, gender identity, and geographical location. My heart's most deeply held (and most beat-down, fragile, and flickering) hope is that, as you read these words, open clinics, abundant practical support resources, loving networks of safety, and access to abortion care in your own community do *not* feel entirely like dreams or memories from a past life. But, if they do, may the brilliance and tenacity of those who have been leading our movements, and those who tell their own abortion care work stories be ever-visible stars on the dark map of your own sky. May those stars orient you toward giving a shit, doing something, point you to the care workers and organizations who are holding us all together, who are imagining and creating and sustaining space for each and every one of us. So that, rather than despair, you see a way forward for yourself, alongside them. So that you may learn from them, invest in them, collaborate with them, fund them, protect them, join them. So that you may come to appreciate and understand and love them.

I love people who have abortions, whether those abortions are legal or not.

I love people who need or want abortions but are denied them.

I love abortion doulas, providers, funders, and care workers, no matter the context or legality of their work. I love the friends and siblings and community members who show up, who hold space, who celebrate and grieve and love with those who have abortions, in all the big and small ways they can.

This book is a love letter. I wrote it for you.

Abortion Is the Beginning

Here we are, together, you and me. Survived and still surviving. Are you comfy? Do you have water? Snacks? Is your jaw clenched? (Mine, too.) Have you had a nice big stretch today? Have you if and when it's possible and safe and easy for you to do so—put your feet on the ground and placed your open hand across your heart? (I love this outfit, by the way. You're looking especially, particularly, radiantly gorgeous, today. Damn.) Have you, by any chance, recently taken four deep slow breaths—inhaling, holding, exhaling, and holding again, for four counts each? No? Let's start there.

I know it's probably chaotic out there, wherever you are. And you're holding and carrying and creating *a lot*, at any given moment, in that perfect brain and body of yours. If you instinctively hunch over books and laptops and phone screens, like I do—clenching the hell out of that jaw the whole time—you likely needed those four breaths as badly as I did.

We should probably talk about positionality, you and I, before we settle in. Let's consider all the facets of our own little prisms of identity (race, gender, geographical location, class, religion, sexuality, citizenship, and documentation, etc.), and what they might reflect back to us, which views they might cloud or obscure. Naming our positionality, or our social location (sociology's term for that combination of factors listed above), is the first step anyone must take toward centering those *most* impacted by issues of abortion stigma, access, and care.

The realities of my body, my positionality, and my social location—and therefore the realities of my life—are these: I am white; I am cis; I am a woman. I am bisexual, as in chaotic. I am queer, as in *other*, queer as in (to quote the artist Nicole Manganelli), "madly in love with the burning world." I am femme. I am chronically ill, and chronically unchill. I am a type 1 diabetic, and I would die in three to four days without a constant and self-administered drip into my bloodstream of the injectable synthetic insulin that my health insurance (almost) affords me. I am a survivor of sexual violence. I am a mother. I have experienced two pregnancies that I know of. One pregnancy resulted in my son, who ultimately made his exit through the sunroof at thirty-seven weeks (my C-section scar is pretty impressive, it must be said, and if you and I ever get drunk together I might ask if you want to see it). My other pregnancy was so stubborn that two separate abortion procedures—a medication abortion *and* an in-clinic aspiration—were required to end it.

I have undergone treatment for an eating disorder and I have cried in doctors' offices from Maine to California and beyond. For a long, long time, I have been in therapy and on SSRIs (shout-out to my girl Zoloft, co-writer of this book and co-parent of my child, partner in crime, builder of scaffolding around my heart and brain, a platonic life partner without whom there would be none of this at all). I have struggled with depression and anxiety since I was a child, and, and, at any given moment, I am probably worried that you're mad at me. (You're not, though. Right?)

Does this seem like a lot of things for my body to be carrying? Our bodies do carry a lot of things, accumulating more and more of them across the wild and difficult seasons of our lives. This can take some work to remember, in the grind and crush and hustle culture of our daily lives, and at a cultural moment when most of us are at our very worst—our least generous, our most traumatized, our most fragile, our numbest, simultaneously exhausted and ready to fight. There are multitudes and layers to the experiences of every person's body—even if those experiences appear, from the outside, to be similar in scale and kind—that will always be beyond our comprehension. Most of them are none of my business, beyond what they mean for the care or support I can provide in any given moment. I realize that, as Octavia Butler said, I don't know very much. That none of us do but that we all have the ability to learn more, and the ability to teach one another. In other words: I am showing up to this book as I am. I invite you to do the same.

Doula work requires curiosity and connection beyond the generalities we've learned to volley back and forth at each other—*How are you?* and *How can I help?* These questions can serve to create additional work for the person we are trying to support. By asking a vague and open-ended *What can I do?*, we are often forcing someone to, in essence, invent a doula for themselves. To identify and name all the methods and means of the care we are providing to them. *What do you need?* and *Let me know if there are any other ways I can support you* do have their places in a conversation, as I partner with someone to seek or create not just the abortion experience they *need* but the abortion experience they *desire*, the exact shapes and colors of the care they dream of. But not everyone has the time or safety or the language to answer those open-ended questions. Not everyone can put their dream to words, even if they feel worthy or deserving of it (they are). Some people need a menu of care.

So I get specific. Often, I ask:

Would you like me to make your appointment?
Can I get you a ginger ale? Do you want ice?
What language do you want to use for this body part? Do you
    want me to tell the doctor not to use that word?
Can I pay for your Uber?
Do you want me to call your partner?
Can I bring you my heating pad?
Do you know if you have health insurance? Do you want me
    to call your health insurance company and find out what
    costs they'll cover?
Can I rub your back?
Does this feel safe? Is this okay?
Do you want to talk about what's happening?
Want me to call the nurse hotline for you and find out if you
    can take that medication?
Would you like me to walk on the outside, between you and
    the protesters?
Can I check on the timing for that next dose?
I looked up some information about that question you had,
    do you want to talk about it?

And by each and every one of these questions, what I mean is:

Is this a way that I can love you through your abortion?
Is this?
How about this?

Abortion Is Mine

My abortion story is a love story.

It's January, icicles dripping in crystalline rows. I take the pregnancy test in the watchful presence of my eleven-month-old. His company is as chaotic as it is inescapable. From the moment he first began to crawl, launching himself on his chubby hands and chubbier knees around the corners and up the steps of our tiny house in perpetual motion, I have not once enjoyed a solo trip to the bathroom. So why should I have any privacy this morning?

It's 7:18, then 7:19, then 7:20 a.m. The pallid winter sunlight stretches its skinny arms farther and farther across the snow-covered rooftops of our dead-end street. We're already running late, the baby and I. Time is moving forward without us, the morning leaving us behind.

The hallway beyond the bathroom's open door, dust bunnies collecting in every hardwood corner, is strewn with Cheerios. An errant half-squashed blueberry lies in wait, ready to adhere itself slimily to the sole of an unsuspecting bare foot. I am perched on the toilet, my teeth and hair unbrushed, the circles under my eyes a deepening shade of plum, a pregnancy test dangling weakly from my hand. The baby sits at my feet, vigorously manhandling some alphabet blocks and yelling his sole (and therefore favorite) word, on a loop—*Dada! Dada! Dada! Dada!*

I watch the second line of pink dye appear across the white plastic window of the test. I blink stupidly at it, squinting, tilting my head like a dog hearing an unfamiliar command.

Nah, I think, the baby babbling and banging away at my feet. *I can't be.* The reality of the urine-soaked piece of plastic in my hand—the possibility I have only just dared to acknowledge in the abstract by finally pulling the package of pregnancy tests from the back of the medicine cabinet—will have to wait. I need to get out of my pajamas and into my scrubs. I need to pack the baby's bag—the milk, the bottles, the sleep sack, the teething rings, the portable sound machine for nap time, the diapers and wipes and butt cream. I need to drop him off at his grandparents' house. I need to get to work.

Numb with denial, I wade through the fog of the morning on autopilot. Pregnant, drinking coffee, pregnant, changing lanes on the highway, pregnant, pulling into my parking spot at the clinic and clocking in for my shift. Feeling shaky and seasick, disconnected and floating, I change into my one remaining clean(ish) set of scrubs, crumpled at the bottom of my locker. I step into my beat-up old pair of wood-and-leather clogs, the clunky and graceless kind that nurses and waiters swear by. I flip on the bright overhead lights of the waiting room. I boot up my ancient work computer, a metal-and-plastic loaf of system errors and turning wheels and work-arounds so complex you'd think its users work for NASA instead of for the reproductive health nonprofit paying us $18.57 an hour to hit CTRL-ALT-DELETE and smash the keys in frustration.

I open the medical records software that dictates every moment of my day: every patient's appointment details and the timestamps of their arrival and departure, every phone call I make or receive, every yeast infection and breast exam and positive chlamydia test and ultrasound and referral. I unlock the cabinets stocked with emergency contraceptives and IUDs. I log the temperature of the birth control storage closet. I keep moving, keep going, checking off task after task, running from the stillness that I know will bring a full-body submersion in the freezing sea of my new reality. The new truth of my body, the answer it has given me to the question I didn't even want to ask. The new story I'll have to tell, the plot of which I am still, somehow, managing to hold at bay.

My boss appears—twenty-eight weeks pregnant herself, and limping wearily toward the finish line of birth in her maternity scrubs. She is moving at her own efficient morning pace, breezing by me with a friendly but distracted greeting. She's on her way to the waiting room, where she will call her first patient back to their exam room and begin to ask them about *their* story and what part they would like us to play in it.

"Katie," I say quietly as she passes, and she slows her pace, pivots. Her face is a cheerful question mark.

"Could you run a UPT for me?" I murmur, unable to make eye contact. "Whenever you get a second. No rush."

UPT—urine pregnancy test, one of so many she and my other coworkers will run today. It is the first step of most appointments at the clinic, of any birth control prescription, or IUD insertion, or ultrasound. The first step of any abortion.

She stops in her tracks, her smile faltering. I watch her face absorb the question.

"Of course." She nods, after a beat. "Just leave it on the counter in the lab for me." I know it's time to look right at this thing, time to stop running away and turn directly toward what's chasing me. I take a sample cup into the patient restroom, its bold-type signs cheerfully directing you to collect certain types of samples for certain types of appointments and tests, its diagrams of genitalia and cutesy illustrations on its brightly painted walls. I pee into the cup; I flush; I wash my hands. I open the door to the little holding tunnel above the toilet, a small box that opens into the clinic's laboratory. On the other side of the wall, the internal secrets of patients' bodies are revealed. HIV tests, STD screenings, metabolic blood panels— we do it all. And in a drawer marked *UPTs*: the stack of individually wrapped plastic cartridges that can tell a body's future—or at least, the future of its next few hours, or days, or weeks. I return my focus to the desk in front of me, where phones are ringing and patients need my help.

As I answer calls and greet the patients trickling in, a circle of coworkers gathers around me behind the desk with their laptops and stethoscopes and thermoses of coffee. Every morning, we huddle to discuss the day's flow, in an attempt to predict and pre-empt all of its potential pitfalls: the logistical hiccups and hurdles, the security threats, the patients we know well and the patients whose needs and preferences we can't yet anticipate, the crises we anticipate and the harm-reduction strategies we feel equipped to employ. I chime in here and there, listening as I move around and between my coworkers, faxing referrals and medical records to local hospitals for mammograms and cervical biopsies, contacting our abortion fund coordinators to cover a $555 or $750 or $1,000 procedure, and greeting patients as they arrive.

Suddenly Katie reappears, at the back of the scrubs-clad crowd, silent and unsmiling on the other side of all the laughter and chatter and discussions unfolding as if everything were normal, between where she stands and where I sit at my computer. Her face is a closed door. I meet her eyes, knowing the answer even before she gives me a tiny, solemn, barely perceptible nod. A yes. A positive. A *you're pregnant, buddy.*

I inhale. As the cold wave of this certainty finally completes its slow unfurling inside my body, crashing somewhere deep in my chest and rolling outward from the site of impact along my limbs, I feel the urge to laugh. I removed my IUD just a month ago, wanting to give my body a break from hormonal contraception and to consider other methods of birth control. Since then, no barrier in place, Will and I have been a little more relaxed. I've been tracking my ovulation, and feeling, foolishly, confident that the odds of unplanned conception were low. The story I've been telling myself, *about* myself: that I am someone too fluent in the language of safe sex and pregnancy prevention, someone too "responsible," for an unplanned pregnancy—has turned out, after all, to be the laziest kind of fairy tale. I feel the mockery of God, the universe, Will's sperm, my eggs.

You got me, guys, I think. The game is over; I've lost. I exhale.

Okay, my mind says quietly to itself. A shoe dropping. A block tower collapsing. A checkbox drawn on paper and a pen-drawn checkmark slashing through it.

Pregnant.

Katie motions for me to follow her into the lab, where we lean against the cold white counters that stand opposite each other—one sink into which the cups of urine are dumped once they've been tested for gonorrhea, chlamydia, UTIs, *pregnancy*, and one sink for the constant thorough washing of our hands. We blink at each other, shell-shocked, as the regular rhythms of the clinic bustle around us, staff and clinicians calling to one another, voices echoing down the hallways on either side of us, a patient laughing in an exam room.

"So," she finally offers, gently, into the heavy silence. "What do you want to do?"

I close my eyes against the bright overhead lights. I try my best to grasp onto a deep, slow breath, but the one I do manage to catch is shuddering, shallow.

"The baby isn't even one yet," I say quietly, more to myself than to her. I want to cry. I feel like I *should* cry. But my eyes are dry.

A clanging sound approaches: Alexis rolls a metal surgical tray into the lab. She is my midwife, one who has reached into my body to find answers and solve problems and create peace where there was chaos, who has inserted and removed my various IUDs over the years, who has prescribed me countless doses of fluconazole for yeast infections and nitrofurantoin for UTIs. She wrote the very first script for the antianxiety medication that keeps the colors and flavors in the world for me, keeps me upright and capable of joy and pleasure, keeps my brain from swallowing me whole. She is a care provider in every sense of the word.

Alexis looks from Katie to me, appearing to sense that she's stepped into some deeper emotional water than all the usual tide pools that soak our feet and ankles every day in these rooms and hallways. It's not at all unusual, in this workplace of ours, to stumble upon a colleague in tears, or to see a shouting or sobbing patient through some acute distress, or just to carry the vague awareness of an emotional crisis playing out somewhere within this rotating and colliding configuration of bodies, as we move through our emails and meetings and tasks. But the vibe in the lab is, at this moment, unusually intense, even for us. Alexis's face becomes a question, asked first of Katie and then, turning slightly, of me.

I answer it: "I'm pregnant."

"Oh!" she cries, her eyebrows leaping upward in excitement. Her smile breaks me open.

"No" is all I manage in response. Then, as I knew they would eventually, the tears catch up to me. I look up at the blinding white ceiling, where the fluorescent overhead lights blur and shift on the rising waters of my tears. I try to blink them back inside my head. It's a technique that's never worked for me, not once, but a girl can become attached to the tips and tricks passed down to her by older wiser cousins and camp counselors and babysitters and then deploy them uselessly for the rest of her life, can't she?

"Okay," Alexis immediately adjusts. Righting herself, she echoes Katie: "What do you want to do?"

* * *

If I were capable of feeling anything in this moment, I know that it would be a warm, fluid rush of something approaching familial love. Something like the wordless, shapeless safety I felt as a child in the presence of my mother. Something like coming home and dropping your keys in a bowl by the door, or entering a room where you know you can immediately remove your bra and unbutton your too-tight jeans, and then doing so. Both of these women, who have patients to see and phone calls to return and complicated lives and families of their own, are dropping everything, in this moment, for me. The fullness and the focus of their presence, their eyes on me and their bodies still, calm, steady, and pointed toward mine, their willingness to face me and hold space for me in this moment, keeping me aloft so I don't fall and shatter.

"I guess I should go call Will," I venture weakly.

"Only if you want to," Alexis says with a chuckle. She grins and rolls her eyes, and she and Katie start to laugh.

Unspoken in their laughter is the view from our collective rear-view mirror: the pregnancy histories already present in this room with us. In that laughter is all the noisy, dirty, up-all-night, potty-training, scraped-knees, and finger-paint-covered presence of the kids we are already parenting, and the absence of the kids who never came to be. The miscarriages and abortions and ectopic pregnancies are here with us, too. The pregnancies that end before we speak of their existence at all.

I want to laugh with them. I always thought I would, if I found myself in this situation. I'm in the safest place to laugh about it, and in the company of two women with whom I laugh the easiest and the loudest. But all I can muster is a weak approximation of a blank and dead-eyed smile.

"Go call him if you want," Alexis says gently. "And take your time. Think about it. You know we can do whatever you need. Just say the word."

I nod. I can feel that I'm still attempting to force my face to express some tiny fraction of my gratitude. My lips move as they're supposed to, my cheeks push up and out. I can tell, though, by the *Oh, honey* looks on the two women's faces, that it must be a pretty bad smile.

A pregnant smile, I think. On my pregnant face. Katie hands me a box of tissues, rubs my shoulder. I tuck the box under my arm, leave the lab, and numbly ascend the stairs to the floor above the clinic, where the offices and conference rooms have been deserted by their occupants at the onset of the pandemic and all its attendants' remote-work safety measures. I half expect a cartoon tumbleweed to roll through the standing desks over the abandoned laptops and the disconnected, rerouted work phones, whenever I flick on the lights up here.

Dialing my phone with one hand, I duck into a small meeting room and toss the box of tissues onto the center of its conference table. I pull the door shut behind me, walk to the window, and wait, staring blankly down at the snow-dusted street, the ice-slicked alleys, the overflowing dumpsters, the parking garage below.

Will's phone buzzes in his pocket, unnoticed among the noise and the non-phone vibrations of his work. A carpenter and woodworker who ferries his lumber-and-tool-filled truck across the harbor every morning, Will is right where he can usually be found—in the air, four stories up, on the roof of someone's half-built seaside home. I call again. I swipe at my cheeks; I'm starting to *really* cry, now that I'm alone, in the naked open way of a child before she ages into the understanding that sadness is secret and embarrassing and something to apologize for.

This time, he feels it vibrating, but by the time he's fumbled his gloves off and squeezed it out of his pocket to answer, the call has ended. He hits the RETURN CALL button and finds his weeping wife on the other end of the line. The floodgates thrown wide now, tears stream down my face and pool on the windowsill where I've collapsed onto my forearms. My forehead rests against the freezing glass of the windowpane. I tell him about the two pregnancy tests. I tell him that it's early, we can take some time, if we want, to consider our choices. I tell him he should sit with the information for a while, feel his feelings, then interrogate them. Think it over, analyze it, make a pros and cons list. Or, I tell him, I could have an abortion right away—Alexis could even do it today.

"'Just say the word,'" she'd told me.

He absorbs this.

"Well," he says, "what do you think?"

In my mind I see his eyes soften and his jaw tense up, the way it does when he's about to kiss me or wrap me up to soothe an ache, take on a burden, help me carry something heavy.

"I don't think we can do this," I say. "We can't have a newborn before the baby's even two." I run my hands through my hair, knotted and limp from a year of neglect, a year of putting my own needs last. "And we can't afford another baby," I add. "We can't even really afford *one*."

"Yeah," he says, quiet and slow. "Yeah, I feel the same way, sweetheart."

Okay. A consensus is reached, heavy and silent except for the background buzz saws and hammers on his end of the call, and the sounds of crying on mine.

That's that.

I will have an abortion. That's the decision. That's the plan. The knowledge of this enters the room, sits at the conference table, stretches its arms and legs.

* * *

Until the moment hours from now, when the mifepristone tablet first touches my tongue, I will move through the world in a strange and hazy liminal state. Pregnant, but not with a child. Not with someone I will meet and name and dress and raise. Not with a baby, whom I will lovingly shepherd through and out of my body, a body that will not expand and rearrange and tear itself apart in pursuit of this shepherding. Not even pregnant with a fetus, who will kick and elbow my ribs, as my son did incessantly in his fetal days. I'm pregnant with . . . an embryo? A barely fertilized egg, maybe the size of an orange seed. *Product of conception*, we sometimes call it at the clinic and in my doula circles. *Pregnancy tissue*. Or, more simply, just *tissue*.

Intellectually, I know this. But the state of pregnancy is not so easily divided and segmented, at least not for me. Having discovered my pregnancy with my son at roughly the same orange-seed stage, and carrying the still-fresh memory of how *that* tiny embryo had grown into the fetus, the newborn, the almost-one-year-old human being now at the center of my world, the existence of *this* tiny embryo doesn't feel like nothing.

It is something to me, I realize. A part of me, and also not. It's made of me and Will, of our materials and our ancestors and our dreams, just as our son is. If I continued this pregnancy, if it didn't end in an abortion or a miscarriage, I know that it would grow into a new member of our family. A son or daughter or child of ours. A sister or brother or sibling of his. A grandchild. A cousin. I hang up the call and set a five-minute timer on my phone. I crouch on the floor of the empty conference room and sob. When the timer goes off, its tinny harpsichord melody repeating and repeating, I stand. I wipe my nose. I dry my puffy eyes with my fists, my palms, the collar of my scrubs. I put on my surgical mask. I go back to work.

ABORTION IS MEDICINE

A few hours after my phone call with Will, my body having steered me through the usual patient check-ins and medical-records exchanges and the routine birth control counseling and HIV tests and small talk, on autopilot, I step into one of the clinic's small exam rooms with another coworker, whose job it is to prepare me for my medication abortion. I extend my arm, palm upward, to receive the blood pressure cuff, I stand on the scale, I share all the details of my consent to this care, my mental state and reasons for making this decision, and my medical history. I answer the questions we ask of patients every day: Am I here of my own free will? (*Yes and no, capitalism being what it is, you understand,* but jokes are not acceptable, so for the sake of this conversation, I just say yes.) Am I safe in my relationships? (Yes.) Do I have a plan for contraception following this abortion? (Yes.) Do I feel sure of my decision? (Yes, I say, beginning to cry again.) Could I sign here, and here, and here? (Okay, is there a pen over there? I left mine in the lab.)

Hannah Matthews.
DOB X/X/XXXX
Established patient.
Fever: negative.
Blood pressure: in normal range.
Prior Tonsillectomy. Appendectomy. Caesarian section.
Diabetes mellitus, type 1
Gravidas [pregnancies]: 2.
Live births: 1.

I ask if it might be possible to skip the standard transvaginal ultrasound.

"We'll have to ask Alexis," my coworker says.

They summon her to the room. She wants to hear my reasons. While carrying my son, I explain, I'd been ultrasounded dozens of times—twice a week, in fact, by my third trimester—because of my chronic illness and the many risks it posed to my pregnancy. On those grainy scans, I had watched him grow and become. I watched him turn into . . . *him*. From an embryo as tiny and nebulous as the one inside me now, to a strange little fetus who sprouted hands and feet, who learned to cough and hiccup and roll over, who once stretched both chubby arms over his head and yawned with boredom as the 3D imaging wand passed over him. I wanted to keep those magical grayscale visions—from the still images of his developing face, to the videos of his first delicate flutters and flickers (and later, of the vigorous boxing matches he would have with my ribs and my bladder)—to preserve them, alone, in the room of my heart reserved solely for him.

Alexis agrees that it's medically safe to forgo, on two conditions: first, if I am certain of my LMP (the clinical shorthand for *last menstrual period*, the easiest way to self-report and roughly date a pregnancy), and second, if I have taken a negative pregnancy test at any point since she removed my IUD a month ago (to ensure that no wily little ectopic pregnancies have sneakily taken root while the device was still in my uterus). Without the proof of a negative pregnancy test, taken at some point since that removal, a scan would be medically necessary. But my urine *has* been tested for pregnancy hormones, at another routine appointment I had just weeks ago. So the presence of that quiet little "No" in my chart, that numbered *Negative Pregnancy Test* diagnostic code, unnoticed and unremarkable at the time it was documented, saves me. It rescues me from a step of the process that can often bring up complex and painful emotions in even the most straightforward abortions, can feel loaded and distressing for even the most confident and joyful abortion havers.

No ultrasound! Okay. My body shakes this off, it gets a little bit free of something; it lightens and loosens and relaxes—slightly—outward. (Little does it know, this body—this cute and chubby little shortsighted, optimistic, naive collection of freckled skin and sturdy bones and crescent-moon-scarred uterus and broken-down pancreas and heart that beats too loudly, this body that keeps no discernible schedule, that has ideas my tired brain must temper and mitigate and negotiate and steer it away from, again and again. Little does it know.) For now, in its ignorance of what's to come, my body simply allows itself to be flooded with warm, liquid relief.

* * *

Yet another coworker enters the room, to draw my blood, so that my HCG levels can be tested before and after I take my abortion pills. If the post-abortion blood draw shows a sufficient decrease in the pregnancy hormone, it will be an indication that none of the tissue responsible for producing said hormone remains in my uterus. That my body knows it's not pregnant anymore. The coworker, now tying off the rubber tourniquet around my biceps, is a steady, quiet presence, a skilled and seasoned phlebotomist who has come to the clinic from a job in the lab of our local hospital. They draw my blood quickly and gracefully, the dark red flash of liquid shooting up through the clear plastic tubing and into the vial, rapidly filling it.

"Feeling generous." They laugh. They apply a wad of gauze and then a neon pink Band-Aid to the tender spot of my inner arm, the light pressure of their cool fingertips on my bare skin anchoring me to the moment, the room, the chair. Without this—the gentle touch and the laughter and the bottomless grace of all these people, rotating in and out of the room to prepare me, to help me, to make and hold space for me and all the functions of my mind and heart and body, to care for me—I feel like I would float away.

Alexis walks me through the risks and side effects of the medications, all the potentialities I know well but only secondhand, like a poem memorized for a graded recitation. I don't yet quite believe it's *me* we are discussing now, *my* fever, *my* nausea, *my* pain. *My* pregnancy. *My* abortion. This room, this conversation—it's for patients. For other people's abortions. I'm meant to be on the other side of this table, helping someone else, writing down someone else's vital signs, offering someone else the All-Options and Exhale Pro-Voice phone numbers, and the educational adoption and parenting materials, and asking them the state-mandated demographic questions regarding their marital status and "level of education." As though anyone is the sum of these answers.

I'm handed the nondescript paper bag containing my prescribed doses of the two medications that will, if all goes to plan, end my pregnancy. Mifepristone, the first: a single round pill to be swallowed immediately. Misoprostol, the second: four white hexagonal tablets to be dissolved in my cheeks, under my tongue, or inside my vaginal canal, within forty-eight hours of swallowing the first. When taken vaginally, they are less likely to cause nausea and vomiting (and I wouldn't have to taste their bitter flavor), but they could also potentially leave a faint residue on or inside my body—important to avoid if I wanted to hide my abortion from my partner, or to tell a health care provider that I was having a natural miscarriage in the event I needed urgent care at an unfamiliar or untrustworthy facility.[1] "Okay," Alexis says after handing me the bag. "You know the deal. Call the clinic or text me if you need anything or you want to talk, okay? No matter what time it is."

I nod, too grateful, too numb, too overwhelmed to speak. I crumple and roll the sack into a wadded-up ball of jagged paper corners, feeling the ridges of the two pill bottles inside. I shove it into the depths of my tote bag, where it will rattle around in the darkness among the teething cracker crumbs and loose Cheerios and pacifiers and diapers and wipes and all the paraphernalia of my diabetes—the used needle caps, the stray bloody glucose test strips, the empty insulin cartridges.

I sling the bag over my shoulder. I leave the room, the clinic, the building, I walk the same streets and turn the same corners I always have. In order to have my abortion, I go home.

* * *

Having a medication abortion is incredibly safe. Barring the presence of factors like an IUD, an ectopic pregnancy,[2] allergies to the drugs involved, bleeding disorders, and a few other exceptions, it's safer than using Viagra, antibiotics, or Tylenol.[3] It is also, increasingly, a method through which one can self-manage their abortion outside of a clinical setting, on their own terms and in the place of their choosing. It usually goes something like this:

First, you obtain the appropriate doses of two medications, mifepristone and misoprostol. You get these from your doctor, from a hospital, or from a reproductive health clinic that performs abortions or provides telehealth prescriptions. Or, if you are going to self-manage your abortion, you may get the pills online, from a mobile clinic, remote prescription service, or international pharmacy, and have them delivered to your home. People also share these medications with one another, with their friends and families and communities. This is illegal, but it's also very common (and increasingly so, as proliferating abortion restrictions and bans drive our health care underground and our pregnancies into the shadows). Organizations like SASS (Self-Managed Abortion; Safe and Supported) compile and share invaluable knowledge of DIY medication abortion care. SASS is the US arm of the international abortion access nonprofit Women Help Women, and maintains a website with comprehensive and accessible information and also provides a secure contact form for any questions one might have about self-managed abortion, or SMA.[4] And as the risk of criminalization grows—especially for those communities and individuals already most impacted by restrictive abortion laws, the Black and Indigenous and Latinx people and other people of the global majority, who already bear the brunt of reproductive violence and oppression by the state—individual self-managed abortion seekers are often turning to protective resources like the Digital Defense Fund and If/When/How, a network of reproductive-justice-focused lawyers with a legal defense fund and a legal helpline.[5] These little pills are not just pharmaceutical wonders, coloring outside the lines of their intended usage and scope. They are life changers, world builders, future makers.

Mife and miso are 95 to 98 percent effective when taken together before twelve weeks of pregnancy.[6] Misoprostol-*only* abortions—in which twelve tablets of miso are taken, in three rounds of four tablets at a time—have a slightly lower efficacy rate, at 75 to 85 percent before twelve weeks of pregnancy.[7]

* * *

When a pregnancy has progressed beyond twelve weeks, a medication abortion is still possible, though the protocols are different and multiple doses are often required. Anonymous hotlines and online resources like the Reprocare Healthline; the M+A (Miscarriage + Abortion) Hotline; Women Help Women, and its US project, SASS; and Women on Web can all be useful for up-to-date medical guidance.

One to two days after taking these medications, there is a 98 percent chance that you are no longer pregnant. That you have been returned to an unpregnant state—yourself again, or still. Or maybe you are in a new, post-pregnant state. Maybe you are a new self. But regardless, you will probably be able to get up on that third morning, as you always do, to go to school or work, or to care for the children you already have. And when you get up on that third morning, no matter what circumstances brought you there, you are still whole, and worthy, and inherently good. You are still you. Or you are a new and different you. I love them both the same.

* * *

I push open the door to our tiny, cluttered mudroom, paper bag in hand, and kick off my slush-covered boots by the door. As I step into the kitchen, removing my coat and dropping my tote bag, the baby is clapping his hands and shrieking with laughter in his high chair, delighted with my husband's airplane-spoon noises. His cheeks and chin are thoroughly coated with the sticky innards of said airplane's vegetal passengers; the pureed carrots and peas also cover his fingers, his tray, and the front of his *Goodnight Moon* T-shirt, his bib long abandoned on the floor and marinating in a pool of the milk that seeps from the sippy cup he's also tossed overboard. Utter chaos, as usual. I kiss the top of his downy little head, breathing in the chamomile and lavender of his baby shampoo. I kiss Will's wind-chapped lips, resting my forehead against his as he holds my face in both his hands. Then I go into our bedroom and drop the paper bag on the bed. I remove my scrubs, running a hand over my bare, stretch-marked, C-sectioned stomach.

"I'm sorry," I whisper to my hip bones and my belly button, the stretched skin of my abdomen, worn down as it is by last year's overtime work to sustain my baby.

I step into some sweatpants and throw an old Planned Parenthood T-shirt over my head. *PROTECT SAFE, LEGAL ABORTION*, the shirt reads, a relic from an era when we thought that might be possible to do.

I open the paper bag, reaching first for the packet of anti-nausea medication that Alexis has prescribed me. Here, distracted and overwhelmed, I make a mistake. Though the drug is one I've taken many times before, throughout my vomit-filled first pregnancy, and also one I've advised many patients and clients to take, for years, I manage to bungle it now. Failing to remember the instructions I've recited and written out in too many love letters to count— *Place each tab, one at a time, on your tongue. Allow it to dissolve completely*—I immediately swallow both of the bitter, chalky tabs, washing them down with the glass of water I'd abandoned on my bedside table the night before. Only then do I turn the packaging over in my hand, read the directions, and realize my error.

"Fuck!" I half shout at myself, and throw the now-empty foil and plastic against the wall, watching it bounce onto the floor. Instantly embarrassed by my own melodrama, I step out of the room, away from the scene I've caused, and back into the kitchen.

Will has one quizzical eyebrow raised. The baby cackles and claps, delighted by this facial maneuver. Will immediately pivots to clowning for the benefit of his son—scrunching up his nose, opening his eyes wide, filling his cheeks with air. My face burns. I'm nearly crying again, I realize. I go to open the other medications before I lose my nerve.

The mifepristone is first. Sometimes referred to as RU-486, or the "abortion pill" (despite the fact that it will *not* cause an abortion on its own), mifepristone was first approved as a pregnancy-ending medication by the Food and Drug Administration in the year 2000. My friends and I prefer to call it by its charming little nickname: mife (pronounced "miffy"). One small white round tablet, reminiscent of a miniature breath mint or a featherlight piece of birthday-party confetti, will block the progesterone in my body from reaching my womb. Without progesterone, that magical little steroid hormone, my uterine lining will begin to break down and dissolve. No pregnancy, including mine, could survive that gradual crumbling, the demolition of the home my body has been dutifully building to shelter, nourish, and protect it.

As I swallow the pill, I focus on my baby in his high chair, now twisting away from the washcloth Will is wielding in a futile campaign to wipe clean his sticky cheeks and his tiny cleft chin. I think of him growing in my womb only a year ago, of the progesterone my body made for me then.

Next come the four misoprostol pills; hexagonal morsels of bitterness, whose acrid flavor I won't have to taste at all, because I've opted to take them vaginally instead of buccally.[8] The drug will soften and dilate my cervix, and cause my uterus to contract, pushing the broken-down pregnancy tissue out of my body. This process can bring along with it some nausea, fatigue, an unpredictable amount of cramping and bleeding, and an equally unpredictable spectrum of complicated emotions. The abortifacient properties of misoprostol—which can also be used in the treatment of stomach ulcers, arthritis, postpartum hemorrhaging, and in the induction of labor in childbirth, and is often called Cytotec or Arthrotec—are said to have first been discovered by Black Brazilian women, who noted the phrase *Could cause miscarriage* on its warning label in the 1990s.[9] They passed this information to those who needed it locally, word spreading among sisters and neighbors and friends, and soon many pregnant people in Brazil, where abortion was illegal at the time, were taking the over-the-counter drug to deliberately end their pregnancies. Eventually, clinicians and researchers caught on to the shared knowledge of these brilliant and radical communities, and developed the abortion protocols described here. My friends and I call the drug miso (like the soup), but many providers and care workers prefer a "mye-so" pronunciation (and in doing so avoid the salty, brothy associations of our version). I can take the miso pills immediately after I swallow the miffy, Alexis told me, because I am just barely pregnant—five weeks, a few days more if that. I remove my sweats and underwear, shake the pills out into my palm, and push them up inside of me, one at a time. I re-dress and lay flat on my bed, though I know it isn't necessary. This, too, calls to mind the seeds that would grow into my son, my first pregnancy, my motherhood. Staring up at the ceiling, I think of the handful of times I lay on my back after sex, the year before last, hoping to lend a gravity boost to Will's sperm in my quest to conceive the little being who is happily blowing raspberries in the kitchen. Though I knew then, and know now, that absolutely no actual data supports this postcoital—and now post-abortion-pill—repose, I need to feel that I'm participating in this, somehow. That my body is not my boss, nor am I hers. She is my partner, my collaborator, and—despite our frequent creative differences—my loving and beloved old friend.

I have asked my body to release this pregnancy, using these pills. They're safe and easy and 98 percent effective, after all, and I have watched and supported their route through a body and their aftereffects play out hundreds of times with no problem, so I consider the matter closed.

My body, as usual, has her own ideas.

ABORTION IS (NOT) SURGERY

"Hey," begins the nurse practitioner on the phone five days later. She pauses, sighs, starts again. "So . . ." she says, in that way that never precedes good news (though that *so . . .* always hopes that you might *someday* be able to laugh about it, whatever *it* is, that piece of information following on its heels).

"Your HCG is rising."

I drop onto the bed, clutching my towel to my chest.

It's my day off. I was planning to catch up on doula work, emails, chores around the house. I've just sprinted from the shower, hair dripping, to answer the NP's call. Adrenaline propelled me, soaking wet, across the bathroom tile to grab my cell phone, fearing that the worst was happening at work: a shooting, a bomb threat, a crisis. It doesn't occur to me that she might be calling to tell me I'm still pregnant. I'm *not* still pregnant, after all, and I know this for sure, because I had an abortion just last week. She was there, too, when I was prescribed the medications! I told her all about the cramping and the bleeding, when she asked! That's how I know that *she* knows this, too, my body's state of unpregnancy. So how can she be telling me, now, on my day off, that my HCG is rising, which implies that there is still pregnancy tissue present in my body?

I can't be pregnant, and I have evidence; in the form of blood clots the size of lemons (normal, in a medication abortion) and the pair of underwear I had to throw away, after a maxi pad had shifted in my sleep to expose a vulnerable strip of the white fabric (that's on me, an unforced error in dressing myself that I have made with regularity since my very first period in the sixth grade, and will likely continue to make until menopause finally arrives in its flaming chariot to rescue me from my innate lack of common sense). Those poor, blameless, mint-green boy shorts, now soaked in stripes of deep red, still lay crumpled at the bottom of my bathroom trash can—they're real. And I know that I didn't imagine the pain of my abortion, either, the cramps and contractions steamrolling over my lower abdomen, radiating through my lower back and down my thighs. I had witnesses to all of this, to my agonizing transition to my becoming unpregnant: Will and the baby.

And of course I am with Will and the baby now—my two constants, my pair of beloved brown-haired heads and handsomely dimpled chins, when I get this phone call telling me that I am still pregnant. The medication abortion has failed. My HCG levels are, in fact, rising, according to the follow-up blood draw performed by my phlebotomist friend on my lunch break yesterday. I'll need an ultrasound right away, to rule out an ectopic pregnancy. If it *is* ectopic, this stubborn little happening of mine, I'll go straight to the hospital. If it's not, I'll likely need to have a suction procedure at the clinic—an MVA, or manual vacuum aspiration—the NP tells me now, to empty my uterus of what remains of the pregnancy tissue. I picture it in there, as she speaks, a little piece of this other future that I'd said no to, that I'd told: not now. But it was still there, still working away, pumping out those baby-growing hormones as if it hadn't heard me.

I hang up the phone, throw on a robe, and lift the baby from his high chair. I bring him into the nursery to strip him of his soaked pajamas.

Wiggling and kicking on his changing table, follows my eyes to our shriveling peperomia plant in its hanging clay pot, the tips of its stems now brushing the windowpane in its desperate search for an escape hatch. We've been joking, Will and I, that if the tropical plant ever did finally make contact with the freezing window, in its yearning for the sun, it would immediately die of either cold or despair. Its little green spirit would be broken by the realization that no matter how far east the easternmost wall of our little house, no matter how determined its growth pattern, it couldn't actually transform a Maine in January into the steaming rain forest meant to nurture and raise it. The jungle meant to be its mother.

Desire—even desire that has a thermostat, a window, fertile soil, doting caretakers who water and tend it—is not enough to change a climate. You need more powerful tools than love to make the weather.

* * *

Surgical abortion is a common and widely used term for the in-clinic procedures that end a pregnancy . . . and I really wish it wasn't. It's a misnomer, one that can be frightening and stigmatizing. It's used, frequently and innacurately, to describe both types of in-clinic abortion procedure: a suction or aspiration abortion, and a D&E (or dilation and evacuation), in which the provider uses both suction and medical tools to remove the pregnancy from the uterus. Both procedures are incredibly safe, and both work 99 percent of the time (slightly more effective than a medication abortion, which works ninety-eight out of one hundred times—I just happen to be one of those lucky two). Later in a pregnancy, someone may also have an abortion through a process of laboring and delivering. *None* of these abortion mechanisms constitutes a surgery.

* * *

Will comes with me to the hastily arranged ultrasound; he holds my hand, rubs my back. I leave my bra on, and my sweater, its holey crocheted shoulders still damp from my shower-wet hair. I lay back on the exam room's bed and turn my face to the wall, tears rolling onto the paper that crinkles stiffly under my supine body. The same nurse practitioner who called to tell me the news stands over me, performing the ultrasound, moving the transvaginal wand—the one I've cleaned and disinfected, after it's done its job inside other bodies—back and forth in me, and squints at the screen. She asks if it would be okay to call in another nurse practitioner, the coordinator of our abortion care program. I stiffen.

"I don't think it's an ectopic," she assures me, seeing my alarm. "But I just want a second pair of eyes."

Into the room comes the second coworker. She takes control of the wand, turns to the screen, and immediately breaks into a smile.

"I forgot you had a C-section," she murmurs to me, her voice so kind and full of understanding that the sound of the words is like a safe, warm bath. She's pointing at the grainy moving images of my insides, I presume to show me what the crescent moon of my cesarean scar looks like from the on the inner wall of my uterus, the sewn-up sunroof through which my son made his reluctant exit from my body at thirty-seven weeks. But I don't want to see. So I just nod and smile sadly toward the wall.

The NPs determine that, in order to rule out an ectopic pregnancy, a vacuum aspiration procedure must be done. The contents of my uterus must be emptied and then examined. If the expected components of my pregnancy tissue can be accounted for, I'll be home free. If not, I'll have to go immediately to the emergency room, where people experiencing ectopic pregnancies receive the urgent interventions that save their lives—in the states where those interventions are still legal, that is, and then within those states, the hospitals not overseen by Catholic corporations or run by cowardly or conservative administrators.

So, an in-clinic procedure. The aspiration. The choice I didn't make. And it needs to happen today. *Right away*, they agree. I'm in a daze. Minutes later, I'm curled up in one of the cushy reclining chairs that line our recovery room, as my concurrent doses of minimal sedation kick in. I feel resigned. I feel scared. I feel tired. I feel sad. I feel cozy, and pleasantly stoned. I feel full of love, for Will by my side, for the care workers buzzing around me (getting me water, checking my blood pressure, setting up the procedure room, preparing the instruments for my abortion). I feel so many frightening, ugly, sharp-edged, hollow things, in these last moments of my pregnancy. But I don't feel alone.

I'm taken to the procedure room. My pants and my underwear come off once again, still slightly sticky from the ultrasound goop that clings to my thighs. My heels go in the stirrups that have held so many feet before mine. I scooch my butt to the very edge of the bed, as I always forget and thus must always be asked, before *every* Pap smear and pelvic exam, to do. Alexis inserts a speculum. She injects a local anesthetic into my cervix, the neck of my womb. She's stubborn, my cervix, introverted and aloof. She often needs to be encouraged, pleaded with. Lying on the table, sharp cramps like electric pulses, I picture her as a grumpy little pink starfish, taking the cannula in through her scowling mouth as Alexis inserts it. This, alongside the pleasant heaviness of my eyes, is how I know the sedatives are doing their jobs. I tell myself not to say it—the weird starfish thing—out loud. *Then they'll know how high you are if you compare your cervix to a sea creature*, my brain giggles stupidly through the pain.

* * *

My two coworkers, close on either side of my body; Will kissing my forehead and smoothing my hair away from my face, whispering that he loves me, I'm brave, I'm doing great; the strangely upbeat dance pop playing on the clinic radio; Alexis between my legs, reaching inside of me as she has done before, but this time with the handheld suction device she'll use to gently, carefully empty me out. These are some of the things I'll remember—and in case I ever do forget, I've written them all down now, here, for both of us.

* * *

Later in a pregnancy—beginning around twelve weeks—the in-clinic abortion may become a longer or more complicated process. The cervix (maybe yours is a grumpy little sea creature, too, or maybe it's a sweet-natured, agreeable flower that opens on demand, or maybe—if these analogies creep you out—it's just a part of your body, through which things pass) may need to be dilated before your procedure.

This can be done with misoprostol, or with dilators. The cer-vical dilators we use at my clinic are made of seaweed—a strange, aquatic little plant that fills my heart with wonder. *Laminaria*, it's called. The brand we use at the clinic is sourced in the Sea of Japan. It's harvested where it grows, before being dried, sterilized, and rolled into a small, dehydrated stick. In this little clinic, having been flown all those miles in the air, the seaweed is then inserted by loving hands into the opening of a patient's cervix. Once placed, the laminaria gradually rehydrates, expanding as it takes on the water of the body holding it. This opens the cervix and can also promote prostaglandins that cause contractions. If laminaria is part of your abortion care, it will usually be placed the day before your procedure, resulting in what my clinic calls a two-day. You can return home and rest, or live your life, as the seaweed expands inside of you. Less commonly, laminaria or other dilators may be placed on the same day as your procedure, with a waiting period to allow for their expansion.

When I explain to patients and friends—that laminaria begins with the long green strands, dancing and bending and rippling, salty and willowy beneath the surface of the sea—they often share my wonder, too.

Abortion is found in nature. Abortion is a miracle. Abortion is tidal. Abortion is life and growth and magic and the elements.

Abortion is the deep blue ocean, not the crashing wave.

* * *

"Do you want to see your tissue?" asks Alexis, as she slides the speculum out of me and covers my legs with the thin cotton surgical sheet.

I glance up at Will, who stands at the top of the bed, gripping my left hand, his large and calloused fingers laced through mine. He shakes his head.

"Not me," he says quietly. "What do you want, sweetheart?"

I'm not prepared to know what my preference is here—how could I be? Sensing my hesitation, Alexis tells me that it will be by the sink, if I decide I do want to look at it. I can get dressed, she says, and stay in the room as long as I need. They'll all be right outside when I'm ready to go.

She says, "We're all right here. We've got you. There's no rush. We've got you."

She hands me a washcloth to clean myself of the blood and the cold medical lubricant sticking gloppily to the skin of my inner thighs. I pull my feet from the stirrups and hold my knees to my chest. Cramps roll through my body. The pain and anxiety medications flow through my veins. One by one, the women file out of the procedure room, leaving the two people who have created this together, alone, in the room with it and with each other.

A few feet from where I sit, pants-less and shivering and no longer pregnant—for real, this time—a glass dish sits by a deep metal sink, draped in a paper towel. My tissue. Alexis has examined it thoroughly, searching for the yolk sac and the fetal pole. She feels certain that she has emptied the contents of my womb completely. The material of my body, which minutes ago still bloomed like algae in that same hot wet lush tropical darkness that grew my son, sits cold and sterile in that pie plate now, under the bright examination light.

I step into my underwear and pull my jeans up gingerly over my thighs, the elastic maternity band hugging my stretch marks, flush against the small pink crescent moon of my C-section scar. Holding me in. Holding me.

"I think I'm going to look at it," I say, more to myself than to Will.

He studies my face for a beat: my tired eyes, the tears that have dried to salt on my unwashed cheeks. He nods slowly.

"Whatever you want to do, honey." He reaches for my hand, squeezes it twice, and lets it drop limply once more to my side. I move to the sink, take a deep breath. I lift the paper towel. Here they are, these not-yet-six-week-old pieces of a future that will never be. I've seen pregnancy tissue before, of course, but this tissue is not the material of an unfamiliar circumstance. Of someone else's marriage, someone else's pain. It is not the result of someone else's sexual assault or changed mind or health condition, or of a broken condom on a stranger's floor. It's made of me, and of Will, and of the baby stacking blocks at home.

Because I was so newly pregnant, the tissue most closely resembles a heavy period. A constellation of tiny clots. Loosely connected pieces of bloody, stringy, matter. Parts of me, and not—they have been in my body, but not of it. Right?

Oh, I think, seeing them now. Not *Goodbye*, as I half expected to, or *Sorry*, though those will arrive later. But for now, it's just me and the remains of my pregnancy and the only word I can assign to this feeling: *Oh*.

I lay the paper towel back over the dish. I think of burial shrouds. I back away from the sink. Will helps me into my coat, my gloves, my snow boots. I walk out of the room, out of the clinic, into the fresh frigid air and the screaming protesters and the racing city traffic, sunlight glinting from rearview mirrors and sirens following my steps. I see my breath in front of me, cloud after cloud of it, my lungs reminding me, again and again, that I'm alive, I'm upright, I'm moving forward.

Interlude:
Abortion Is a Story
(Some Notes on Language)

I killed my baby, the stranger writes, the words cold and clear. I feel their impact like a punch.

Once a week, I spend a few early-evening hours on my couch with a glass of cheap rosé and a bag of Trader Joe's cheese puffs, replying to strangers' text messages about their abortions. On the private and anonymous hotline, one of several such services[1] in the United States, volunteer counselors like me are on standby to hold a free, open, nonjudgmental space for callers and texters, wherever and whenever they need to talk. Over our six weeks of training, my fellow counselors and I role-played for hours on end. We practiced scenarios in which the stranger on the other end of the line would use language and describe circumstances that provoked intense discomfort or emotional responses in us. We pushed one another to examine our biases, our values, our ability to offer support outside the borders of our comfort zones. To draw on the expanse of our collective knowledge of how abortion can look and feel, rather than the narrow roads of our individual contexts. We prepared, in other words, to receive texts like this one. It comes through my screen one night in June, my baby long asleep and my husband out working in the garden. It's been a long, cold spring, and the earth is still skeptical, distrustful, just now warming to the radical new ideas that we, its tenants, have been proposing: of open windows, blooming flowers, sundresses and bare shoulders not buried under jackets or sweaters. The idea of summer.

The sun is beginning to set, and the lilac tree in our backyard is just barely waking for the season, just beginning to stretch its fragrant purple arms and yawn into the fading golden light. I'm curled under a woven blanket, the dog a snoring, fur-shedding lump at my feet, when the text message arrives.

I killed my baby.

Recovering from this blow, I sit up straight. I release the breath caught in my chest. I type, aiming for a tone that is calm and collected (but is likely landing somewhere slightly more robotic than I'd like): *It sounds like you're holding a lot and you might need some support. Can you tell me a little bit about what happened?*

The cultural powers that be have wrested control of the narratives around who has abortions, and when and why they have them. (Implicit in those narratives: who *deserves* to have abortions, and when and why.) The language and tone we adopt when we discuss sex and reproduction in general, and abortion specifically, either serves to praise compliance to these narratives or to lash out in rejection of them. We use the loaded and inaccurate language of our antiabortion oppressors (*late-term abortion, mother kill, life, baby, child, heartbeat,* and its natural descendent, *heartbeat ban*) or we use flippant terms and jokes in order to defy and disrespect those oppressors, and either way, we often fail to center and honor the individual person having the individual abortion—the only rightful author of its story.

I don't often engage in debates over abortion rights, for the same reason I don't sit down to share a meal at any table where *I* am on the menu. My body is not a theory or a talking point, and neither is yours. But the invitations I *do* accept are those to speak with other people about their own abortion experiences, and how they feel about them, on their own terms. Even when those terms frighten me, or make me uncomfortable. Even when someone tells their stories in a language I don't like to speak.

Language is a river that never stops flowing, its waters always shifting and changing and moving forward—whether we can keep up or not. Should any of the terms and phrases and labels used in these pages be outdated by the time this book reaches your hands— as I accept that they inevitably will—please feel free to take a red pen to my sentences and correct them. I promise I don't mind. I am down for *all* the discussions and debates and arguments playing out, as we speak, over what we should call this or that aspect of pregnancy, of care work, of abortion, so as to cause the least amount of harm.

This glossary refers only to the language that I use. The people you will find describing their own pregnancies, abortions, and care work experiences in this book may use different language than you or I—for a variety of personal or cultural reasons. That's okay.

In my care work, I honor, mirror, and use whatever language is being used by the person having the abortion, or telling the story of that abortion. But while we're alone here, just you and me and all these pages, I'll be using the following terms:

Pregnant person/pregnant people: This is how I refer to

people who are currently pregnant. It is a pretty specific subcategory of human beings at any given moment, who are in a temporary state of being, and it includes some—but not nearly all—of us female, male, nonbinary, intersex, gender-nonconforming, and gender-expansive people. People of all and no genders can become pregnant. Referring to "pregnant people" does not exclude women, while using "women" or "pregnant women" *is* exclusionary. "Women," in the context of abortion havers, erases many of the people who are, as you read this, having abortions. Pregnancy and abortion are common human experiences among all genders. Women are just one subsection of the pregnant people who are moving through the world around you.

Pro-abortion: I'm writing these words to you from the flaming legislative hellscape that is the year 2022. We find ourselves, at this point in the fight, in a place of needing to be very clear about our personal and political stances, a place *far* beyond the reach and the usefulness of the term *pro-choice*—especially considering that in our country, actual reproductive *choices* are made available to very few of us, by design. "Choice" does not factor into the equation for many pregnant people at all. If you cannot afford to raise a child, if you are incarcerated or experiencing homelessness or food insecurity, if you are undocumented and do not see a safe way to bring a child into the world, if you are someone for whom racism, ableism, transphobia, abuse, trauma, or some combination of these has made carrying, birthing, and parenting a child dangerous or impossible, the basic human rights that you are being denied can no longer reasonably be called "choices"—decisions that you are making or not making of your own free will.

As Monica Simpson, the executive director of the SisterSong

Women of Color Reproductive Justice Collective, wrote in a 2022 *New York Times* op-ed: "Reproductive justice has always been more than just being 'pro-choice.' To be pro-choice you must have the privilege of having choices."[2] I believe that nobody should have to be pregnant against their will, or give birth against their will. This makes me, simply, **pro-abortion**.

Antiabortion/Antis: While people who take this stance often prefer to label themselves "pro-life," they are generally and demonstrably never acting in support of actual human lives.

The things they claim to be "pro-": children, parents, families, "life" as a concept of existence and survival, benefit in no material ways from their activism (and in fact are harmed by it, on a massive and multigenerational scale). That the "pro-life" contingent mobilizer on masse to support policies that decimate the environment (in ways that irreparably damage the fertility and health of pregnant people or people who may become pregnant in the future), strip poor children and families of the benefits and support that would keep them fed and clothed and sheltered, and keep assault weapons in the hands of any would-be school shooter who wants them? Well, those are just details.

Antiabortion people and organizations are not pro-life. They are not even particularly pro-pregnancy or pro-fetus, when you examine their practices and the language and ideas they wield, and they are certainly not pro-mother or pro-family, when you zoom out to place abortion within the larger context of their politics and worldviews, the bills they vote for and the measures they lobby against. In one breath they will tell you that a pregnancy is a "blessing" and in the next, that it is a punishment—a responsibility to be borne by someone who has dared to have a body that can become pregnant. They offer "adoption" as an alternative to abortion, as if (1) forced birth is an acceptable occurrence in any context and (2) adoptees themselves have not been telling us for years that our adoption systems are violent, racist, coercive, and traumatizing. (Note: **adoption is an alternative to** *parenting.* **It is** *not* **an alternative to abortion, in that it still requires pregnancy and childbirth, with all the attendant physical, emotional, and financial impacts.**) They are in opposition to abortion, and to sexual and reproductive freedom and autonomy. They are, simply, Antis.

Later abortion care or **Abortion later in pregnancy:** You may have read or heard the phrase *late-term abortion* (among its uglier and more violent cousins *partial-birth abortion*, or *born alive*) used by pundits or lawmakers, but medical experts and providers oppose its use as inaccurate and politicized. The term is intentionally provocative and inaccurate, implying that abortions are taking place after a pregnancy has reached "term" (thirty-seven weeks) or "late term" (over forty-one weeks), which is false. In fact, the American College of Obstetricians and Gynecologists (ACOG) has written that "late-term abortion" has no medical meaning and should not be used in clinical or legal settings.

People need later abortion care for all kinds of reasons, and will increasingly find themselves having to seek abortions after twenty-one weeks of pregnancy, as states pass near-total or total abortion bans that force them to travel and endure weeks, sometimes months, of waiting for their appointments. An abortion is necessary and good and your right, regardless of when you seek or are able to have it. There is no point in a pregnancy at which your body, health (including mental health), autonomy, or life cease to matter.

"Viable pregnancy": "Viability" is a constantly shifting, cultural-context-specific, and thus generally meaningless goal post, both medically *and* legally. To put it simply, as a wise physician once told a doula I know: "*Any* pregnancy that the pregnant person cannot or does not want to carry is a nonviable pregnancy."

If we talk about *viability*, we must refer also (or only!) to what is viable for the person who is pregnant. Forced birth, a violently racist and abusive national foster system and adoption industrial complex, parenthood without resources or support—none of these are truly **viable** options, for any human being. A viable pregnancy is one in which holistic care (for the mind, body, *and* soul), safety, autonomy, power, community, and parenting resources are freely and readily available to the pregnant person. And because the presence or absence of these elements are not for me to decide in the case of any pregnancy but my own, I simply do not say "viable" unless that is the language used by the pregnant person.

Another thing I don't say: **"Using abortion as birth control,"** a strange and judgmental little phrase that belies the speaker's claims of authority on the topic. Just as an IUD or hormonal implant is birth control, just as a vasectomy or tubal ligation is birth control, abortion is—quite literally—a form of birth control.

Doula: It's a noun: what I am. It's a verb: what I do.

A doula is a person trained to provide practical, emotional, physical, and informational support. There are childbirth and postpartum doulas, death doulas, full-spectrum and pregnancy loss and infertility doulas. And there are abortion doulas. The etymology of the word is Greek, originally meaning "female slave" or "female helper," which is one reason that many people who do this work grapple with it as a title—and some eschew it altogether, in favor of "companion" or "care worker." Some of us struggle with the associations to chattel slavery and to the Atlantic slave trade that the word may call to mind, and/or with its gendered origins, and some of us have moved away from the label altogether. I still use it for myself in many contexts, but I acknowledge that it is a complicated term and that some folks might not want to hear it come from my mouth. I also self-describe, in different contexts, as a support person, a companion, or an abortion care worker.

Doulas perform a wide range of tasks that can range from intensive pain management and recovery care to running a simple errand or two; from spending days or weeks providing intensely intimate physical and emotional support to making a ten-minute phone call or sending a few text messages. Many abortion doulas also work as birth and/or postpartum doulas, and call themselves *full-spectrum doulas*—meaning that they provide support for *any* outcome of a pregnancy, an adoption, or a life transition. Many are also lactation consultants, death doulas, sex educators, chaplains or clergy members, counselors. Many come to doula work as I have— gradually, as we move through the world and connect the dots: God, love, care work, human rights, community and connection, justice, our responsibility to one another.

An abortion doula (or companion, or care/support worker) is someone who supports you—physically, emotionally, spiritually, practically, and logistically—through your abortion. This work can take so many shapes, so many colors and sizes and ever-shifting, nebulous forms. This work can look and feel so many different ways. The work of an abortion doula can be done, in one form or another, by anyone, no matter how stretched thin across jobs and obligations and methods of survival. No matter how well-read or well-resourced. It can be done by you.

Abortion Is Yours

We file into the clinic conference room, a gradual trickle of tired bodies, in our scrubs and our street clothes, yawning behind our paper surgical masks. Our eyes are bloodshot, watering, irritated by being rubbed, by staring directly into the glow of a laptop screen for too long, or by the plastic safety goggles required in exam rooms or other circumstances of close patient contact. We're carrying mugs of bitter break-room coffee, or $9 iced lavender oat milk lattes from the coffee shop around the corner, or giant water bottles covered in rainbows of stickers. Some of us have our laptops and phones on hand, in case of urgent patient need or in order to respond to the communications that may come through—from other clinics, other laboratories, other tired people in scrubs.

We take our seats around the table, most of us slouching or hunching or curled up and clutching our knees to our chests. At the head of the room are some clinic managers and our medical director, Dr. Brown, a sharp and funny mom of two young boys with a dark and spiky pixie cut (and a darker, spikier sense of humor). Before each one of us sits a tableau of three plastic cups—green, yellow, and red, from left to right—and a stack of index cards.

Not acknowledging these rather strange props, Dr. Brown begins to take us through some legal updates and some details about the expansion of our clinical services to accommodate the oncoming tidal waves—the first of which is now just beginning to crest on the horizon, its shadow creeping over the room, the clinic, the city, the region—of the patients who will be traveling to us from other states for their care. The doctor delivers these updates as simply and straightforwardly as possible, eliciting as few fresh tears from us as she can.

It's spring, 2022, and we are awaiting the imminent overturning of the *Roe v. Wade* decision by the Supreme Court—thanks to a leak, we know the contents of the ruling—and the subsequent tidal wave of suffering to follow. When the ruling does come down, the trigger bans take effect, and dozens of states across the country begin to go dark, we know what we're about to witness. So many people—including children—will immediately begin to die of the sorts of pregnancy complications that can only be resolved by the terminations of those pregnancies. Many other people—including children—will be forced to carry pregnancies and give birth, and, should they survive that, will then be plunged into unplanned or unwanted parenthood (which, in this country, is likely to bring with it the whole variety pack of state violence: poverty, food insecurity, lack of access to education, neglect of postpartum complications, injuries, and illnesses, a systematic denial of adequate health care and thus poor physical and mental health outcomes . . . the list goes on and on). And because abuse and intimate partner violence are exceedingly common in the lives of pregnant

Americans—murder being the number one cause of their death, according to a 2021 study published in *Obstetrics & Gynecology*—those rates will skyrocket, too.[1] Providers and clinic staff will be forced to not only watch this suffering bloom and grow, the ripple effects of abortion bans reaching far and wide into families and communities, but will also, monstrously, be forced to participate in its propagation—turning patients away, withholding or delaying information as it becomes illegal to disseminate, weighing our compliance with these illegitimate and unjust laws and our complicity in their violence against the safety of our children, our families, our livelihoods. This is to say nothing of those of us who will instantly lose our jobs, as clinics close and abortion doula work becomes aggressively surveilled and prosecuted in our states.

While we wait, we work, rushing around the decks of our sinking ship. We see our patients and we have our meetings. We draw blueprints for the lifeboats we will try desperately to build from our sparse reserves of sticks and seaweed. We try not to spend our limited time and resources pre-mourning all those we know will drown—all those we know we won't be able to reach or save. We move on and move on and move on, to our next agenda item, our next topic, our next little task. Which, today, is this: it's time, Dr. Brown tells us, gesturing to the cups and cards around the table, to do a values exploration.

* * *

My abortion values did not suddenly arrive with the delivery of my clinic name tag or my doula certifications; they did not appear, fully formed and ready to be articulated, overnight. They

emerged—and are still emerging—gradually, deepening and dis-
tilling and coming into focus over years and years of witnessing,
absorbing, processing, and doing the work. Before I can hold space
for other people's complicated and ever-evolving feelings about
abortion, I have to get clear about my own. Values work is basic
upkeep and requires our ongoing attention, our constant mainte-
nance; it's like washing the dishes. You can empty the sink and fill
the drying rack today, but there will inevitably be more dishes to
wash tomorrow. If, as Ursula K. Le Guin tells us, love is like bread[2]—
always needing to be made and remade anew—then values are the
ingredients (a list, always being edited and refined), the recipe (in
progress, taste-tested, and tweaked again and again), the bread pan.
The container in which the love rises and the vessel that must be
washed and dried and buttered and flour-coated, for each new daily
loaf, every single time.

Values explorations, also sometimes called values clarifica-
tions, are exercises for anyone who is interested in any form of
abortion care or related work. Each and every doula training I
have experienced, as a student or a facilitator, has featured a values
exploration, often as the very first agenda item following intro-
ductions and a grounding.[3] It is a project involving introspection
and mutual understanding. It helps us to meet ourselves and one
another more deeply, to see more clearly where we are coming
from and where we have arrived, and how far in which directions
we still may need to travel. It encourages vulnerability. It makes
space to safely hold ourselves and each other accountable for the
stigmas and biases we carry while being gentle and loving toward
ourselves and each other for carrying them—as it was not a con-

scious choice we made to pick them up in the first place. It helps us shake off our anxious need to only ever hold—and express—perfect politics. Our desperate yearning to have all the answers, to be always and fully imbued with the moral clarity and authority that might cut through the fog of being human, short-sighted and self-centered as we are. The pressure, self-applied or otherwise, not only to *do* no harm, but to *think* no harm. But bodies and hearts—"gut feelings," fight-or-flight instincts and cortisol levels and the memories we carry in our bones and blood and cells—don't work like that. We've all absorbed messaging around abortion since before we've even understood its definition, and we've been made to feel certain sensations and emotions that may be wildly misaligned with the articulated views and opinions we profess.

The emotions that arise in you, the reaction your body has to a trigger: these are not the whole story of who you are, of your values and your character and your abilities. Who you are is the willingness to feel, to ask questions, to interrogate, to examine and learn. Who you are is what brought you into this room and onto these pages to explore your values around abortion in the first place. It's the way you meet yourself in the mirror. It's what you do next.

* * *

On each index card is printed a simple statement, with no context and no qualifiers. We are asked to sort the cards into the appropriate cup, based on the following key:

GREEN

I will provide care or support
to this person with no   OR   **I agree with this statement.**
hesitation or concern.

YELLOW

I am feeling some kind of   **I'm not sure if I agree or disagree**
way. Something is coming   **with this statement.**
up for me here, but I'm not   *("IT DEPENDS!" we humans*
sure where the discomfort is   OR   *love to shriek, when presented*
stemming from or if it would   *in public with an overly*
not stop me from helping this   *simplistic hypothetical and*
person.   *asked to define ourselves by*
                                                    the stark choice it demands.)

RED

I don't feel that I am the
best person to provide care
or support in this scenario,   OR   **I disagree with this statement.**
as there is a fundamental
misalignment with my values.

Silently, we pick up our cards and begin to shuffle through them, tossing them into their green-yellow-red categories. We are hesitating, worrying, thinking, reading and rereading, agonizing, and then, finally, we are sorting them into the color categories. We know the cups symbolize our respective comfort levels with what the cards say—and what they don't—about our ability to provide abortion care to anyone, in any circumstance. One of us reaches for a box of tissues; another briefly leaves the room to take a break.

The people in this room, reading these index cards, have a wide range of reactions and emotions. And that's okay. If a hypothetical abortion—or a real one, unfolding right in front of you—causes something to happen in your body, if it feels "sticky" to you, as my doula friend Cait would say, that just means you're human, moving through a messy world and carrying all your very own messes with you, like all the rest of us. You may feel that perfect-abortion-politics pressure, when you come to this work, ashamed that you cannot intuitively and immediately live those perfect politics in perfect ways, expressing your perfect thoughts in perfect language.

But perfect abortion politics are not what make you ready to do community abortion care work. Sitting still in the discomfort, naming your feelings honestly and openly and asking questions about where your gut reactions may be coming from, and where they align with or diverge from your values and who you want to be, and how you can meaningfully engage with them—that's the homework that will come up, again and again, over our lifetimes of learning to love us through our abortions.

The statements printed on *these* cards, written more neatly than any I could ever make, include the following:

A thirteen-year-old is too young to have an abortion.

A thirteen-year-old is too young to have a baby.

A person who went through fertility treatments in order to conceive has changed their mind, and is now seeking an abortion at twenty weeks.

A patient tells you that she is not being coerced but that having an abortion is the only way she will be able to "keep" her boyfriend.

A pregnant person should be allowed full autonomy over their body, including the use of alcohol and drugs.

*Someone should be able to have an abortion at **any** stage of their pregnancy for any reason.*

*A patient says they will continue their pregnancy **unless** genetic testing returns a diagnosis of Down syndrome.*

Someone tells you that they are not informing their spouse or anyone else in their life of their decision to have an abortion.

A twenty-five-year-old patient comes to you for an in-clinic abortion; you see in their chart that this is their sixth procedure. They decline LARC⁴s or other birth control counseling. A family should be able to choose an abortion for purposes of sex selection.

The conference room is nearly silent, save a random cough or sniffle and the echoes of the sharp-cornered index cards landing one-by-one in their plastic cups. Sun streams in through the windows and car horns sound in the distance. After five minutes, the table is bare and the cups are full. It's time to share. To own up to our shit. To be vulnerable and honest and to reflect, together, on the places where our own stigma and biases rub up against the values we want to live out in our work. To ask questions about how we might address and repair that friction. We sit in the uncomfortable quiet. Finally, a medical assistant clears her throat. She opens her mouth. She begins to speak, flushed and uncertain: she is—and she feels shy about this, she tells us—sometimes troubled by the work of supporting abortions later in pregnancy. She occasionally experiences a twinge of judgment, she admits. She thinks, "Why didn't you come to us sooner?" The head of our abortion care program, a nurse practitioner who works closely with Dr. Brown, nods supportively.

"Thank you so much for sharing," she says in her calm, even tone. There's no surprise, no scolding, no condescension in her words. "Let's get into it."

There is no universally understood or accepted definition of "later" when it comes to abortion. More than 90 percent of abortions take place in the first trimester of a pregnancy,[5] though that balance is rapidly shifting, as abortion bans, restrictions on sex education and accurate medical information, and deprivation of reproductive health care (and health care in general) do their work. People are discovering their pregnancies (and receiving diagnoses of related health conditions) later, have scarcer access to prenatal care or counseling resources like the All-Options Talkline,[6] and are faced with logistical, legal, and financial barriers that can delay their appointments by weeks or months. Enter all-trimester clinics like Partners in Abortion Care, the Boulder Abortion Clinic, and the DuPont Clinic, and activists like Erika Christensen and Garin Marschall. Christensen and Marschall, later-abortion patient advocates and founders of Patient Forward, an abortion advocacy organization that focuses on the total decriminalization of pregnancy including unrestricted access to abortion throughout pregnancy. Together, they also created the public education resource WhoNotWhen. After her third-trimester abortion in 2016, in which she was forced to travel thousands of miles and pay thousands of dollars to end her pregnancy, Christensen realized that her story needed to be told. And—luckily for all of us—it has been, from a 2016 *Jezebel* article that went ultra-viral to hearings on the Senate floor. She has been fighting against later abortion stigma and against the "viability" standards and clauses that are often accepted or promoted even by pro-abortion legislators and advocates.

Viability, a nebulous and ever-shifting legal and medical term, refers to the moment at which a fetus becomes able to survive outside of the pregnant person's body. But there are many problems with that one-size-fits-all definition of the term, and with lawmakers' insistence on slapping it onto an endless spectrum of different pregnancies as they unfold on different timelines in different bodies and over the courses of different lives, and all of those pregnancies' potential outcomes. Many providers and abortion doulas feel like viability should be retired as a concept, altogether, because, again: *any pregnancy that is not viable for the pregnant person to continue is not a viable pregnancy.*

And Christensen wholeheartedly agrees. "I wish people understood," she says, "that pregnancies require consent in order to be viable."

And who is most likely to need an abortion later in their pregnancy? People in places where abortion is banned, people of the global majority—especially, in the United States, Black and Indigenous people and other people of color, youths, people living in poverty and people without access to regular care or reproductive education and support. People who can't just easily make an abortion appointment for the following week, take a day or two off, and get to a clinic. People who—for a wide variety of reasons—may not even realize they're pregnant.

"I've read about later term abortions and stuff, and most of the time there's something medically wrong with the baby," Christensen remembers a twenty-one-year-old from Florida telling her. "[It seems like] nobody has a pregnancy that long and doesn't want it. Most of these are like one percent of women and it's always a woman who wanted the child and then something went wrong. It's never just this person didn't know they were pregnant, and it makes me feel stupid and dumb. It makes people think *people like me don't deserve an abortion*. I wish I had known I was pregnant earlier. But people who don't know how far along they are during pregnancy, they do still deserve an abortion."

(Consider just how granular the management of these artificial schedules can be, and how arbitrary—the division of a pregnancy into twelve-week "trimesters," for example, is an invention of the judges who wrote the *Roe v. Wade* decision.[7] Trimesters are neither a medical fact nor a natural bodily occurrence, but merely a legal framework, designed to allow state governments to enact their own restrictions on a pregnancy at various stages of it. Consider the privileges and resources it takes to know how pregnant you are, down to the week and the day, and to access care within a narrow time frame.) "It's hard to explain how it felt to hear her say this," Christensen tells me of the young woman, "and understand that stories like mine"—here, she is referring to later abortions that are determined to be "necessary" "lifesaving," or medically indicated—"contribute to this master narrative/myth about later abortion. Of course she *does* deserve care, and patients like her are literally why we do this work and refuse to entertain *compromise*."

When we attempt to "compromise" on human rights, when we impose means-testing and judgments of worthiness (who *deserves* an abortion? and when?), we make ourselves into dictators, ruling over countries we've never inhabited, countries whose citizens we've never met and whose languages we could never learn to speak. Why and when someone seeks an abortion, the circumstances of their pregnancy, their emotions and experiences surrounding all of this: there are vast and uncrossable oceans between those complicated coastlines and your own shores. If invited, you may visit them. But you do not live in that country, know its infinitely complex histories, understand its street signs—let alone make its laws.

I am always in the process of becoming that soft landing place—learning where my sharper edges are (and finding that new ones form and emerge all the time). The edges I could sand smooth, I have; and the ones I couldn't, I've gradually found or been taught the language to acknowledge and describe, learning to draw an honest map around them and put up warning signs when I haven't yet forged a route through an interaction that successfully avoids them.

But being pro-abortion—that is to say, loving and fighting for the human right to bodily autonomy—is just like anything else. You can, for example, feel that clean air, water and food, and housing are human rights, without having a simple solution to every single problem on the tip of your tongue at all times. It's okay not to have the answers. It's okay to feel uncomfortable, inarticulate, unsure. It's okay for activating ideas and situations, when you encounter them, to pull you away from your focus on caring for the other person, to pull you out of their experience and into your own. It's okay to need more time, more reading, more self-reflection. It's okay to be learning alongside the loving.

"I think with every new person that I talk to," says Camila Ochoa Mendoza, the creator of the podcast *Abortion, with love*, "they open up a window that had not been open for me before." On her podcast, Camila interviews people from all over the world about their abortion stories and/or their work in pro-abortion spaces. Often, upon hearing these stories, she finds she has to revisit her opinion about something, readjusting how she thinks or feels about an issue in light of new perspectives.

One of the pod's most moving episodes invites the listener into a room with Ochoa Mendoza and her mother, to hear an emotional and complicated conversation about these forms of abortion stigma, and where the two women differ, and the places where they hurt or anger or misunderstand each other. The gaps between mother and daughter are generational, philosophical, and deeply personal.

"I like to think that I'm quite open to learning, and I would love to be corrected on the issues that I hold stigma around," says Ochoa Mendoza. "I want to unlearn those things that we've been fed through our lives around abortion, which we never realized are stigmatizing until we're confronted with it. Even around sex-selective abortions, or young people having abortions, or abortions around fetal abnormalities, those are really difficult conversations with no right answer," she tells me. "I notice myself being nervous to have those conversations, because I'm worried of saying something wrong . . . but also, recognizing that I'm human."

And as a fellow human, grappling daily with the inevitability of causing harm, of misunderstanding and being misunderstood: I cherish the reminder. Wherever we are, you and I and all the rest of us, there are mistakes and evolutions and changing tactics. There is curiosity and shifting and adjusting and clarifying and apologizing. And there is learning, like it or not, for the rest of our lives.

* * *

An hour after the values exploration meeting, I'm downstairs in the clinic checking in on a patient who is here for her third abortion in two years. She has multiple partners, no plans for parenthood in the next five years, and is not interested in discussing contraception today. I help her through the first and last steps of her appointment, share a laugh with her about the wealthy summer tourists currently clogging the streets of our neighborhood, and tell her to call us if she needs anything else.

A few hundred miles to the south of me, a doula named Jay sits at a hospital bedside, supporting someone who is twenty-four weeks pregnant and uses opioids. Jay holds their client's hand, stroking the back of it gently with their thumb. Two doses of naloxone are safely nestled in the messenger bag at their feet. Jay explains some basic harm reduction concepts to the hospital's doctors. Later they will pull a nurse aside to correct the stigmatizing language she has been using about their client's drug use.

Three states over, to the west, a redheaded doula in her early twenties, IUD-shaped earrings dangling from her ears and freckles scattered delicately across the bridge of her nose, walks into an exam room to greet a patient, who looks at her and says, with no hesitation: "No. I want someone Black." The doula doesn't flinch. She smiles, nods, and tells the patient that she'll try and get one of her collective's Black doulas on the phone right away to see if they're available. She leaves the room and makes the call.

Somewhere near the Texas-Mexico border, R. is on the phone with someone who is undocumented and cannot risk crossing an immigration checkpoint to get to an abortion clinic. The caller is a minor, with no money, no means of transportation, no line of credit in their own name. R. is trying, desperately, to troubleshoot their abortion, to make suggestions that might feel safe and feasible, to find a safe and healthy option that will not put them at risk of deportation, arrest, violence, separation from their family.

"They just kept saying, 'What can I take that's in my house to stop this pregnancy?'" R. tells me. "'Is there anything I can take that's in my house? Please help me. What can I take?'"

Abortion Is Sex

If a pregnancy is evidence that a person is having sex, then an abortion (for any reason) is evidence that sex does not have to lead to procreation, that it does not exist in our lives solely to bear children. That we might disentangle the act of sex from morality, or "consequences," free it from the cultural structures of marriage and parenthood. That sex might be pursued and enjoyed freely, for the sake of our own bodies and our own pleasure and joy: this is what the antiabortion movement fears. Claims that "life begins at conception" or statements that begin, "I'm pro-choice, *but...*" go hand in hand with an assertion that we should be monitoring and policing each other's sex lives.

What kinds of sex would you feel empowered to have, if you knew that any and all pregnancies that might result from that sex would be met not with judgment, fear, shame, criminalization, and secrecy, but with openness, kindness, respect, and support?

Sex happens. Pregnancy happens. Miscarriage and infertility and stillbirth happen. An unintended pregnancy is not a weakness or a moral failing; it is not a consequence; it is not a punishment. It is an inevitable occurrence in a culture hell-bent on keeping sex a secret and thereby keeping you as vulnerable, uninformed, and unprotected as possible. You didn't fuck up. You're not irresponsible. You don't need to suffer because you had sex. You didn't earn pain or struggle, or the financial burdens of daycare and diapers, by having a human body.

You are whole and good and worthy and deserving of whatever sex you seek or desire, whatever pregnancy outcomes you seek or desire, whatever family structure and future and life you seek or desire.

Abortion is an act of imagining, of building worlds in which that truth is never questioned or denied.

Abortion Is Justice

I can hardly believe it's happening, but the sound is unmistakable: Loretta Ross herself is laughing on the other end of my phone line. Her laughter is infectious, the smile in her voice a honeyed salve applied directly to my bad mood on this sunless November morning. I'm looking out the window, over city rooftops and alleys of overflowing dumpsters, from the darkness of my small and depressing "office" of the moment— a storage closet full of birth control pills and hot pink clinic escort vests. My notebook, open in front of me and ready to absorb Professor Ross's wisdom, is full of my hastily scribbled notes and questions.

It's 2021, winter creeping toward my hemisphere. I don't yet know how soon *Roe v. Wade* will be overturned, or that I'll find myself in need of my own abortion even sooner. For now, I am unpregnant, raising a busy child and working two day jobs and laboring endlessly to research and write, to pitch and publish articles and essays for extra money. I'm spending my thirty-minute lunch breaks conducting interviews from this grim little closet— beginning with Professor Ross herself.

Loretta June Ross is a scholar, professor, and activist. Her

legacy is capacious and far-reaching; active in anti-apartheid and
anti-gentrification movement work, organizing for racial and gender justice, and founding the DC Rape Crisis Center. And, until
her retirement from community organizing in 2012, she was also
the national coordinator of the SisterSong Women of Color Reproductive Justice Collective, an organization she cofounded. Ross
and eleven other women,[1] in the tradition of the Combahee River
Collective,[2] cocreated the framework of reproductive justice in
1994, in response to then-First Lady Hillary Clinton and other
Democrats choosing to omit reproductive care from their health
care reform proposal. Reproductive justice ("RJ" in many abortion
care circles' shorthand), is a world-changer. It is a paradigm shift.
Both rhetorically *and* materially distinct from the frameworks of
"reproductive rights" (which places the power over our reproductive lives into the hands of judges and legislators) and "reproductive
health care" (which confers much of that same authority upon doctors and medical corporations, and which assumes access to clinics
and providers), reproductive justice places the power back into the
hands of the people. It acknowledges that reproductive lives play
out in complex and marginalized *individual* bodies and identities,
within families and communities, at the intersections of so many
other social justice and human rights issues. SisterSong defines it
as "the human right to maintain personal bodily autonomy, have
children, not have children, and parent the children we have in safe
and sustainable communities."[3] Reproductive justice centers those
most impacted by the systemic and violent denial of this human
right—namely, women of color. Each and every one of us have
the right, reproductive justice tells us, to access every pregnancy
outcome, and to parent or not parent, in ways that are reflective of

our human dignity. Access to drinking water and fresh food, safety from violence and the police, access to health care and education, prison abolition, climate justice, housing justice . . . *all* the things that make it possible for families, for human beings, to survive and thrive.

We're talking about the joy and the pleasure to be found in person-to-person abortion care and support work, and about the unexpected places in which she's been finding it. "I've served as an abortion escort, when people fly to Atlanta," Ross tells me. "We became a destination for people from other states that had shorter (gestational age) limits. It was always a joy to pick them up at the airport, to welcome them, to escort them to their hotel rooms, take them to the clinic, pick them up after the clinic, take them back to the hotel, pick them up the next day for the aftercare visit.[4] It's a small thing," she says, "but it's an important thing, that I take *a lot* of joy in doing." Our ideas about abortion, sex, pregnancy, parenthood, and bodies in general come to us long before we understand just what we are believing (and repeating) and why. As a little girl, I absorbed the abortion stories shared and the discussions of reproductive rights frequently held around my dining room table by my mother and her friends, a brilliant and loving group of mostly white, middle-class, second-wave feminist academics. These women passed down to us, their children—explicitly and implicitly, in all the usual big and small ways that parents will do—the white feminist "pro-choice" lens typical of the era and context in which they were parenting us: namely, that abortion rights were an issue of male domination, of men versus women, boys versus girls.

But as legal scholar Dorothy Roberts reminds us in her seminal *Killing the Black Body: Race, Reproduction, and the Meaning of*

Liberty, that is simply not the real, whole, true story. What I didn't learn, in those early and formative framings of sex and reproduction, is that restrictions on abortion are inextricably tied to the horrors inflicted upon Black women at every other step of their reproductive lives: incarcerated people forced to give birth in shackles and separated from their newborns; the criminalization of drug use, poverty, and pregnancy outcomes, a weapon of the state that tears families apart and places Black children in state custody, effectively legal kidnapping; soaring maternal mortality rates and infant mortality rates; obstetric violence and abuse. Eugenics and forced sterilization, as in the unnecessary and nonconsensual hysterectomies performed on poor Black women and girls, some as young as nine years old, at teaching hospitals in the South—a practice so common it was nicknamed the "Mississippi Appendectomy."

"The systematic, institutionalized denial of reproductive freedom," Roberts writes, "has uniquely marked Black women's history in America."[5]

* * *

Communities of color in the United States are systemically and violently robbed of the economic, social, and political power required to build their families and lives as they choose. National policies, and those who enforce and uphold them, see to it that these inequities and oppressions continue, and in some cases—as in the context of reproductive rights and abortion laws—that they escalate. But community care efforts—doula collectives, community-led harm reduction initiatives, mutual aid projects, abortion funds, collaborative art and storytelling programs, grassroots leaders, and spaces in which to gather, even if only virtually or remotely—are at the heart of reclaiming and expanding this power, freedom, and abundance.

The National Latina Institute for Reproductive Justice's tender and powerful "Yo Te Apoyo / I Support You" campaign, launched in 2013, emphasizes this need to explore and hold space for "the nuance we see in our communities," the organization says, "that regardless of your personal opinion about abortion, the Latina/x community would support a loved one in their de-cision. This video series reflects the various ways that individuals show up for their loved ones."[6] This project is an extension of the Latina Institute's transformative centering and lifting of Latina/x voices on sex and sexuality, gender, pregnancy, contraception, birth justice, and abortion. The National Asian Pacific American Women's Forum (NAPAWF), meanwhile, has designed an "Asian Abortion Glossary," a resource of useful words (such as *abortion*, *gender equality*, and *bodily autonomy*) translated into eight Asian languages—a connective and invaluable tool for inter- and cross-community conversations and care work. A national RJ organi-zation, NAPAWF fights abortion bans and restrictions, publishes research and reports, and arms care workers and organizers with tools like the NYC Asian American Organizing Blueprint for Re-productive Justice.[7] *You* are the expert on the RJ needs of your own communities. And if you're working in and with communi-ties of which you are not a member? If you're supporting people whose identities sit at the intersections where you'll never stand? It is wholly your responsibility to seek out, listen to, learn from, honor, support (and, when you can, to *pay*)[8] the leaders already working in those spaces, because they are the experts there.

* * *

"I'm a part of the Reproductive Justice *and* the Black Liberation movements, and I do not think they are separate," says Jordyn Close. "They both flow into the other, more often than not." Close is an organizer, advocate, abortion storyteller, and activist in Ohio, and has spoken and written extensively about her experiences. Now the board president of the Abortion Fund of Ohio, Close emphasizes that she is an abolitionist, and that her organizing is also focused on decriminalization, pro-abortion policy and stigma busting, and on Black feminist political education.

"Political education, I think especially on the left, sometimes is very inaccessible for the communities that we say we do this work for," Close tells me, in our discussion of the places where her RJ activism intersects with her own abortion care experiences. "No one should have to read a thousand pages of theory before being taken seriously about their lived experiences. I did not go to college, I have my GED, and I believe organizing from a place of lived experience, rather than academia, is what is going to bring us (closer) to liberation."

Sasha, a queer Black full-spectrum doula in New Jersey, agrees. "This is very ancestral for us," they tell me when I ask them about their process of coming to abortion care work. "We've always been doulas, and at births, and assisting pregnant people. It's always been ancestral. I've been at births since I was, like, eight years old. So I've kind of been doing it, never really had a name to put to it."

Sasha became a doula nine years ago, supporting folks through *all* pregnancy outcomes, and RJ was her foundation. It remains a North Star for her, the beating heart of the center of her practice nearly a decade later. "I got into this work because I really wanted to make some changes in the reproductive justice systems of this world," she tells me. "Just seeing how marginalized communities are treated, and not getting the care and the access and all the resources that they deserve. So that was my calling, I had to get into it."

While white doulas and care workers may aim to ground our abortion care work in a reproductive justice framework, the limitations of our whiteness make us, at best: RJ students, allies, accomplices. Not leaders.

And talking about whiteness is essential for white care workers: naming it, perpetually interrogating how whiteness and white supremacy function in our movement spaces, our work, our lives. Tannis Fuller, the white codirector of the Blue Ridge Abortion Fund, in Virginia, describes her ongoing frustration of engaging with other white folks in leadership and direct care roles, who are quick to lament the white supremacy baked into the policies, operations, and cultures of their own organizations and workplaces. But when Fuller then asks how they are addressing it, these white leaders generally go on to describe to her their long-term, slow-moving, lip-service-heavy plans: to hire DEI (diversity, equity, and inclusion) consultants, read books, take trainings—to do anything, in other words, except to cede an inch of their power. Anything but to hire and invest in Black leaders and other leaders of color—and then to actually be led by them.

"The only way to fix it," Fuller says, when these other white leaders bemoan the dearth of Black coleaders and collaborators who trust them (and who feel safe, respected, and fulfilled enough to *stay* at their organizations), "is to fucking fix it."

* * *

In *The Turnaway Study*, Diana Greene Foster and her team of researchers learned that, of the reasons people give for seeking abortion in the United States, 40 percent of respondents say they are "not financially prepared" for a baby.[9] Doulas are called to fund people's abortions when we can, to support them materially when we can and practically when we can't—providing childcare, a ride, a crowd-funded hotel room or plane ticket, a connection to an abortion fund or practical support organization with deeper pockets than ours. Help navigating the bills that may arrive after an abortion—from a hospital, clinic, or health insurance company. Economic justice is reproductive justice, and until the larger problems are solved through the enactment of reparations, equal pay legislation, and so many other policy shifts, we take care of each other.

When Syd comes to me for abortion support, her face is flushed, and tears stream down her cheeks. I don't know her very well, but she works with a friend of mine at a local coffee shop. "They've cut my hours down so much because of COVID," she says, "I don't think I'll even have enough in my bank account to pay for diapers." She buries her head in her hands as I sit across from her, the iced matcha latte she's made for me on the table between us. I reach into my bag for a pack of tissues and slide them across to her.

"I already did the math," she says softly as she takes one.

In the US, federal assistance programs for families don't acknowledge a need for diapers. According to the website for the National Diaper Bank Network (NDBN), American families cannot use SNAP or WIC assistance on diapers, and though TANF

(Temporary Assistance for Needy Families) may be used to purchase them, many families don't receive this benefit. In fact, the NDBN reports that only twenty-three percent of families living below the federal poverty level nationwide receive *any* cash assistance through TANF. In thirteen states, it's fewer than ten percent. And even when families do receive TANF assistance, the funds are often insufficient to buy diapers on top of the many other expenses (utilities, rent, hygiene essentials, clothing, etc.) that the money is meant to cover.[10] And babies go through a lot of diapers in the first few years of their lives. Like three thousand diapers a year,[11] if we're talking disposables. (White feminists with money and time might argue, here, that cloth diapers are a cost-effective and environmentally friendly alternative to disposable diapers—a perfect example of the gaps and weaknesses in their racial and class analysis of feminist issues, gaps that RJ enables us to fill. For example, as Dr. Jennifer Randles noted in a 2022 issue of the journal *Gender & Society*, most US daycare facilities will not accept cloth diapers, and many states have laws prohibiting families from washing them in public laundry facilities.[12]) And, of course, diapers are just the tip of the iceberg. The absence of federally mandated paid parental leave, piled on top of jobs that pay sub–living wages, piled on top of no paid sick leave for prenatal or pediatricians' appointments, no affordable (or often, even available) childcare. Astronomical health care bills for even the lowest-risk and most straightforward pregnancies and births can bring families with relatively good health insurance to our knees—and *those* families are the lucky few and far between.

Reproductive justice–aligned care workers and organizations have *always* supported families, children, and parents. All Options, known for its secure and anonymous hotline providing information and resources in support of all pregnant people and all pregnancy outcomes, also operates a Pregnancy Resource Center in Indiana. The All-Options PRO provides local families with diapers, supplies, parenting support, and community—*alongside* their Hoosier Abortion Fund.[13] Indigenous Women Rising and the Alabama Cohosh Collaborative, two collectives that fund and support abortion care, both run programs distributing breast pumps and supporting postpartum and breast-/chestfeeding parents in their communities. The reality is that 75 percent of US abortion patients are poor or low-income,[14] and 49 percent live below the federal poverty level (which, in 2021, meant a family of two subsisting on $17,420 or less a year; a family of four, $26,500 or less).[15] So it's easy to see why access to abortion care is a necessity for economic survival in this country, especially if the person seeking it is already a parent when they have their abortion, like almost 60 percent of US patients.[16] As Loretta Ross and Rickie Solinger put it, "the reproductive options that fertile people have are always structured by the resources they have—or do not have."[17] The fight for universal access to good sex education or birth control is inextricably connected to abortion not because those things would serve as "prevention" of abortion (there's no need to prevent something that is safe, normal, and good!), but because all tools of reproductive freedom and power are needed for the world we are trying to build. Support for parents and children is essential and critical, not in order to influence people's choices to procreate (or not), but because everyone is entitled to the basic human rights to birth and parent *if* and *when* and *how* they choose. We must have the information and the resources to make informed decisions about what we do with our bodies, our lives, and our family structures. *That* is reproductive justice.

* * *

When we ground and sustain our community care within a reproductive justice framework, we can begin to unlearn individualism and ego. While we still must operate under capitalism, navigating all of the wealth-hoarding, fame-and-glory-seeking, personal-achievement-obsessed traps it has set for our us—and while we are all still human, with our lifelong need to be seen, heard, and understood for who we are as individuals—viewing abortion care or any other work through an RJ lens can show us, over and over again, that intersectionality[18] means interdependence.

In my conversation with doulas D'andra and Qiana, they emphasize that they do not wish to be cited individually. They work collectively, through the Afiya Center (TAC), a Houston-based RJ organization that serves, in these doulas' words, to "meet each Black womb-holder exactly where they are," and as such, they prefer to be *credited* collectively for their ideas and their words, too. They endeavor to surround themselves at all times, the doulas tell me, with other safe, supportive women, "who are committed to the work," and training more Black community doulas is a major focus of their practice. Individualism and ego have no place here.

TAC, created and run by Black women and for Black women, offers its community peer-driven projects that address birth justice and maternal health, abortion care and access, HIV/AIDS, and intergenerational salons, film screenings, and book discussions. "We really are the women we serve," D'andra and Qiana tell me. "Trust Black women, we know what's best for us."

Because I spend much of my week doing paid clinic work and freelance writing, and because I live in a dual-income household,

I'm able to offer my abortion doula services for free. This allows me to turn no one away, to be accessible to any and all members of my communities without a single question. But I also know that it's a choice borne of privilege, and one that can contribute to a volunteer model that only rich white ladies—a population not reflective of most abortion doula clients—can afford to practice.

Many doulas need or want to be paid for their labor, but *also* need or want to partner with poor and under-resourced, housing-unstable, and unhoused clients in their communities. If a doula cannot do their work for free, and if they don't have access to a collective that fundraises to pay its doulas a salary, such as the Alabama Cohosh Collaborative or the Baltimore Doula Collective, sliding scale models can be used to determine who pays what, and in what circumstances. Such a model creates many access points, allowing for many different price points and funding the offering of our services at no cost to those who cannot pay at all. Many doulas find a sliding scale to be the most essential tool of economic justice in their work—a method of honoring the financial realities of the people they are supporting and also their own. One such framework, used by many care and support workers all over the world, is Alexis J. Cunningfolks's Green Bottle Scale. Even if you never plan to charge money for your care or support work, models like the Green Bottle Scale can help you to locate *yourself* on a socioeconomic map and place yourself in relation to the people around you. A community healing practitioner and herbalist, Cunningfolk and has made their scale widely available online, intending for free usage and sharing across disciplines and communities.

By remaining mindful of what resources we can each bring to the table, and of the lived experience and the expertise of people in the reproductive justice needs of their own bodies, families, and communities, we can resist the white supremacist veneration of hierarchies. Just as trainings and degrees are not what make someone an expert care worker—doing the care work is. We can recognize that the *true* leaders and authority figures, when it comes to a pregnancy or an abortion, are not the CEOs or the lawmakers or the theologians, not the judges or the doctors or boyfriends or parents, not anyone but the person experiencing this pregnancy, this abortion, in this body, and in this moment.

We can follow each other, the people who have experienced pregnancies and abortions of our own.

We can follow us.

Abortion Is Indigenous

As I'm sitting down to interview Q.—the warm and magnetic Mescalero Apache/Laguna Pueblo/Xicana abortion funder of the powerhouse that is Indigenous Women Rising (IWR)—my husband is driving my sleeping baby around and around the block, the portable white noise machine blasting from the belly of its stuffed teddy bear disguise. Both of us, Will and I, are hoping to squeeze just thirty spare minutes from the stone of this day, so that we may do some of our own work; and I couldn't be more grateful to be spending my entire precious half hour of baby-free time on this conversation. Q. appears on my screen, with a radiant smile and a sun-gold Southwestern sky moving across the frame behind them. I hear a little peal of laughter from somewhere just out of frame—there's a child in Q.'s back seat, too.

"You're obviously familiar with land acknowledgments," Q. says when I'm done giving them my standard white-girl disclaimer; acknowledging the tribe on whose unceded land I live and work. "So, within Indian country, we're kind of making fun of those now. Just because it feels very superficial. It's supposed to be a call to action, you know, how do we rematriate lands back to that particular group? Or: Can we figure out how to redistribute resources and push for Indigenous people to take on leadership? Whether that's part of abortion care or anything else."

Which is not to say non-Indigenous people shouldn't begin with that basic information, if they seek to avoid replicating colonialist violence in their care work: "I really think it's important to note that there are five hundred and seventy federally recognized tribes, and two hundred to three hundred state-recognized tribes," Q. tells me. "Starting locally, I do really encourage folks to use [the Native Land map[1]] as a resource to figure out where are you, and who might be there. *Whose land am I on?*"

Q. and their colleagues at IWR have changed the abortion care game, providing a space for Indigenous people to access care, to practice resistance and self-love, and to share their own experiences, on their own terms. The organization was founded in 2014, originally intended "as a campaign to bring attention to the fact that Indigenous women and people who rely on Indian Health Service for health care were being denied access to Plan B, a form of emergency contraception," according to their website.

"This was a huge issue considering the disproportionately high rates of domestic violence and sexual assault on reservations and the limited capability of tribes to prosecute non-Native offenders." Its projects now include an abortion fund,[2] which serves Indigenous and undocumented people nationwide, community breastfeeding support and breast pump access initiatives, and comprehensive and affirming sex education programming. The arms of IWR's activism, advocacy, and community care work reach into *every* part of life impacted by issues of reproductive justice—which is to say, every part of life, period. "A lot of states have an Indian affairs or tribal liaison under the state government," Q. tells me. "Those pages on the state government's website are usually really helpful in showing what tribes are there, the history of them, contact information, their tribal leaders. If a tribe has a website, it's really helpful to see what they have—their community health page. A tribally run clinic, or Indian Health Services. Some of those seem kind of small, but they really are effective in asking if a tribe has a clinic already, a tribal clinic, if they might already have family planning resources. What is your community's stance on abortion, or is there anything we can share, resource-wise?"

The Indian Health Service (IHS), an operating division within the US Department of Health and Human Services, is the only health care available to Native people living on reservations. It is also notorious for denying its Indigenous patients not only Plan B, but also other forms of contraception, adequate sexual assault resources or treatment, and abortion. The Hyde Amendment, since its passage in the 1970s, has barred federal funding for abortion care—disproportionately impacting the ability of low-income people and people of color to end their pregnancies, and discriminating specifically against the Native people who had no choice but to receive their care from a federal agency—IHS. And elsewhere around the globe, Indigenous people are cut off from their own cultural and community practices of sexual and reproductive health care while simultaneously denied the "modern" medical care with which colonizers have supplanted them.

As interest in abortion care work grows, sacred Indigenous knowledge is being repackaged and sold by non-Indigenous folks without acknowledgment—as has previously happened with so many other white-and-monied-people "trends" across multiple disciplines and fields, from *gentle parenting* to the concepts of *foraging* to Carol Dweck's growth mindset theory—originally (and arguably more skillfully) explained by Dr. Martin Brokenleg's Circle of Courage model. At this very moment, a white organizer is teaching (Wabanaki) basket weaving and permaculture workshops to other white people in my rapidly gentrifying city, for profit, without payment to the techniques' originators, on whose land he skateboards and self-promotes. White doulas, midwives, and herbalists are charging hundreds of dollars for access to the (uncredited, uncited) knowledge of wild abortifacients that Indigenous herbal medicine practitioners perfected and preserved.

But Indigenous communities around the world are fighting to retain and expand their forms of doula and companion work, as laws and colonizers seek to forcibly erase them or render them impossible by depleting and destroying the natural resources those forms of care (and the communities who practice them) rely on. Indigenous people in Latin and Central Americas are partnering their ancestral and regional knowledge with the acompañamiento model of supporting someone through an abortion process. This model is practiced all over the globe, from Argentina to Nigeria. An anonymous Indigenous birth worker and abortion companion, who lives in a region where abortion is both illegal and a cultural taboo, tells me that she has led trainings and workshops remotely for several cohorts of abortion companions in her—and neighboring—tribal communities, and she doesn't plan to stop.

"Even for ourselves," Q. says, "we have to remind ourselves: How do we include the communities that *we* come from? It's not meant or built to be easy for us, whether it's feminism or anything else. Name an industry, we were always meant to be left out of it."

Abortion Is Nature

I kneel in the garden; the knees of my jeans soaked through and the cold wet dirt spreading its darkening stain outward, down my shins and up my thighs. It's March, two months after my abortion. My daydreams have been vivid lately, as the ground thaws: I imagine my pregnancy tissue—those scarlet little bits of me, and Will, and our ancestors, and a future I'll never know— absorbed into the earth, under the snow, nourishing the soil around it and maybe even beginning to sprout now. Will this be the week its tiny green buds break through? This particular daydream plays on a loop these days, though I know it to be a fantasy. I have deliberately avoided looking into where or how the clinic disposed of my tissue, in particular, but I have a general sense. I know it involved harsh industrial processes, and medical waste containers composed of materials and dyes not found in anyone's garden. My pregnancy's destination was sealed, sterile. It did not return directly to the earth, and it doesn't grow from it now.

None of this gardening stuff comes naturally to me—not the grit accumulating under my painted fingernails nor the hunchbacked posture I've assumed here, in plain view of my neighbors. I've never had what anyone would call a "green thumb," nor an aptitude for anything that demands a mixture of patience and hard physical labor, nor a good memory for the difference between an annual and a perennial. But when my hands are this filthy, I (probably) won't touch my phone. When the computer's in the house, where I can't see my browser's forty-five open tabs there's a chance I'll be able to close a tab or two inside my brain. And when the sun or the wind or the first raindrop hits my face, I might remember something unnamable, something Very Big and Very True from long before I or any of my ancestors were born. When the birds are out and singing, no walls or windows between us and near enough for me to note the short little phrases that bubble up again and again from their jewel-feathered throats—that's the nearest I can get to it, here on this page.

One of the most potent tools for activating the vagus nerve— the calming mediator of our parasympathetic nervous system—is the sound of birdsong. Evolutionarily, birds only chirp when no predators are around. So birdsong—in all the glory of its chatter and whistles and melodies that dip and soar along the scale— communicates to our bodies that, in this moment, we are safe.

Reproductive justice begins—as all things do—with this violated, exhausted, abundant, living, and breathing earth. I often say that humans have been having abortions for as long as there have been humans, but the truth is, abortion is bigger than our little species could ever conceive of, and older, I think. Mice and monkeys have abortions. Trees abort their offspring; plants abort their unripe fruits. Abortion is older than plastic, and hospitals, and laws, and the Catholic Church. Abortion is older than us.

* * *

Jada's herbalist, a woman she has known and trusted intimately for a long time now, leaves a glass jar on her porch in the blue light of early morning. There is no note attached, no message or instructions. The unlabeled jar sits silently in the freshly fallen snow, waiting patiently for Jada to open her front door, shivering, look around at the empty street, the vacant yards and porches of her neighborhood, and then to discreetly retrieve it. The jar, she knows, contains a mixture of blue cohosh, angelica, juniper berry, bay leaves, and calendula. There may be others—she doesn't remember.

"She just mixed up an herbal blend for me," Jada says. "There are two different types of herbs that she uses—an abortifacient (the actual herbs that terminate a pregnancy) and an emmenagogue, that sort of gets the blood flowing again. So those combined help push everything out and hopefully prevent any complications."

Abortion is not a recent idea, nor a traceable invention of modern medicine. People have been using plants to end pregnancies for as long as we've existed. Herbal abortions often happen so early after the fertilization of an egg that they are simply referred to as "bringing back a missing period." (Not to be confused with "menstrual extraction," a type of manual vacuum aspiration technique that arose from underground abortion care networks in the 1970s.)[1] Enslaved Black people famously used cotton root to induce abortions, and Indigenous communities all over the world have practiced their own herbal abortion and contraception methods for thousands of years. These days, books like *Natural Liberty: Rediscovering Self-Induced Abortion Methods* and community-distributed zines with names like *Wildseed Feminism* and *Hot Pants:*

Do It Yourself Gynecology and Herbal Remedies are widely available, often stocked by (cool) bookstores or passed from doula to doula, midwife to midwife, and friend to friend, all over the world. And there are many other names for the act of ingesting herbs and plants to end a pregnancy and/or induce menstrual bleeding, across the countless cultures and spiritual traditions in which herbal abortion care is widely practiced.

"Humans have used these herbs for a really long time," says Jada, when I ask if she would choose an herbal abortion in the future. "They're tried and true."

* * *

It may not surprise you to know that I—the girl who can kill the heartiest houseplant in a week or less (that's the Hannah Matthews guarantee!), who flunked out of Girl Scouts with nary a single wilderness badge, and who has been one misspelled Google search away from consuming a poisonous berry or mushroom on more than one occasion—am not an expert in herbal abortion care. For that wisdom, an endlessly fascinating body of remedies, recipes, studies, and stories, I turn to zines, to books, to the Indigenous midwives, care workers, and doulas who offer paid courses and workshops and take part in community knowledge-shares. And, of course, I turn to the internet. I turn to folks like daena horner.

daena horner, who uses both she/her and they/them pronouns, is an herbalist, educator, and abortion doula, who I came to know and admire through their wildly popular Instagram account, Holistic Abortions. They work independently and in coalition, partnering with the Abortion on Our Own Terms campaign and collaborating with other experts to create training materials, research, and classes. horner is a font of information, practical skills, ancestral and traditional wisdom resources, and clinical experience around self-managed abortion.

"I came into this work through lived experience. I was the friend people asked to come with them to their abortions," horner tells me. "My own clinical abortion left me feeling uncared for and unseen by the medical system, [so] I sought to avoid going to a clinic for my next abortion. I sought herbal remedies and community-sourced misoprostol. I combined these methods and the experience changed everything for me. I was lucky to find the knowledge and support I needed in that moment." Experience is power, as many of us learn in ways we never plan or wish to— and horner's own experience is the foundation of the community they've built.

"Community-led care shouldn't be about luck or privilege (or desperation from lack of clinical access)," says horner. "Abortions are more than releasing tissue. People are often processing complex emotions, like the intergenerational shame and traumas our mothers and grandmothers went through, and bearing witness to that growth is beautiful."

I ask horner what they tell the people who come to them in search of starting points or inroads—whether looking to become proficient at herbal abortion care themselves, or just hoping for some basic plant knowledge. "Start talking to your friends and communities, start building a strong in-person network, share your stories together, practice exams, build a safety plan together, eat meals together." But, horner reminds me, when she speaks of community, relationships, she does not only mean those shared between humans. "When I say that in order to get through this we need one another, I mean our plant and animal friends, too. I mean our land and soil. Build *those* relationships. Find where supportive plants grow in your garden, town, or region, and start visiting them. Bring them gifts, leave some water, plant some seeds, start the slow process of building healthy, fertile soil."

Above all, horner wants us to dream. To ask ourselves not just *How will I support people?* But to get creative, expansive. To use our imaginations.

"As a dear friend of mine reminds me often," horner tells me, "*we cannot go to a place we cannot imagine.*"

Abortion Is Care

On June 24, 2022, Alabama's total abortion ban—its so-called Human Life Protection Act—will go into effect. The law allows no exceptions for rape or incest. It will force many sudden closures of reproductive health clinics across the state—the sole providers of *any* form of affordable health care, in many communities—and will trigger fresh waves of the suffering, violence, and dismal health outcomes already faced by its population—not coincidentally, one of the poorest and Blackest populations in the nation.

But right now, the sun is shining in Huntsville. A warm golden light filters through the leaves on this autumn afternoon of 2021, in this place where—with many caveats and restrictions—abortion is still legal. The yellowhammers sing to one another from the trees. I'm speaking with the doulas of the Alabama Cohosh Collaborative (ACC) about their lives, their children, their pregnancies, their abortions, and their work supporting the six hundred to eight hundred people who still come through the Alabama Women's Center for Reproductive Healthcare (AWC) each year for their in-clinic abortion procedures, as they will continue to do until the moment it becomes illegal, on that Friday morning seven months from now.

But we don't have a clear view to that day yet, and right now, a doula named Catessa is laughing.

After she pulls into her parking space at the AWC, but before she walks into the clinic for her doula shift, Catessa listens to upbeat music. She practices cycles of deep and calming breaths, holding her limbs loose and her body relaxed and still, and repeats a series of positive affirmations to herself. The doula sits alone, her car's air-conditioning and sound system still shielding her from the oppressive Alabama sun and the clinic's protesters screaming their threats and prayers at the staff, patients, and families arriving and departing. She steels herself for the swirling, hours-long rush of emotional intensity that will be, for the abortion doula, just another workday. She turns off the car. She takes one last deep breath, smiles, meets her own calm eyes in the rearview mirror. She steps out onto the pavement, into the angry heat, the chaos and the noise.

More often than not, these days, Catessa finds herself supporting people for whom an abortion is not a "choice" in any real sense of the word. Many of the AWC's patients are here in hopes of accessing the *only* viable option available to them and their families, within the systems determined to make pregnancy, birth, and parenting as dangerous and difficult as possible for Black women, poor women, trans folks—anyone other than those whom white supremacy deems deserving of survival. Catessa first came to this work through the Alabama Cohosh Collaborative, and through it she has found a home like none other she's ever known.

"I'm kind of a ball of bubbly happiness," Catessa says, when I ask about her pre-doula-shift state of mind, "so I try not to be too too *too* happy, like"—she throws her head back, away from the phone and yells—"*HEY, YOU'RE GETTING AN ABORTION!!!*"

The noises of her kids playing, echoing shouts in the background, weave through our laughter. "So sometimes I have to hold it in, like: *Okay, girl, calm down, yes, we want to be positive, [but] we don't want to be tossing up confetti or anything like that.*"

As Catessa—who is also a labor and birth doula, an entrepreneur, and a mama of four—walks me through her pre-shift rituals in her soothing Alabama drawl, I feel my own shoulders and jaw relax, the smile on my face expanding reflexively and unforced, my breathing slow. "I just need to be kind, and to exude love . . . in those moments, especially for those clients who take it the deepest, to be able to be that pillar of light for them."

Importantly, the doulas of the ACC are paid for their hours spent providing care and support, a decision that was made with intentionality by the collaborative's founders, who include Dr. Yashica Robinson and Kirsten Clark. "We were really passionate about sustainability and doulas being paid for their work. And we had worked with volunteer collectives before, and it's not to say that those shouldn't exist, but there are barriers to access for people who want to be doulas. It's rich white ladies who are able to donate their time, and people who don't have kids. And *that* is problematic on another scale."

Volunteer work has never been sustainable in the long term for Clark, who has a family to support and financial burdens of her own to carry. So donors, she says, were an important piece of the puzzle. The doulas of the ACC get paid $25 an hour, and anyone who comes to the clinic can receive their services at no cost.

"And we're able to have more cultural congruence," Clark says, "because most of our patients are *not* rich white ladies."

According to the Alabama Department of Public Health, more

than 60 percent of people who have abortions in the state are Black, and the majority of them already have children. Moreover, nearly two-thirds of Alabama counties lack hospitals that offer obstetric care. Nationally, pregnant Black Americans are nearly three times as likely to die of pregnancy-related causes than are non-Hispanic white women, according to the CDC,[1] but in Alabama, they are five times more likely than white women to die. An abortion ban, by definition a racist and classist tool of state control, can be more than just oppressive, cruel, and dangerous. It can be a literal death sentence. So many of the patients who will need Catessa's support at the Alabama Women's Center today are here to terminate pregnancies that they might have been able to meet with joy and excitement were they not violently and systematically denied access to the tools and resources necessary for prenatal and postpartum health, parenting, and survival. The grief that can accompany an abortion sought of necessity, rather than desire, the grief of a decision to end a wanted pregnancy, can be bottomless. Alabama Cohosh Collaborative doulas frequently witness and hold space for unspeakably painful loss and mourning.

One very young patient of the AWC remains present—alive, but frozen in time, moving and speaking—in the doula's mind, to this day. The smallest details of this high school student and her abortion experience are still vivid and sharp-edged, holding their form for Catessa even now, several years and hundreds of patients later.

"She wanted to actually give birth to the baby, but I don't think that she felt like it would have been the right thing to do. [She was there] so that she could have a better chance at life. Which is exactly how I felt," says Catessa, referring to her own first pregnancy, which she'd experienced as a young and frightened student herself.

"But she was strong enough to sit there, and she went through the whole entire procedure." The girl clung to Catessa, in need of shelter, softness, strength. In need of a still point as the room turned. In need of mothering.

"She's crying, she's holding my hand," Catessa remembers. "There are clients who . . . a lot of times, they don't want to be touched. They want to completely dissociate from the whole entire thing. But I still at least like to ask if I can have my hand on their shoulder. Or (if not) just talking them through the procedure, asking them if they're okay, and just reinforcing and letting them know that they're strong." Catessa closes her eyes, the face and mannerisms of this young patient still vivid in her mind—her family and her circumstances, the clothing she wore, the sound of her cries. "But she wanted to be touched. She was squeezing my hand very tightly, and she would even lean her head into my shoulder. So then I would just lean in closer, too." Tears encroach, Catessa's voice becoming softer and thicker with emotion. "Heck, if I could have, I would have just held her, through the entire thing."

"That was another one of those times that I really needed to talk to someone afterwards, too. More than the procedure itself, it's for me more about the emotions that the clients experience when they're going through it," says Catessa. "And half the time, I just want to take them home with me. To say: *It's okay. We can eat ice cream. I understand.*"

* * *

"You know, a lot of people don't really see the *point* of abortion doulas." Scarlet is half smiling, squinting up at the sky as her dog, a pit bull mix, loops around us in a particularly joyful case of The Zoomies, kicking up a track of grass and dirt in her sun-drenched backyard.

I feel each syllable of the statement land in my body with a heavy thud. Sounds rush in to fill the quiet between us, as I absorb this blow, try to consider her stance—a chickadee calls, a squirrel chatters and scrambles noisily, the sweet-faced dog's collar jingles as he does his enthusiastic laps. "Clinic staff already provide such amazing support, you know? It just seems like this extra, unnecessary thing, and like it adds to the stigma and the perception of abortion as some horrible difficult trauma."

It's not the first time that someone has expressed this skepticism to me, these laughing doubts about the usefulness of my work, and it won't be the last. The nebulous understanding of just what a doula even is, exactly, and what role we could possibly play in what often *is* a brief, straightforward, and routine medical process. The suggestion that even a fraction of the trauma or the danger inherent to childbirth is necessarily present in an abortion (it's not). The very existence of an "abortion doula" implies, to some, that abortion clinic staff and abortion providers can't or don't provide sufficiently holistic care on their own—a suggestion at which my own clinic coworkers sometimes bristle. And I get it. I really do.

But the plain truth of being a clinic worker is that, in those hours when I'm wearing my scrubs and my name tag and answering to nurses and doctors and managers: I am generally responsible for making a few parts of one appointment happen smoothly, over and over again, for twenty patients a day. I'm a cog in a wheel. And while I often do support these folks in other, less rigidly defined forms—fetching coloring books and crayons for their kids, or calling a taxi company and walking them to the corner, communicating at length with those patients in the hours and days before and after their abortions—I will shore up against the limitations of the job every time. Not the human limitations of my own body, mind, or heart; not the limitations of my capacity and will, or those of the person having their abortion. But corporate policies, federally mandated procedures and protocols, the twin engines of the medical and nonprofit industrial complexes—these things chip away at our capacity for community care with low wages, long hours, under-resourced clinics with under-trained staff, and overwhelming patient volumes. When I take off my scrubs and name tag at the end of a clinic shift and become just a community abortion doula again, I'm free (and not just because the bra comes off, too).

As a doula, I answer only to the person I am supporting. They write my job description and my employee handbook, though I may help to give them some of the language and parameters and ideas required to do so. Together, that person and I, we make our own rules, our own space for something singular, something new, something that may be strange, or beautiful, or life-changing, or all of those things, or none of them. And, sometimes, it's something no one else needs to ever even know about. Something no HR department could ever pin down, design a slide deck for, contain within the boundaries of a job description. Something that can and may always be just between us.

* * *

Were I to hit PLAY on a cool training montage here, it would be a lot less *Rocky* stair running or sexy *Dirty Dancing* choreography and a lot more me, hunched over in bed, eating peanut butter M&M'S

and underlining passages and opening yet more tabs in my laptop's browser. I discover online communities of doulas, the trainings and spaces created collaboratively, for us and by us, all over the world. I pore over *The Radical Doula Guide*'s blog, with all its joyful revelations, its radical, new-to-me work and organizations and people and ideas. I feel the flutter of wings in my chest. From interviews with doulas on Miriam Zoila Pérez's blog, I am led to some essential sources of knowledge, doors and windows opening into concepts and books and talks and classes and workshops and music and art. All of it whispers, or shouts, or sings: *doula.*

Why aren't we talking about this at the clinic? I wonder. *Why isn't an abortion doula present in the room for the appointment of every patient who wants or needs this type of community, witness, companionship, and support?*

The bird inside my chest learns to stand. It rises up on its shaky little spindles of legs.

I begin to learn from a local doula, whom I'd known vaguely through my local circles of abortion care and activism folks. She is a full-spectrum doula, with years of knowledge and wisdom about birth, abortion, harm reduction, supporting pregnant people in our local communities. She is intimately familiar with all of our city's strange little municipal quirks, the ever-changing weather of state laws and regional politics, and with the burdens and barriers and loopholes and workarounds specific to our own small time and place.

The bird opens its wings. It takes flight.

I find my way to Dopo, an international cooperative that takes its name from the Italian word for "after" (a nod to the fact that there is no term equivalent to "postpartum" to describe what is often an incredibly rich, complicated, and transitional period of time that follows an abortion). The bird spreads its wings wider and soars above the clouds. The air becomes perfectly clear. Zachi Brewster, Dopo's creator and co-facilitator, is a doula who found the lack of support available to her following her own abortion startling and unacceptable. What sparse resources and organizations she *did* find seemed to be concerned primarily with people mourning miscarriages and planning future pregnancies.

"I hoped for a space that understood what I was going through without needing to justify, overexplain, or gloss over the delicate orb of contradictory emotions I was holding. I wanted advice on how to be compassionate towards myself, and reconnect with my body," Brewster wrote of her experience, in a blog post on Dopo's official website. "I needed someone to just be there for me."

Just be there for me: an ask that doesn't require you to have a medical degree, a position of power, a decade of experience, or a surplus of material resources. A plea that sits at the heart of a doula's purpose and day-to-day work. A reason to deal with all the bureaucratic bullshit and the inconveniences and to work as hard as you can to be honest about, to set aside, and to work to destroy your own biases and stigmas and fill the gaps in your knowledge. To rest, to nourish and water and feed, to be there for *yourself*—so you can then show up for someone else.

You don't need a 501(c)(3) status, a degree, or a state license to help your sibling, your neighbor, or even a stranger. You can, simply, at any moment: learn about what they need and want, consider the specifics of what is safe and accessible for them, and identify your role(s) in assisting them. And then you can take action. You can make yourself a house, and you can just be open and safe and comfortable and there for them. Solid and steady and still.

A house needs a foundation and comfortable furniture. It needs space for someone to move through, and peaceful quiet for them to speak. What you should try to have in order to just be there for someone (including yourself) before, during, and after an abortion:

- Basic knowledge of the laws and the parameters of care where the abortion is happening. I have found the websites abortionfinder.org, abortionpillinfo.org, and ineedana.com to be helpful, as well as Reproaction's Fake Clinic Database,[2] an up-to-date map of all the discoverable antiabortion crisis pregnancy centers in the United States. Robin Marty's *New Handbook for a Post-Roe America* is an essential resource, too. An understanding of the bodily processes involved in the different types of abortion (in-clinic procedures at different stages of a pregnancy; medication abortions— both self-managed and clinically supervised; herbal abortions if that is something that is provided in your communities), and of what they may look and feel like as the person undergoes them.

- An active desire to identify, examine, and unlearn the stigmas, misconceptions, and biases that you've collected over the course of your life and that you may still be harboring now. Their roots can be deep and strong, and they can break ground in unexpected places, so it's essential to be aware of them and prepare for them to trip you up.

- A fluid, always-evolving understanding of your own strengths and limitations, a fluency in communicating them, and an ability to orient (and continuously reorient) yourself and the person you are supporting toward pleasure, joy, and connection when possible.

- An understanding of abortion as an issue of reproductive justice, and of how intersecting identities and lived experiences can shape a person's reproductive life and determine their ability to access and exercise their bodily autonomy. An understanding of your own social location and how it shapes your worldview and your cultural competence.

A patchwork of needs and abilities necessitates a patchwork of care and support, and there will be times you can only provide someone with a simple piece of the quilt. A ride to an appointment, or a donation to a fund, or a casserole baked for someone's family, or a few hours of time spent with the person as they recover and heal; these are all essential jobs, and they can each be done by a different person. There may be times you can't provide them with anything—because of their safety or yours, financial limitations, a lack of capacity, or a need to focus your time and attention elsewhere. But if you *can* help connect someone to trusted resources that will fulfill their other needs, or even if you just contribute your one small part—you are doing the work of a doula.

Doulas, as I said, are *not* doctors (anyone who's ever caught me in the act of googling "red bump on wrist itchy NOT a bug bite" or "how do you know when a headache is cancer?" can most certainly attest to that). I am not a medical expert of any kind (though I have worked in clinical reproductive health care settings), nor am I a scholar of public health or sociology with a PhD. I'm just a person who has seen abortion up close and from many different angles, who is passionate to the point of evangelism about protecting your (and my!) bodily autonomy, whose purpose on this planet is to provide care and support for other human beings, and who is endlessly angry and heartbroken about the ways in which abortion care has been deliberately stigmatized, politicized, and made so needlessly traumatic for all of us—and especially for those of us who are already marginalized and traumatized at every turn. Abortion is routine health care, a procedure that is simpler than a root canal or a series of medications safer than Tylenol. And yet, the sheer amount of interpersonal and structural support that can be required for someone to get this care in the way they need, in the way that is safest and healthiest for them, can be enormous.

Care worker is my role in the revolution. The importance of finding your place—flexible and adaptable as you may still need to be, over the years—and staying in your lane came up in nearly every conversation I've had with folks about the different forms of community abortion care they're practicing in their lives. When I close my eyes and envision *my* lane, I think of James Baldwin making the distinction between the roles of *writer* and *spokesman*: "I am a witness. . . . A spokesman assumes that he is speaking for others. . . . I never assumed that I could." Baldwin described himself as "a witness to what I've seen and **the possibilities that I think I see**."[3] There are places you haven't seen yet, places you've never been or even imagined, where you already belong.

* * *

River does want their pregnancy, and they want it very, very badly. But a fetal anomaly renders that pregnancy unable to survive, which they and their partner have just learned at twenty weeks. After an anatomy scan, River is told that the anomaly is virtually guaranteed to create a life that wanting cannot save. The love that River feels for the fetus growing inside them is real and overwhelming. But no depth, no volume, no amount of love and desire for the fetus will relieve its future suffering, or prolong its brief and agonizing time on earth. So River has made an appointment, devastated, distraught, swallowed by anticipatory grief. We communicate via text messages and phone calls, mostly. They cry and cry on the other end of the phone. It is 2020, and our state is awash in its first wave of COVID-19 infections. No one is allowed to accompany River to their appointment, not even their partner, and they sit alone in the clinic waiting room, staring down the barrel of a panic attack. Their grief and anxiety—descending alongside the nausea and the intense hormonal shifts that occur in any pregnancy—are threatening to bury them alive, they tell me.

Were I sitting next to them in this moment, I would ask to rub River's back. I would offer my hands for them to squeeze. I would breathe deeply with them. I would talk them through the ebbs and flows. But, from my little apartment on the other side of town, I can only give them words. So I do. I tell them how proud I am that they are already a parent and a damn good one at that. I tell them what a loving and powerful act of parenting this is—to make this personal sacrifice, and take on this pain, to prevent the suffering of the being that would have become their child. I do a little mantra with them, one I first learned from a doula of my own, though she likely wouldn't have called herself that at the time.

"You are the deep blue ocean," my doula-who-was-not-a-doula said to twenty-six-year-old me, and I hear my thirty-four-year-old self say it to River in turn. "You are not the crashing wave."

"You are not the crashing wave," my doula-who-was-not-a-doula repeated, reversing the order of the statements as she brushed a strand of sweaty hair away from my temple. "You"—she kissed each cheek and folded me tightly into her arms—"are the deep blue ocean."

I pass this to River now, across time and space. They are the deep blue ocean, too.

* * *

Three months later, the seasons changing and life running rough-shod over me as usual, I run into River, unexpectedly, at a backyard potluck. Their full, smiling mouth is a jewel, painted in a deep berry shade of lipstick, and they've baked a delicate three-tiered chocolate cake. They sing and joke and ask questions and do impressions and argue playfully, late into the evening. They're the life of the party. Eyes full of laughter, they regale us with tales of their chaotic three-year-old; her hellish sleep patterns, the complicated games she invents for the family—designed so that there may only be one winner: her—her penchant for pterodactyl-pitched shriek-ing when she becomes enraged, or excited, or bored. Friends and community members surround River on all sides, passing them full steins of cold beer and bowls of ice cream, and handing them wool blankets to drape across their shoulders and their lap as the sun dips below the trees. River moves seamlessly in and out of full-chested laughter and intimate conversations, answering questions about their work, their garden, the books they've been reading and the books they want to read next.

As the party winds down, the fire sparking and crackling as it dies, the orchestra of voices becoming thinner and thinner as guests drop away into the night one by one, River approaches me. They look into my eyes, reach out for both my hands with both of theirs. They give me a private smile. "I'm in such a good place now," they say, weaving their fingers through mine and squeezing. "Thank you."

We both know what they're referring to: the minutes and hours and days and weeks that they're holding in stark contrast to *this* moment of their life, this "now." They open their arms, we hug tightly, we say goodbye. I don't know when or if I'll see them again, but I'm so grateful to have witnessed them both then and now.

We go forward, our paths branching away from each other, but in parallel and with two shared memories now. I give a little wave as River climbs into their car, backs out of our friends' shared driveway, wheels spitting gravel. They pull out onto the long, pine-flanked, star-lit road, heading home to the little house in the woods where that whirling dervish of a three-year-old daughter is, finally, mercifully, asleep. I watch River drive, moving forward and away from me.

You are the deep blue ocean, I think, as I watch their taillights retreat into the darkness. *You are not the crashing wave.*

Interlude:

Abortion Is All the Stuff

in My Doula Bag

Every person's needs, resources, and abilities are different, of course, but here's some of what I like to try and gather, if I know in advance that I'll be accompanying someone.

TOOLS FOR THE BODY

- **A notebook/journal and pens,** to keep track of symptoms and sensations, timelines, notable events, and medical information. An abortion experience can be a blur—especially if sedation is involved—and it's always safest to have a basic record of what exactly has been happening in a body and when (and then to burn or shred this record afterward).
- **Heating pads!** There are some brands that stick to your underwear or clothing that are disposable and allow for freedom of movement. But one of those big old-

fashioned plug-in babies always works, too. And you can make your own, if you're crafty—more on that later.

- **Disposable gloves.**
- **Fold-up emesis bags,** like the kind you'd find in a hospital or on a plane.
- **Maxi pads.**
- **Ibuprofen/Tylenol.**
- **Snacks,** especially nausea-friendly ones, like crackers, pretzels, Cheez-Its, ginger ale, herbal teas.
- **Water.**
- **Tissues.**

TOOLS FOR THE MIND AND HEART

- Paper for journaling, drawing, coloring.
- Laughter and jokes (when the vibe is right).
- Guided meditations, verbal anesthesia, and breath work/guided imagery experiences (e.g., "This part of the process may be painful or overstimulating, so let's focus on that painting on the wall. What colors are in the painting?" etc.).
- Questions designed to ground the person and zoom out of what is happening in a moment (e.g., "Are you reading any good books right now?" or "What are you doing this weekend?").
- Mantras or affirmations to do the same (e.g., "You are the deep blue ocean, you are not the crashing wave," or verbal breaths. A verbal breath can mean slowly breath-

ing in on *I am loved* and breathing out on *I love.* Or an inhale on *I have enough* and an exhale on *I am enough.*).

• Resources for so-called self-care—I love to send folks home with copies of the Doula Project's free *DIY Doula* zine,[4] which anyone can download and print out, and which frankly and honestly acknowledges the perspectives on the very concept of self-care from those who must stay focused on *survival.*

Abortion Is Survival

Abortion was my liberation, that's how it touched me.
I needed both those abortions. . . . I cannot imagine
what my life would be today if I had not had abortion.
I would have chewed my leg off, like a wolf in a trap—
whatever that translates to, I would have done.
—Viva Ruiz

"You're on the schedule," P. says, her hand warm and gentle on my shoulder. "Four o'clock. Alexis can see you as soon as her last patient leaves."

We have been working in parallel roles at the clinic for only a few months, but P. is like a lantern swinging in the dark for me; her long blond hair and big smile a warm glow cutting through the bleakness of the news cycles and bad-news-filled meetings, her arms a respite on the increasingly frequent days when one of us would leave an exam room or rise from a desk chair, turn to the other person and offer, "Hug?" Like me, P. feels things deeply; like me, she's been raised to apologize early and often. Like me, she sometimes has to step away from our work—to cry in a supply closet, or stretch her limbs in a hallway, or take some deep slow breaths alone in whatever darkened office she can find.

"Thank you, buddy," I manage quietly, placing my shaky hand over hers. I know there is still one more favor I have to ask of her, my lovely friend who's already moved mountains in order to squeeze me into our packed patient schedule. My medication abortion will cost me $555 up front. My bank account balances flash across the screen of my thousand-tabs-open mind. Personal checking: $142.70. Family checking: just barely enough for mortgage and groceries. Family savings: recently depleted by payments to the medical providers and collections agencies still flooding my mailbox with their clear-plastic-windowed envelopes. The old pickup truck is in the shop accruing new charges every day on an itemized bill we haven't seen yet, our kind but gruff mechanic up to his elbows, at this very moment, in its years of oil and grime. The station wagon needs four new tires, and soon, new brakes. The baby is growing too tall for his car seat, though its packaging had made us emphatic promises that it would "grow with" him when we bought it. Its capacity and height limits proving to be no match for our off-the-growth-charts Paul Bunyan of a child. His feet, clad in baby Crocs or rainbow grippy socks, or (more likely) chunky and grass-stained and bare, already dangle off the seat's bottom edge.

My medical insurance plan categorically denies any coverage of abortion care. (Other gems excerpted from my PPO's Explanation of Benefits include: *Your newborn will be subject to their own cost-sharing for covered services beginning on their date of birth*. And in the section explaining that I am responsible for 20 percent of the full cost of any prenatal care, the coverage bizarrely defines any and all pregnancy-related services as *maternity care for mother and child*, despite the fact that an embryo or fetus is—medically! prescriptively!—not a child, and despite the fact that many pregnant people (a) are not "mothers" in any sense of the word and (b) need medical attention that is not "maternity care" . . . whatever that term even means.)

I burn with shame as I open my mouth and let the bird of what I hope will be my last Big Ask fly out, the beat of its wings my strained, embarrassed whisper. "Any chance of funding, you think?"

P. laughs, "On *our* salary? Big chance, love."

She sits down at her keyboard, takes a sip from her coffee mug, and—as she and I have both done countless times before—opens a new instant message to our clinic's abortion-fund coordinators. We wait in silence for an answer, a percentage, a dollar amount. *OK*, comes the response from one of the coordinators after a moment, *let me see what we can do.* A few minutes later: *We can cover it. One of the funds will give us $385, and we can use $170 from another fund. The patient won't have to pay anything today.*

My shoulders drop. I want to sob with relief, to grab P. and squeeze her delicate frame in a tight rough hug, to do a humiliating dance of some kind. But another patient is at the door. I need to get back to work, to make money, to pay for all the other life-and-death things that aren't this abortion.

Abortion funds are autonomous collectives of people—sometimes paid staff, but far more often volunteers with full-time jobs, who squeeze this work into lunch breaks and late nights and weekends—who raise and distribute the money required to have an abortion. The cost of an abortion can vary wildly, depending on your geography, gestational age, provider, and other medical, legal, and logistical circumstances. The average cost of a surgical abortion at ten weeks was $508 in 2014, according to the Guttmacher Institute, with location- and circumstance-dependent price tags ranging from $75 to $2,500. A medication abortion at ten weeks or less cost an average of $535 that year, according to the same source, but what patients must pay for their care can range from $75 to $1,633 or more.

Funds are, by and large, local and independent, though they often collaborate with one another, across city and state lines, to get people their abortions. Increasingly, as draconian laws force patients to travel farther and farther from their lives and communities, to cover more and more ground in their journey to obtain their five pills or their ten-minute procedure from a clinic, multiple funds are partnering to provide one person or one family with the money and the practical support they need. (Of course, there are some barriers that cannot be funded away—by design. If people have no source of trusted childcare, no work leave, no freedom or documentation or safe way to travel, they are forced to stay pregnant and give birth against their will, no matter how much money can be raised and pledged for them.)

Abortion funds give someone $500—or $750, or $2,000, or $443.68, or $20—and in doing so they create whole futures, whole people, whole lives, whole worlds. The funding that paid for my abortion came not from my government or my health insurance company or my employer. It came from people, like you and me, from individual human beings who make up yet another village of care.

This village was paying for my son to have all the food and clothing and books he needs, for his health care and toys, for him to have a living mama, in a healthy body, with capacity and joy to spare. They paid for me to avoid falling behind on my mortgage and student loan payments. They paid for my parents to receive flowers on their birthdays. They paid for my car to have its oil replaced and transport me safely to work. They paid for me to write these words to you. That may seem like hyperbole, but the plain fact of the matter is this: without that $555 for my abortion, there would be none of this.

*　*　*

When SB 8, Texas's draconian six-week abortion ban (with a wildly unconstitutional bounty-hunter enforcement mechanism tacked on to it for good measure), takes effect in September 2021, Martina is twenty-five years old. She becomes, in an instant, one of the millions of Americans of reproductive age who are, suddenly, hundreds and hundreds of miles away from the nearest source of in-clinic abortion care.[1] She will need thousands of dollars, she comes to understand, for the travel, lodging, supplies, and the actual health care costs incurred. Thousands of dollars she does not have, and cannot hope to earn at her minimum-wage job. She can't think of a way to safely crowdfund her abortion, as any one of her family members, coworkers, or neighbors, any acquaintance or stranger who might happen upon her GoFundMe or hear about her predicament through her small town's grapevine—has a new state-funded incentive to punish her for seeking care. Any bystander or casual social media browser could be awarded a bounty of $10,000 by the state of Texas for successfully suing anyone found to have "aided and abetted" Martina's abortion by providing her with resources, shelter, transportation, or even advice.

Enter the National Network of Abortion Funds, an expansive and powerful collective of local and national organizations. As of October 2020, nearly one hundred abortion funds across the country (and three international funds[2]) were listed as members of the network on its site. Of course, other funds exist outside the network, and many practical support organizations and doula collectives also give money and resources directly to abortion seekers in their systems of care, whether they technically consider themselves to be abortion funds or not. The local fund that ultimately paid for Martina's abortion costs in full has helped hundreds of other people in Texas in the handful of months since I spoke with her.

And that lifesaving, world-changing, future-creating money that flows through abortion funds every day? It isn't coming from the pockets of venture capitalists or the estates of famous philanthropists, with the rarest of exceptions. It's coming from community members, neighbors, providers, and clinic workers, from people who are often barely making ends meet themselves. ("All of us abortion folks just digging in our couch cushions," one fund's executive director says, "passing the same two quarters back and forth forever.") It's coming from me when my paycheck has stretched beyond my family's needs. It's coming from the advance I received from my publisher to research and write this book. And it's coming—if you paid for the copy you're reading right now—from you.

"I think that anybody can send money to an abortion fund to make sure that access is maintained," Loretta Ross tells me on the phone. **"I think that's the minimum a feminist should do, even if** they can't do anything else—support access by sending money to an abortion fund." (Emphasis mine.)

THE TEXAS EQUAL ACCESS FUND / TEA FUND

"I was doing repro work before I knew I was," says Kamyon Conner, the director of the Texas Equal Access Fund. "Like, as a kid. Teaching people about menstruation and how to actually use a tampon. Or I knew where they could get free birth control and free condoms when I was a teenager, so . . ."

We both laugh. I'm laid up in bed with COVID, and Conner's assistant has squeezed our conversation into a packed schedule. Exhaustion is palpable, on both ends of the call. Texas funds are reeling in the months following SB 8's passage and enaction. Conner, a queer Black activist and a former vice president of the National Network of Abortion Funds' board of directors, is exhausted but not slowing down.

The Texas Equal Access (TEA) Fund provides financial assistance to people living in north, east, and west Texas who cannot afford their abortions. According to their official website, nearly half of TEA Fund's clients are already parenting at least one child, and 70 percent are people of color. "Quite a few of our callers are from rural communities and have to travel to access abortion," the site reads. Through their helpline, the fund supports people with Medicaid, private health insurance, or no health care coverage at all, paying grants of $300 on average to the clinics that have provided their care. And the TEA Fund has long been filling the emotional and practical needs of Texans who have abortions, too.

TEA Fund's PATH (post-abortion truth & healing) group provides a confidential space for emotional support and connection for people who have had abortions. Anyone who has had an abortion is welcome to join.

"The PATH group was thought up by our social worker," says Conner. "It's one of the first things that she wanted to bring to our organization."

Some of the fund's staff members connected with other folks who'd had abortions in the area and wanted to keep in touch. From those seeds grew the garden of the PATH group.

"It's only people who have had abortions, those are the people that come, those are the people who facilitate the space. They talk about abortion, but it's more about having a sense of community," Conner explains. "Because we'd heard from a lot of folks that they were the only person that they knew, because no one talks about it, because of stigma. So now they all know other people."

Conner explains how they trained volunteer abortion doulas for TEA Fund, initially for both in-person and textual support. When COVID-19 struck, the text line became the main component of the program. At first it was for resources and abortion funding, but now it has bloomed into so much more. "They can text anonymously with anyone who just wants support, who wants to talk through the day, and if they have questions about what's happening, their procedure, if they want to talk about *Bridgerton*." Conner chuckles. "You know, whatever it is."

I burst out laughing. Of the last three people I've supported through abortions or options counseling, I tell Conner, all three have mentioned the soapy, steamy historical drama series. *Bridgerton*—the gorgeous cast, the choreographed dances, all those heaving breasts that spill out of Regency-era gowns, and those unlikely rendezvous in marble-columned gazebos—is a great unifier of abortion patients and workers, it turns out, from Texas to Maine, from five-week procedures to twenty-five-week procedures.

Conner's path to directing the fund has been steady and straight beginning with consistent volunteer shifts and joining its board in 2013. They've held numerous positions, from intake coordinator to treasurer, with crash courses in leadership and grassroots fundraising along the way. "Nobody taught me how to fundraise." Conner laughs. "TEA Fund taught me how to fundraise, the real way."

We talk about the discomfort of fundraising, the complicated social and political dance of it.

"And being in this position, in this nation, in Texas, being someone who's looked at racially as someone who asks for help, right?" says Conner. "It's probably one of the places where I, in this role that I'm in now, have experienced the most amount of racism."

The space of philanthropy has always centered the wealthy white people who flex their power at will, and those who are socially connected with them. To be forced into that racist dynamic, over and over, against the backdrop of Texas's shifting legal landscape and escalation of state control over its citizens' bodies—in particular poor Texans, immigrants, and the Black, Indigenous, and other Texans of color who are the majority of the state's abortion seekers—has been compounding stress in what is already an acutely stressful job.

"The conditions in which we are being forced to work are extremely unideal," Conner says, referring to the collective trauma of community abortion care workers and funders everywhere, and to the specific trauma of funding abortions in Texas, as the state begins to strip away abortion rights and to aggressively prosecute those who would continue to exercise those rights. "Just having this constant anxiety . . . and that became really apparent at first. I mean, there's no way to prepare all the way for how something's going to make you feel, until you're living through it. So I don't know that there's more we could have done to prepare. But after living through it, I was like . . . I gotta take some space."

Space and distance are, for those who do the work of caring for their communities, like oxygen or water. Nonnegotiable. But they are also the first sacrifices we make at the altar of our work—because it calls to us on a soul level, because it calls to our bank accounts on a reality level, because we love deeply those who, we know, will have to pick up our slack if and when we do step away, and because in abortion work specifically—there is so much unmet need, such large-scale and visceral pain and suffering, and so many people who are not abstract statistics or political slogans to us. When we step away, we are stepping away from the real human beings—their bodies and faces and children and struggles and lives—whose physical and emotional spaces we have the wild privilege of entering, sharing, of helping to repair and to build.

"But now, I tell folks: I can tell you what we're doing, what we've been doing, but this is not sustainable. This is no way for folks to be accessing health care. And it's not sustainable to force us to work this way, either," says Conner, of the funds and providers and care workers who have been looking to Texas for guidance, reaching out to TEA Fund and asking for help, advice, a playbook for continuing our support work as states go dark, one by one.

"We can keep doing this," Conner says, "but it's like plugging up leaks in the dam."

* * *

In a perfect world, abortion doulas and care workers would be free
to focus on emotional support. We would never have to figure out
how to get a community member to a clinic hours away, or how
to transport them across the country. We wouldn't lay awake at
night wondering how we were going to help fund people's health
care and childcare and transportation costs, how we were going to
help keep them safe from criminalization, incarceration, violence.
Care workers would not have to cosplay as lawyers or accountants
or businesspeople, just to play our role in keeping our communities
alive and afloat.

But the realities of the world we *do* inhabit demand that much
of our time and energy *is* spent on these practical, logistical, and
indirect forms of support. Before we can do the work of emotional
support for someone having an abortion, some basic needs must
be met first. Practical support organizations (PSOs), like the Brigid
Alliance (which helps fund and coordinate travel and lodging for
people forced to leave their states in order to receive their abortion
care), are scattered throughout the country and are a vital part of
this basic-needs-meeting scaffolding. A list organized by Apiary
collects the practical support organizations by geography, for easy
reference.[3] They call this gathering of resources "centralizing information without centralizing power."

PSOs are getting more specific and more creative all the time:
Elevated Access, an organization of commercial pilots offering free
flights to abortion seekers forced to travel, and the Haven Coalition,
a New York City collective of volunteer residents who provide safe
housing and transportation to appointments for out-of-towners,

are two examples of the operations created to identify and then fill very specific gaps in support.

And while funds are an absolutely essential piece of our patchwork of care in this country, the role they play is not always as straightforward as it may seem. They aren't vending machines, or ATMs. Most don't operate from a physical location, as a clinic would, and many have few or no paid staff members. Abortion-fund folks are often working through nights and weekends to get people assistance, around day jobs and families and responsibilities of their own.

Many of us don't have the disposable income that would allow for regular donations. And the needs we have can go far beyond funding. Folks who answer calls and texts and online requests for these organizations are engaging in yet another form of doula or community care work. When H., twenty-five, was working on an East Coast abortion fund hotline, they noticed that simply providing money didn't seem to *ever* be enough, when it came to the callers' needs and well-being.

"I was working on the hotline for over five years, but it was very quickly that I realized that there was this gap in the community that was really prominent," H. tells me. "I would stay on the phone with some of these people for *hours*." Their perspective of what was needed in the role expanded, immediately and dramatically, as they saw that callers were leaning on the fund for more than just the money they needed to pay for their appointments.

"I was really just providing active listening and compassion skills. Thankfully, those were skills that I—socialized mainly as a woman and in a Jewish community—was kind of used to. But I wasn't trained. And I felt I should be, and I wanted to be, and I wanted other people, who may not have been as comfortable in those conversations as I was, to be trained." So H. developed that training for their fellow fund volunteers.

Fund workers' interactions with abortion seekers are not purely transactional; they are loaded with emotion, with complexity, with layers upon layers of human need and the many unpredictable ways in which it will always express itself. Fund workers are care workers, too. Doulas, in their own right.

THE COLORADO DOULA PROJECT (CDP)

"You know when people are patients at the Boulder Abortion Clinic, and they are coming in from out of state, they're typically here for about five days, and they don't have money for food," says Gina Martínez Valentín, a longtime abortion doula and the executive director of the Colorado Doula Project. "We heard about somebody who was eating the free popcorn in the hotel lobby, and we were like, *Oh, fuck.*" That was the moment when she and her fellow doulas first realized that their model of care was lacking something desperately needed by many of their clients, though they'd never been explicitly asked for it: direct cash support, and essentials like toiletries, clothing, and food.

"People are embarrassed," Martínez Valentín says. "And they don't want to ask, because they're like, *Well, they just helped me with this, they're not going to help me with these other things.* So then we started doing meal support."

The Boulder Abortion Clinic, where the majority of CDP's clients are scheduled for their appointments, maintains a small pantry of nonperishable foods for patients in need and also distributes preloaded credit cards. "So if someone doesn't have Cash App or Venmo, they can take one of the cards, to order takeout or delivery or whatever." Groceries, cigarettes, anything the person deems necessary for their survival, and their family's survival, for joy or nourishment or comfort in that moment—*nothing* is off-limits, and Martínez Valentín is crystal clear about this in her communication with any and every client who comes to CDP for financial or material support.

"'We sent this money to your Cash App,'" she explains to them. "'It's earmarked for food, but you know, if you need it for something else . . . we're not here to police what you're using it on. You know best what you need and what the money should be used for.' Which just comes back to a really central ethic of the way we treat our clients.

"A lot of us have been poor ourselves," says Martínez Valentín. "Usually, poor people are a lot cleverer with money than anybody telling them to stop buying Starbucks or whatever."

The doulas of CDP often shop for clients who are traveling, who are trying to care for children in motels and hotels between their medical appointments, and who may not have the time, capacity, or emotional bandwidth to acquire their own supplies with the collective's funds. "We had somebody come to Colorado, in the winter, with Florida shoes. Our doula went to Target and got them new shoes. And then, at the end of their week here they were like, 'Here, take these shoes back and put them in the closet for somebody else.'" And the spirit of mutual aid often extends into a client's life far beyond their trip to Boulder. "If someone has a bill coming through—a lot of these people are moms—and is really sick with stress over it, we're like, 'Okay, we'll just pay that bill.' Or, if someone is coming from Texas—you know, we've had a few people lately who are, like, five minutes pregnant. And they can't get in in Texas, so they have to come all the way here for what is a very simple medication abortion that they should be able to do at home." After racking up thousands of dollars in costs for their plane tickets, bus tickets, gas, childcare, and the medical expenses of the care they often access far later in their pregnancy than they wish, thanks to the added burden of cross-country travel and long clinic wait times, CDP's out-of-town clients are often left completely broke.

Recently, Martínez Valentín remembers, wincing and shaking her head, the CDP funded a room in a hotel and an airport shuttle for a patient who had no extra money and nowhere to go between her abortion procedure and her flight home on the following day. The woman did not ask directly for shelter or resources, but let it slip that she was nervous about sleeping in public and on hard services while cramping and bleeding.

"I found out," the doula says, closing her eyes, "that she was going to sleep in the airport. Overnight."

THE BUCKLE BUNNIES FUND

"Our demographic, I feel like, is largely Hispanic, cis women," says Makayla Montoya-Frazier, a founder of the Buckle Bunnies Fund, a self-proclaimed loose confederation of young queer folks in San Antonio, Texas. "They're probably in the age range of eighteen to thirty. A lot of these girlies are single (I love that for them)! I would say it is majority young Latinx women and a lot of sex workers. Hold on—"

She goes off-screen for a moment, then reappears with a paper bag in her hands. "There's a girl outside my window who needs Plan B, so I'm just going to drop this out the window real quick."

She leaves my screen again; I hear greetings being called, laughter. Two friends, strangers to Montoya-Frazier, got her phone number from a community member and asked to pick up some of the repro supplies that the Buckle Bunnies Fund is known for distributing throughout San Antonio. Montoya-Frazier responded with her home address, and when the girls appeared on her lawn, she simply dropped the bag down to them, Rapunzel letting down a long braid of home pregnancy tests and emergency contraception.

"Since we are sex workers," she tells me, reappearing in my Zoom window once again, "we have friends who are sex workers; we're telling them. And we're handing out our cards at the clubs, the strip clubs. The privacy thing is a huge part of it for sex workers." Montoya-Frazier settles back into her seat. "There are so many people who don't want the publicity. . . . There are people who have come to me who I know, for years, or know of. And they're trusting *me* to not say anything to other people. Gaining that trust means you have to be on the same level as them."

Montoya-Frazier knows exactly what it is to be a pregnant sex worker—it's something she's experienced herself, more than once. "I remember being in the club, back when I was, like, eighteen, and I would see other pregnant strippers. And people were judging them; they would talk shit about them. And I felt so sad, like: *This is when they need more support than ever.*

"And there were some strippers who'd be like, 'I had an abortion a week ago and now it's time to get back in the game.' So then when I was a pregnant stripper, I was like, *Damn.* Now I'm in the exact position that I've seen so many times. What could make this better for me? You know there are so many people in the sex industry who get pregnant and need abortion support or who need care and compassion.

"And you know, like: you can be pregnant, and be dancing, or be doing sex work, and be a parent! I'm not going to tell you that you have to get an abortion because of your lifestyle. And it's shitty, because the CPCs [Crisis Pregnancy Centers, the antiabortion facilities that masquerade as legitimate clinics in order to coerce, deceive, and trick pregnant people in order to prevent them from accessing abortion care] won't even tell them about their choices. Nobody's being honest. There's so much judgment.

"So, yeah, being in that position myself, I know how important it was to be able to trust whoever I was going to."

Now, dropping bags of Plan B and pregnancy tests out her window, and answering anonymous Signal and Proton Mail messages to connect her San Antonio communities to the resources and support they need, Montoya-Frazier *is* that trusted person, for local sex workers and so many others.

Our conversation takes place in the spring, half a year after SB 8 has taken effect but a few months before the *Dobbs* ruling triggers Texas's pre–*Roe v. Wade* total abortion ban. It is months before Whole Woman's Health, the clinic that cared for Montoya-Frazier through her own abortions, will be forced to shutter all of its Texas clinics and begin crowdfunding a move to New Mexico, leaving millions of the poorest and most vulnerable people in their home state with no in-clinic abortion access at all.

When I ask her what's next, on this bright San Antonio morning before any of this becomes our bleak reality, Montoya-Frazier tells me: "I just want to really just put our hearts into it, just run it until *Roe v. Wade* is gone, and we have to cease our public work. I just want to get as big as we can . . . and then die." She laughs. "But even dead, we'll keep going."

I ask her about the toll that's taking on her, knowing that at least one kind of death is on the horizon, that she and her fellow organizers can hold their fingers in the dam for only so long. She sighs.

"I'm just tired all the time . . . you know, I get up, and wrangle my six pets. I try to get to my abortion work, you know, looking at messages, who needs what. I have clinics emailing me that they need funding for people. I have my friends, my community members, you know: *Someone needs Plan B! Who needs a pregnancy test? Who needs period supplies, miscarriage stuff, support . . .*"

She trails off, the collective grief and exhaustion of this moment thick in the air between us and our screens.

"Buckle Bunnies forever," I say, raising my right hand to place it over my heart in allegiance. Montoya-Frazier laughs and does the same.

"Fucking Buckle Bunnies for-fucking-ever, bitch!"

Abortion Is Pain

Hey. You. Where does it hurt? And how does it feel to talk about it? Any and all of your pain is welcome here. We don't relativize in this book. Maybe that's a coping tool you've used in the past, or a learned behavior, that *I'm okay, really, it's not that bad*, or *I shouldn't complain, he/she/they have it so much worse*, but I want to be clear: your pain is as real and true as anyone's.

And: you do not need to be in any certain degree of pain to ask for help. Asking for help does not imply or necessitate trauma. Asking for help is our most basic and most essential human skill. The only one we're born with. Remember?

"How will I survive this?" Patients and doula clients sometimes ask me before their abortions. Or, its cousin: "How will I get through this?"

And I respond, every time: "You already are. You're surviving it right now. The way you need to survive it might change, and we'll figure out a new way then. But right now, you're doing everything you need to do. You are surviving this already."

Robin is someone I've met only once, and—like many other people I've only met once—Robin is someone who has changed me on a cellular level. What Robin wanted during her abortion was to feel no physical pain. She wanted comfort, softness, numbness, sleep, ease. And in order to create and maintain these things for her body and mind, she wanted drugs. Whichever drugs would do the trick, in the largest doses and at the highest frequencies available to her.

"I don't need this pain, and I don't deserve this pain," she kept saying, over and over, with conviction, a mantra that moved me deeply then and still does now. The force and clarity of her sureness pushed the words forward again and again. I was stunned and impressed, the first time I heard it from her mouth. It was her fuel, a motor of defiance pushing her through the scary and uncomfortable first step of her abortion at twenty-one weeks: the dilation of her cervix. It was her reason to advocate for herself each and every time she wanted more pain medication, or a break from the sensations she was feeling to take deep breaths and give her body a reprieve.

You don't need this pain. You don't deserve this pain. If you feel any measure of pain, anywhere in your body, you are allowed to ask for help in easing it. There is no such thing as "the wrong kind of" or "not enough" pain.

ANESTHESIA, SEDATION, AND COPING TECHNIQUES

Physical pain during an abortion exists on a spectrum, whether it's a medication-induced miscarriage or an in-clinic aspiration procedure. Every body produces and responds to sensation in its own unique way. It's widely said, among doulas and providers, that the level of discomfort that one experiences during an abortion may correlate to their body's responses to menstruation and ovulation. Do you tend to experience intense cramping and heavy bleeding during your cycles? If so, an abortion experience may bring more physical discomfort than it would for someone with lighter and less noticeable cycles. Our bodies all carry memories and fears that create and respond to physical sensations differently. Because I have experienced sexual violence, for example, my body wants to clench down on any penetrative instruments or contact with my cervix—this can start as soon as I even so much as *see* a speculum leave a drawer. My knuckles curl reflexively into tight fists, my jaw locks in place, I bare my teeth and bite into my bottom lip, and my shoulders and back tense up, in unconscious attempts at self-protection. The anticipation of the pain and the dread that accompanies *knowing* all these things will happen—feeds these physiological responses, in a feedback loop of pain-fear-pain-fear-pain. When I have managed to interrupt that circle, it was with medications, deep breathing, visualizations, and support from my partner and doulas and midwives and friends.

Over the three days of induced labor that (eventually) resulted in the birth of my stubborn and enormous baby, I endured a series of cervical checks—in which a doctor inserts their fingers through the cervix to determine how much progress has been made in its dilation. The number of fingers equals the centimeters your cervix has opened. I knew to expect these checks, and to brace for the physical discomfort described by friends who were midwives or doulas, or who had given birth themselves. What I did not anticipate was the wave of fear that swallowed me each time; the heart-pounding *No*

No No reaction that left me weeping or cowering when the doctors would finally remove their fingers.

Confused by the intensity of my body's response to each check, and vaguely embarrassed and ashamed, I'd compulsively offer into the silence that followed, *I'm a baby about pain,* or *Sorry, I'm so dramatic.* I'd say this to the rotation of OBs pulling their hands out of me and removing their rubber gloves after yet another agonizing exploration, and to the nurses fixing my IV and increasing my Pitocin drip after yet another disappointing cervical measurement. I'd even say it to my husband. I would offer a feeble laugh, at myself. I would apologize for the pain *they* were inflicting. I try not to judge myself too harshly for this now, looking back. I strive for self-forgiveness, as always, but still: I'm horrified that these were my reactions to my own pain. That my instinct was to make my suffering into a joke, myself the punch line, my body an object of derision. I wanted to align myself with everyone else in the room, to abandon myself and join them to smile with sympathy and concern at the woman writhing and sobbing in the hospital bed.

Only later, in writing about those three long days of my body's struggle to give birth, did it occur to me that the cervical checks had served as physical echoes, to my body, of when it had been violated in the past. Of bracing for a penetration it didn't want, trying desperately to put up some defenses, and then being penetrated anyway.

I'd forgotten a crucial piece of my own most basic knowledge, a cornerstone of my doula work: a reaction, whether it's tears or a tightened fist or a scream, tells us something important about what's happening in our body. Pain has something to say. We must listen, try to translate, and either counter or agree with it, as best we can.

* * *

After her aspiration abortion, Khadijah tells us, she'll have to get to class. The student has already secured a ride back to campus from the clinic and might even have a little time to rest in her dorm room if she's careful to watch the clock. But she'll need to be sharp and alert by the time her afternoon lecture starts; the subject is statistics—difficult enough for her on her best days. But Khadijah also wants some pain medication. The clinic's baseline eight hundred milligrams of ibuprofen, taken orally, to help reduce cramping and bleeding; and the lidocaine, injected into the cervix to numb it before dilation and aspiration, don't feel like enough.

So when it came to pain management, Khadijah tells me, she would also like some of our minimal sedation—a dosage that will give her a soft place to land "but not wings that fly too high." This tier of sedation involves the combination of two oral medications. First, she is given lorazepam (also known by its brand name, Ativan), which floods her nervous system with "a happy kind of calm." She says that she feels her anxiety dissipating, slowly, at first, then all at once. Benzodiazepines like lorazepam are sedatives, and their mellowing effects can be felt immediately. Khadijah then swallows a dose of Tylenol with codeine, chasing it with a can of the cold ginger ale we keep in a mini fridge by our nurses' station.

"Oh, I feel *good* now." She laughs.

She gets her abortion. She takes a quick power nap in our recovery room before catching her ride back to campus. I'll never know if she makes it to class on time.

Sam, a slight and scruffy-haired twentysomething, requests moderate sedation when we schedule his appointment together.

He tells me that he doesn't want to remember his abortion procedure at all, if possible. His explicit desire is to be "knocked the
fuck out," but I know that there is no local clinic that can offer him
the general anesthesia that would render him fully unconscious for
his procedure. So he goes with the next best option—an IV drip
that will administer fentanyl and midazolam directly into his veins.
Sam drifts in and out of a dreamlike state during his manual vacuum aspiration, and—sure enough—now, some months later, he
doesn't remember much of his abortion at all.

He *will* always, however, remember the post-abortion tacos he
eats several hours later, and the specificity with which we lovingly
discuss the taqueria's menu while in the waiting room, distracting
him from his anxiety by helping him design his own guided medi-
tation through salt-sprinkled tortilla chips and warm queso, plates
of citrusy, garlicky elotes, "and a *fat* margarita," he reminds me, his
eyes squeezed tightly shut and a tight smile creeping across his face.

"And a *pitcher* of fat margaritas," I respond.

We manifest this feast together, from the ice-cold tequila
(which he doesn't actually end up ordering, as it's safest to avoid
alcohol for twenty-four hours after any in-clinic procedure involving sedation) to the glistening, syrup-drenched flan that jiggles
on its plate as he and his friends carve their spoons into it, and
the rich, spicy hot chocolate they drink under the red glow of the
restaurant's chili-pepper string lights. It's the first thing he asks me
about when the sedation wears off, a disposable heating pad still
clutched to his abdomen and his aftercare paperwork folded in his
hand.

"Tacos?" he asks.

"Tacos," I agree. "Definitely tacos."

Abortion Is a Crime

It's strangely quiet for an early Friday morning at the clinic—even the street noise from our regular protesters seems muffled, subdued, as if underwater. Later, the clinic escorts and patients will report that the group has added plastic baby dolls to their arsenal of weapons and are brandishing them at passersby as they threaten, "WE WILL ADOPT YOUR BABY!" and "GOD MADE YOU TO BE A MOTHER!"

In our morning huddle, usually a raucous gathering, we are solemn. Someone goes, quietly and unsmiling down the list of patients, listing their procedures and any relevant details we know—if someone needs an interpreter, if someone has reported that an abusive partner might show up at the clinic today. We discuss contingency plans, preparation needs, safety questions for each and every person on the list, hoping to get each and every one of them in for their abortions, and then out to live their lives—and to do it as quickly, as safely, and as thoroughly as we can. To be both their soft landing place *and* their fortress-secure, swiftly moving, well-oiled machine of care. To move like water and adapt to any and everything that comes up. Someone goes to make another pot of coffee. The phone rings. It's 8:00 a.m., on June 24, 2022. The first patients are arriving.

The ruling comes down after 10:00 a.m., just as we expected. The first thing I see is a nurse practitioner crouched in the hallway outside of an exam room, crying. Then my boss emerges from her office, cell phone in hand and tears in her eyes. She extends her arms, wraps me in a tight hug.

"I really thought we had until Monday," she whispers.

That's when I fall apart, too.

Our clinic operates in a state where abortion access is protected, so we will continue seeing patients as if it is any other Friday. We have a full waiting room, and eleven in-clinic abortion procedures left to go. Some patients call us from their cars, their bus rides, or their homes, confused and afraid, asking if they can still come for their appointment. Others don't show up at all. I say a silent prayer, each time an appointment time comes and goes, that it's because the person has made a different decision. Not because they're scared or think that their appointment is now, suddenly, illegal.

In other clinics, across other states, it's chaos. Patients pulled from their exam rooms and told that they must go home, still pregnant. Staff making hundreds of phone calls, telling shocked and weeping mothers and teenagers and partners and all the other people who can't be pregnant for one second longer, that their appointments have been canceled. *Don't come*, they have to tell their distraught and terrified patients. *Don't come*.

Elliot, in Ohio, speaks to two separate patients who tell her that they would rather die than have another baby. In the background of one conversation, she hears an infant wail and wail, inconsolable. In Texas, when the announcement is made that everyone in a clinic's waiting room must leave—that none of them will be able to have their abortions today—a patient clutches at a nurse's arm and begs her for abortion pills. She offers money, pleads and pleads. It's a crime now, the nurse tells her. There is nothing she can do.

Increasingly, community care work will mean supporting people through continuing the pregnancies that they wanted, or needed, to end. Supporting them through the fetal diagnoses and miscarriages and stillbirths and complications and dangerous births and injury and suffering and the violations and the theft of the futures they dreamed, the futures that rightly belonged to them. And we will know, as we do this, that they should never have needed *these* forms of care at all.

Abortion Is Safety

In May 2022, on the day the draft of the *Dobbs* decision leaked, Rafa Kidvai was moving into a new apartment. The attorney, who serves as the director of the Repro Legal Defense Fund (RLDF), had been schlepping furniture and organizing their family's transition into a new home all day, when panicked communications began to flood their phone. The implications of the leak—that the federal right to abortion was about to disappear, that wildly unconstitutional state abortion laws, with all their wildly unconstitutional enforcement mechanisms and penalties, would not only stand but would proliferate, and that pregnant people would be criminalized en masse—knocked the wind out of an already-exhausted and overwhelmed Kidvai. They sat down among the boxes of unsorted belongings, cradled their head in the heels of their hands, and burst into tears. That's when their two-year-old—a naturally gifted doula in their own right—snapped into action.

"My kid is so sweet." Kidvai laughs. "When *they're* crying, we have a list of questions. So they went down the list for me. They were like, 'Mama, are you hungry? Are you frustrated? Do you feel safe?'"

"*I'm so grateful for you right now*," the attorney and activist remembers thinking of their toddler, laughingly mimicking the wailing and sobbing of their own response to the child's question. "Because I actually *am* hungry, and I *am* very frustrated. And I *don't* feel safe."

The Repro Legal Defense Fund is a project of the reproductive justice lawyers' network If/When/How through which Kidvai oversees the provision of resources like bail money, legal advice and counsel, and representation, and it is a beautiful bulwark for folks who are investigated, arrested, or prosecuted for self-managing their abortions outside of a clinical setting. In partnership with If/When/How, a network of lawyers working against reproductive oppression, the RLDF envisions and builds toward a future of safety—in our bodies, in our pregnancies, in our families and communities and lives.

* * *

While threats to our physical safety—abortion seekers and providers and care workers alike—are escalating, police surveillance of our individual communications and online behaviors are ramping up in kind. Enter the Digital Defense Fund (DDF), which was established in 2017 in response to the abortion rights movement's increasing need for security and technology resources. A multidisciplinary team of organizers, engineers, designers, abortion-fund and practical-support volunteers, DDF brings "our own personal histories with abortion access and technology together to build for the people we love working with and learning from" reads their website. "We work to support and expand the capacity of abortion rights and provider organizations, and individual organizers." The brave and brilliant folks behind the DDF know that technological advice and support—connecting with and protecting one another virtually—can be community abortion care work, too.

"So now folks often come to us [at the Digital Defense Fund] with online privacy and doxxing prevention help," says Kate Bertash, the organization's director. ". . . You'll have these basic tips, tricks, an understanding of how the economy of information moves around the internet." The DDF encourages a practice called Threat Modeling, by which an individual or organization assess the potential risks and consequences they face when engaging in specific actions or communications within specific contexts.

And obviously, says Bertash, those consequences are not the same for everyone. People who are not white, for example, are more likely to be surveilled by their devices and also more likely to be the targets of abuse that is severe, and abuse that *does* make a meaningful impact on their day-to-day experience of using the internet.

"And it reflects what we already know, unfortunately, about clinic harassment," she says. "Black providers and patients are more likely to be targeted not just for harassment, but of course for racialized abuse and threats."

The three big evergreen pieces of abortion digital security wisdom Bertash wishes to impart, regardless of location or legality:

1. **"Be aware of your paper trail,** things that get transferred across the internet. Like: What does it mean for your browser history to come up? Google search history comes up in a lot of these (legal) cases. So (I mind) my

browser search history, things that come to my email, what device I use. Do I want to make a separate email account just for this and then delete it? Do I have a trusted friend, can I use a different device? . . . Be aware of how you search and browse, and what information is collected." Disabling your mobile ad ID, which ties together and tracks your online activity in order to share it with advertisers and app makers, can be an essential step. As can using a secure and privacy-prioritizing app like Euki to track and learn about your reproductive health, and deleting any other period or fertility trackers on your devices.

2. "*Always* use an encrypted chat platform (such as Signal or Proton Mail). Be careful who you're talking to about it. Ask the other person, 'Can you please delete all my messages when we're done talking?' Or set your messages to auto-delete . . . use an encrypted, disappearing chat to talk . . . with *trusted* people." When it comes to phone calls, one could consider using a Google voice number, which costs nothing, or a paid app like Hush or Burner.

3. "Understand that you have the right to refuse a search if you feel safe doing so. A lot of times in these cases, when people have been confronted by law enforcement, they say, 'Can I have your phone?' And people feel intimidated into saying yes. And they take it, they make a copy of the drive, they hand it back to you, and then they can search through the drive copy for incriminating information. And we forget that our phones are

like a little avatar for us. They move through the world with us, they're with us everywhere all day. But know that you can refuse a search, and that you have the right to an attorney. Know your rights, for yourself *and* your devices."

The most basic piece of our work to keep each other safe, says Bertash, is just communicating to those around us that we are doing so. Learning enough to be trustworthy, to be a contact or support who can help someone turn on certain privacy settings, download certain programs, watch out for certain risks. Another pair of eyes and ears, or a mouth that can stay closed. We can be secret keepers, connectors to the sources of safe legal and medical advice, drivers of the digital getaway cars.

"Just make it known," says Bertash. "Like: *If you or anybody you know need information or help . . . I'll help you stay safe and private.*"

Abortion Is Parenthood

I wear maternity jeans to my abortion appointment. They are the only pants I own, other than my work scrubs, that come anywhere close to fitting my eleven-months-postpartum body— organs rearranged, extra room and stretch marks where there used to be taut skin and a regular old innie of a belly button. *No one can tell these aren't normal jeans*, I often tell myself, though sometimes I do roll down their conspicuous stretchy belly panel in order to inspect or run my fingers along my healed C-section scar. I often see abortion patients at the clinic, or meet doula clients in their homes, with that same telltale stretch in their waistband, that same black panel peeking out below the hems or between the buttons of their shirts. The sitz bath in their medicine cabinets, the leftover maxi pads soaked in witch hazel crowding their freezers and their post-birth pelvic-floor therapy appointments scrawled in their planners and calendars. If they mention a child, I'll always ask about them. *Four months old*, they'll tell me. *Fifteen months. Eight months.* Or: *My youngest is turning one next month. It goes so fast.* I'll nod, and smile, and agree.

Selena brings her son's favorite toy car to her appointment.

With tears in her eyes, she produces the little red sedan—miniature license plate detail and all—from her backpack and places it on the clinic desk in front of me. "We just dropped him off at daycare," Selena says quietly, giving the car a few pushes back and forth, just as a child—probably her child—would instinctively do. I watch its tiny metal wheels spin.

"My son would love that one," I say to her gently, imagining his chubby fingers finding its wheels, its headlights, the *toot-toot* sounds he is learning to make.

Selena's eyes light up, one tear spilling over the crest of her cheek as she raises her head to ask me: "How old?"

The majority of people who have abortions are parents of at least one child already.[1] This statistic has been something of a stigma-busting, loneliness-killing talisman for me, a stone I keep in my heart's back pocket as I move through my *own* post-motherhood abortion. Self-condemnation runs on a loop in my mind—as I make my appointment, as I take my pills, as I bleed, as I throw a flower onto the waves of the Atlantic Ocean or crumple a letter and toss it onto a fire, whispering, "Goodbye, I love you, I'm sorry, forgive me." There is an erosion in my view of myself as a mother. Even as I kiss the top of my infant's downy head after swallowing my mifepristone, and even as I build precarious towers with his wooden blocks and cradle him in my lap as I wait for the misoprostol to dissolve, I feel an unbearable cleaving. A separation from my most dearly held identity: his—or anybody's—*mama*.

C. scrolls through photos of her two-year-old daughter as she takes the first pill. It feels necessary to have the little girl, her dark curls and chubby arms and moon-shaped face, with her as she swallows the medicine that will trigger the end of her current pregnancy. To remember her reason for doing this.

As the nurse closes the door behind her, clicking down the hallway of the clinic in her clogs to attend to all her other patients, C. shakily pulls her phone from her bag, laying it flat across her lap before opening the small white paper bag that holds the two hundred milligrams of mifepristone needed to set her abortion in motion. She opens the photo app, many iterations of her daughter's tiny face beaming up at her from the glowing squares. She'll turn two this coming summer, the age at which C. has always imagined preparing her for a younger sibling's imminent arrival—reading "I'm a Big Sister" books to the toddler from her ever-shrinking lap, increasing the frequency and intensity of conversations about the (nebulous and unpleasant) concept of "sharing," bringing the newborn swings and swaddle blankets and breastfeeding pillows up from the house's basement, where they've been waiting patiently in the dark, nestled in their big plastic storage bins. But it was not to be. Not this year.

After her abortion, C. finds herself rocked by grief and shame. Though she has no regrets concerning the financial or logistical factors in her decision, and though she is in many ways deeply relieved to no longer be pregnant, she feels an enormous sense of loss. The loss of the potential second child, of course, but also, temporarily, the loss of her own identity as a mother. Suddenly, she can no longer bear to listen to her favorite songs about motherhood, or read the books on parenting and child development she usually devours and discusses with friends, as she feels so alienated from that part of herself.

"My favorite song is 'The Mother,' by Brandi Carlile," she tells me over the phone as we process her experience together. "I used to sing it to [my daughter] as a lullaby, and I would listen to it when I needed comfort myself."

It's July, and C. is speaking to me from her home, a few hundred miles south of mine. I listen from my driver's seat, in the hot little coffin of my compact car. I am parked in my own driveway, with the engine off and the windows rolled up, so that my own child won't know I'm home, won't hear my voice from the nursery where he plays happily with his grandmother. I press my forehead against the steering wheel, absorbing the pain that radiates through the phone as C. talks.

"But after I had the abortion, I couldn't bear to listen to 'The Mother' anymore. I felt like what I had done . . . it was the opposite of being a mother."

Abortion is often painted this way: the antithesis of loving and parenting children, the opposite of motherhood. That's a big reason that people who already have kids, or who want them someday, can feel confused and ashamed about their desire or need for an abortion, as C. is experiencing. A place where our intellectual understanding of reproductive science can fail, miserably, to stack up to emotion in our perception of what pregnancy is: if C., from the first moment she was aware of her daughter's conception, thought of the "cluster of cells" inside of her uterus as her child, then how could *this* cluster of cells, growing two years later, be any different?

* * *

But abortion often *is* an act of parenting, of mothering, of creation, of loving and protecting one's family. It certainly is for C., who breaks her own heart and sets aside her own desires in pursuit of her family's well-being, her daughter's flourishing. And reproductive justice means supporting families and individuals at *any* stage of their reproductive lives—their well-being and their freedom to procreate, adopt, build the families and communities they want, without governmental or societal interference.

Even if you are not yet—or never will be—a parent, abortion can be an act of parental love in and of itself.

* * *

One winter long before I became a doula and even longer before I became a mother, I signed up for a community effort that an activist/doula friend of mine had shared on social media. Volunteer drivers were needed, to transport an incarcerated new mother's breast milk from the state prison where she was being held to the house where her baby was staying with a family member, in a small rural town an hour to the north. There was a schedule with detailed instructions, and a plea for support from the new mother's caseworker. I signed up for my first shift right away and loaded my car with a picnic cooler and some bags of frozen peas, planning to keep the milk on ice as it made its journey across the state.

Many of the volunteer drivers who participated in this effort were also, to use our shorthand, "abortion folks"—doulas, providers, advocates, and activists in the reproductive justice movement. And the vast majority of the group were also parents. I felt a similar warmth in my bones when a provider at the abortion clinic froze and stored *her* breast milk for me to feed my own baby when my body couldn't make enough to sustain him. There was no cognitive dissonance, for me, of going into an abortion clinic to pick up this frozen breast milk, bags of it lining the break room's freezer alongside the ice packs we use to mail our patients' blood and urine samples to the outside labs who perform many of our medical tests. There is no contradiction when patients and clients breastfeed or chestfeed as they have their abortions, as they rock and soothe their babies in the clinic's waiting room, on the exam table, in the back seat of my car, at the bus stop on their way to their appointment.

The work I do to support a person feeding their child—the chips I feed them as they struggle to help their baby latch on to their nipple, or the special "lactation cookies" I bake them, or the nursing bras and pump supplies I sanitize and pass on—that work is no different from that of loving them through their abortions. Assisting someone in the use of their own body, for exactly the purposes they need or want, and in exactly the *ways* they need or want—that is a doula's mandate. And often, people want to use their bodies in pursuit of their *children's* bodies surviving and thriving.

It is only after writing about my own abortion and my motherhood online that I've received the most vitriolic hate of my career—despite having been public about my work in abortion care for a long time. Strangers calling me a devil, a monster, a horrible mother. Saying my son will hate me for "murdering his baby brother" (though my embryo is fewer than six weeks in existence at the time of my abortion, with no developed genitals or sex yet assigned to it). J. D. Vance, the future Republican senator from Ohio who has recently branded himself "a champion of the unborn" in his effort to court ultraconservative voters, retweets a photo of me reading the (brilliant) children's book *What's an Abortion Anyway?*[2]

to my son, and the floodgates open wider still. Thousands of people share and share and share the photo, adding their own frightening commentary on what should happen to me, a young mother of an infant.

If she killed her other baby, one crucifix-and-American-flag-branded account's retweet reads, *this one might be next.*

Evil cunt, the messages to my personal email in-box, my work email, my Instagram and Twitter DM requests, read. *That poor kid deserves a real mother. Fuck off and die. You deserve whatever's coming to you.*

I read a few of these tweets and emails before deleting the rest. I apply some security filters to my in-box. I block a couple dozen Twitter accounts, report a few of the particularly abusive or threatening messages. I close my laptop, I text my friend about the baby-led weaning book she's asked to borrow, and I go to run my child a warm bath.

Abortion Is Community

Being proprietary about our work and our knowledge
isn't going to liberate us. Comparison isn't going to liberate us.
The more we drill down into the very specific needs
of our individual communities, and connect as much as possible
with other people and organizations . . .
that's how we're going to push our liberation forward.
—Gina Martínez Valentín,
executive director of the Colorado Doula Project

I should tell you, now, that there is something special to me about some of these pages: they've been written in someone else's house. I cross the peach-tree-and-dandelion border that bisects our gardens, I retrieve the spare key from its secret hiding place, I let myself in through my neighbors' side door, and I make myself at home; it's a home with no baby, no sink full of dishes made dirty by me or anyone related to me.

"If you need a quiet space to write," one of those owners called to me, "use our house! We'd love it!"

I nearly fell to the ground and kissed her feet.

To say that I feel good within the walls of this home—covered as they are in photos of these two beautiful neighbors of mine and the life they have built together—would not be sufficient. Look: here they are kissing on a beach; here they are paddling a canoe; here they are smiling down at me from the summit of a scenic mountain hike, as I labor endlessly to arrange and rearrange all these words in a way that might hopefully, someday, be useful.

This is community care. It doesn't always look urgent, or dramatic, or overt. adrienne maree brown writes beautifully of a "political home"—a place that activists can return to for connection, accountability, community. This need exists for care and support workers as well—we need networks of peers and comrades and trusted mentors. And community may not always mean "friends," either. It often means people who challenge you, who critique your work, those with whom you share movement space and values, but not necessarily close interpersonal relationships or unconditional intimacy. Loving conflict—and intentional cooperation, collaboration, and cocreation with folks you don't personally *like*—is an essential part of social movements and of human relationships in general.

* * *

As daena horner, the herbalist and expert at the helm of the Holistic Abortion Instagram account and its attendant webs of care and community that stretch across the globe, says: "When you consistently show up to classes, fundraisers, and other events, [your] connections grow stronger. We need each other, and strong, trustworthy relationships. We need to be connected [widely], but we need strong *core* communities, too."

* * *

Many abortion doulas and companions work within collectives, which often organize local *and* virtual doula trainings, seek local volunteers or staff members, organize local events, and partner with local clinics, abortion funds, and advocacy groups. To name just a few such collectives:

- DC Doulas for Choice
- Cascades Abortion Support Collective
- Bay Area Doula Project
- The Bridge Collective
- Baltimore Doula Project
- Alabama Cohosh Collaborative
- Colorado Doula Project
- SPIRAL Collective (based in Minneapolis)
- The Doula Project (based in New York City)
- Boston Abortion Support Collective
- Mountain Area Abortion Doula Collective (MAADCo, based in Western North Carolina)

While my own doula work is usually done solo, squeezed into the hours outside of my day job in the homes and text messages and encrypted chats and email in-boxes of the folks who seek my support or companionship, it is, by definition, not time spent alone. When I am not physically with someone, supporting them through their abortion, I am talking them through their processes on the phone, or seeing their names light up my screen with texts and emails. I am spending my time and energy inside the space we share together, the space they have invited me into or asked me to cocreate, even if that looks like hunching over my laptop while alone in my room, or schlepping a care package to the post office on my own.

And this doula has her own doulas, of course. You probably have doulas, too. I have my fellow clinic workers and local care workers and providers and organizers to grieve and question and imagine and build futures with. I have fellow writers wrestling with the stories they tell and how and why, and struggling with what it means to speak and be heard, to take up space with our words. I have regular clinic patients who show me their wedding photos and tell me about their new jobs and pets and sex partners and ask about my family and notice my haircut and want my advice. I have the people who reach out to me on social media, and the fellow party guests who mention, in passing, that they've been searching for a resource or a way to get involved in filling the reproductive justice needs of their communities.

I am a stranger, as June Jordan says, learning to worship the strangers around me.

Organizers with some regional Planned Parenthood affiliates have found great success in opening voters' minds to the abortion stigma and biases they may not realize they have through their Bridging the Gap project. BTG is a deep-canvassing initiative, in which volunteers are organized and trained to visit the homes of their (prewarned and consenting) neighbors and community members. Once a canvasser is at someone's door, they speak openly about their own abortions, in a way that emphasizes the commonalities between them and their neighbor. When someone realizes that a member of their community—someone with similar or familiar values and life experiences, someone whose family is known to them—has had an abortion, their perception of abortion bans and restrictions can change radically. Once they are confronted with the tangible, visible, easily understandable realities of a person's reproductive life and the consequences of being denied the care they need, the needle moves.

Canvassing can be a great way to get comfortable speaking about abortion—saying the word aloud to people you may or may not know, depending on how big your town or city is. And it can be a good springboard to other forms of organizing, too—maybe you'll meet volunteers who are deeply plugged in to reading groups, care collectives, local reproductive justice organizing. Or maybe you won't. But you'll be showing up, and making abortion part of your life, and doing the essential work of *talking* about it with those whom you align with and those you don't. If community is a bonfire, a single conversation can be a lit match.

Buying and wearing an abortion fund's branded shirt or hat in public or around friends can light a match, too. If it feels safe for you to do so, a laptop or water-bottle sticker can signal to your future community that you're here, you're showing up, you're ready to make plans and listen to what they have to say. And it can signal to people who've had abortions that they're safe with you. That, if invited to do so, you might be trusted to enter their spaces.

When I see someone with an abortion bumper sticker on their

car, or overhear them speak openly about their abortion experiences or work, or when they recognize one of my abortion-related tattoos for what they represent, I get the same feeling as in the moment I see someone wearing a glucose monitor or an insulin pump, the accessories of my illness. Or when someone sees mine, points at it, and asks if I'm diabetic, too. *Oh!* I think, though I may never have seen them before in my life, strangers moving separately and unknowingly through the world, but in this one small way, together: *There you are.*

Abortion Is Power

I have never felt safe, but that didn't take away my power.
—Bonnie Bainbridge Cohen

Cora's porch steps creak beneath my feet. Her narrow old Victorian stands, a tall and vivid plummy purple, among the peeling paint of the many-colored homes, the wind chimes and stained glass and fluttering rainbow flags, the sparrow-crowded feeders and birdbaths of the sparse and sleepy end-of-winter gardens lining her street.

Cora greets me at the door, towheaded Nathan on her hip and an exhausted smile on her face, dark curls twisted and knotted messily on top of her head. Without a word, she pulled me into a grateful embrace. We step through the dark entryway, its old wood and narrow staircase, into her kitchen with its colorful vintage stove and the sun streaming through the cheerfully ruffled curtains onto its bright tile floor. The baby, with his long eyelashes and the blond wisps swirling onto his forehead and curling around his tiny ears,

is set down. He is only a few days older than my own son, their
midwinter births forming two knots in the thread connecting their
mothers to each other, and then to six others down its length. Cora
and I are in a community parenting group together, a tight circle of eight women with December and January due dates. Several
times a month, we'd congregate in a backyard or a beer garden or a
Zoom meeting, to laugh and bleed and cry and lactate (the ambient
whirrrr-whirrr of at least one breast pump a frequent soundscape
of our gatherings). We've passed around clothing, books, stories,
questions. We've shared our half-formed, sleep-deprived, constantly
shifting strategies for continued postpartum pandemic survival. It's
like a low-pressure, love-filled, traveling commune on which to
raise our children together.

Now, in Cora's kitchen, I feel that same warm homecoming.
Under my paper surgical mask, I grin stupidly down at her son—
this beautiful little being I know that she has long dreamed of,
through miscarriage and fertility anxiety—in adulation. *So much
bigger now! Look at those* cheeks! All the other things one says when
a baby is present. Nathan, comfortable in his cherubic beauty and
accustomed to such fawning adoration, is bored by my cooing. He
crawls off on a quest for more interesting pursuits.

"Okay," says Cora. "Let's do this."

* * *

Few people can speak to the power of doula-supported MAB (our
shorthand for medication abortion) like Poonam Dreyfus-Pai, MPH,
MSW. "I do think that the thing that felt really unique that was happening [in Northern California]," says the former coleader of the Bay

Area Doula Project, "[is that] there were so many home-birth mid-wives, and home-birth doulas, and a culture of birth at home. So to be offering abortions in the home, and say: *There are doulas for that, too, if you want.*" This was powerful and far-reaching love.

Dreyfus-Pai, now the deputy director of All-Options and emeritus chair of the board of the National Network of Abortion Funds, is an Indian American, cis, bisexual woman living in Oakland with her family. She has a magnetic warmth and a vast body of knowledge and experience—from birth and abortion doula work to research to directing and managing some of our most essential and wide-reaching advocacy and care organizations.

"It feels harder, because you are just in someone's space, and they are a stranger," Dreyfus-Pai says. "Unlike with birth, where you have the chance to get to know someone and develop a relationship over several months beforehand, and talk about their values, what they want for the experience, build a plan, all of that. With abortion you just don't have that kind of time frame. So even with a nonviable—like I did support someone relatively recently who was a friend, but a lot of the same skills came into play, it was a nonviable pregnancy, and basically she was just waiting for it to pass.

"And I remember being like, *Right, there's like this period of time where I'm just kind of in this liminal space between finding out that I'm pregnant, and knowing what I'm going to do, and waiting for it to happen . . .* but it's not long. It's not a long liminal space, it's like a day or two. So you're in a stranger's home, amidst all of their very private intimate things and experiences. So that feels different, and in some ways a little harder than being in the clinic space."

* * *

The mifepristone and misoprostol, rattling around in their opaque little vessels, had been delivered to Cora by Aid Access. They'd arrived in a large plastic bag with cheerful packaging and instructions. The supplies I had brought along—pads, ibuprofen, and those all-powerful, age-old anti-nausea potions and prophylactics, Canada Dry ginger ale and saltines. One by one, I removed the medication bottles and the official guidance pamphlets and lined them up alongside the schedule I had written out for her. I'd printed it as neatly as I could—my handwriting as large and untidy as ever despite my best efforts, looping and folding over itself excitably.

> *Dear Cora,*
>   *This is hard.*
>   *You are loved.*
>   *You are powerful.*
>   *And you are so far from alone.*
>   *Mothers all over the world are doing this exact thing at this exact moment, for their babies and themselves. Nathan is so lucky to have you for his mama.*
>   *You are not just what is happening in your body at this moment. You are also and no matter what: gorgeous wonderful brilliant CORA. You are an incredible parent and daughter and sister and human. A beautiful example of a growing joyful vivacious gorgeous shimmering person. Someone I am so proud to call a friend. I'm so honored to witness and support you in this moment of your power.*
>
> *All my love, your doula.*
> *H.*

Following this are the instructions, potential side effects and symptoms to watch for, and the basic timelines we've already discussed, and some SMA resources: the Reprocare Healthline and the Miscarriage and Abortion Hotline, and the SASS (Self-Managed Abortion; Safe and Supported) website. And at the bottom of the letter, as I always add, though abortion remains legal in our state, for now: the phone number for the Repro Legal Helpline.

844.868.2812, I write for Cora, having memorized it myself.

844.868.2812, I write, and I underline and circle it in red.

844.868.2812, I write, as I have so many times before and probably will for the rest of my life.

* * *

Cora takes her pills. She feels well enough—sad, but relieved, and the physical effects of her medication abortion are minimal. She drops off her son at daycare. She goes to work. She makes dinner. She asks questions about follow-up care, and keeps me updated on what's unfolding in her body. She goes camping with her family. She is alive. She is healthy. She is safe. She does not have to have another baby. No one has power over her body but her.

Abortion Is Hope

We'll keep fighting, I text a friend and colleague one night in May, after the draft of the Supreme Court ruling in the *Dobbs* case leaks, stating in no uncertain terms that federal protection of the right to an abortion will soon be gone—which will kick the doors wide open for a barrage of aggressive, invasive laws violating citizens' rights to privacy, bodily autonomy, marriage, religious freedom, and virtually every other facet of that life/liberty/happiness pipe dream we've all been sold.

Yes we will, she replies.

No choice but to.

Even without the looming Big Bad Supreme Court Ruling, things have long been feeling unsustainable. We are, all of us abortion patients *and* doulas, emotionally, mentally, physically, and existentially exhausted. We're two years deep into the fear and isolation of a global pandemic, mass death via illness and gun violence having been fully accepted (if not embraced) by those in power. White supremacist fascism is demonstrably on the rise in the public square that is our media platforms, our megachurches, and our streets; the vines of transphobia and racism and anti-Semitism are creeping swiftly up the walls.

My coworkers and the staff at other clinics across the country, with whom I keep in constant touch, can't keep going on like this. Mya is crowdfunding their top surgery—the gender-affirming health care they have needed for years—while working overtime hours at their understaffed clinic to accommodate the overflow of out-of-state abortion patients. Zadie holds space for abortion patients' trauma and loss on the anniversary of her mom passing away, but has no time to process any of it, because she has to hurry across town to get to her second job at a restaurant, where she will work late into the night only to be back at the clinic changing into her scrubs at 8:00 a.m.

E.J. is being trained to assist with ultrasound-guided second-trimester abortions (procedures which can bring an increase of stress, intensity, and labor—both medically and emotionally). She is fielding daily harassment and death threats from the armed protesters who congregate outside the open-carry state's clinic where she works for the same salary she could make rolling burritos at a Chipotle. She and her coworkers have recently been trying to unionize, mostly in the desperate hopes of bargaining for more paid sick leave as the COVID-19 pandemic rages on. E.J., who is the primary caretaker for her elderly high-risk grandmother, must work in close physical proximity with patients who are symptomatic, who wear flimsy paper surgical masks, and who have tested positive for a variant of the virus as recently as five days prior to her contact with them. Her clinic's management refuses to voluntarily recognize its staff's union, and so a contentious election is upcoming. E.J. has recently begun having panic attacks, at work and at home and—once—while driving on the freeway.

I document, in our patients' medical charts, all the ways in which *they* can't keep going on like this, either—suicidal ideation, intimate partner violence, the daily abuse they experience in their homes and temporary shelters and schools and prisons, the obstruction or outright denial of the health care they need, by health insurance companies, parents and guardians, the state. The holes that COVID-19 has blasted into their lives, their local and federal governments offering *no* materials with which to patch or fill them. The pregnancies they cannot bear or tolerate, the pregnancies making them sick or broke or unsafe or unable to care for their children or themselves or all of the above.

Often, my job is to deliver the news that they must continue to be pregnant. To deny them the incredibly safe and routine ten-minute procedure or bag of five tiny pills that would save their life. To say that, no, I cannot help them end their pregnancy today— because we need to find more money, or because their pregnancy has progressed too far for the medications they were planning to use, or because there are no nearby clinics that can accommodate them for weeks and weeks. These patients, too—vomiting from morning sickness, struggling to work and parent, sometimes feeling fetal movement, a flutter or kick that sends ripples of grief through their body and their life—just keep going on. *No choice but to.*

* * *

I come home, I feed and bathe and *shhh-shhh-shhh* the baby until he's in a deep sleep, sprawled in his crib with his arms thrown wide open above his head in a touchdown pose and his rosy little lips parted—this is the most trusting and vulnerable he will ever be, and every day he spends on earth he becomes a tiny bit less so.

Incrementally, as much as I desperately wish it away, fear is introduced into his life. Money. Violence. Power. I belly flop onto my own unmade bed. My thumbs do as they're trained—I open Twitter. The abolitionist scholar and activist Mariame Kaba has helped to fundraise $250,000 for the Partners in Abortion Care clinic, and the two women who run it, Morgan and Diane—two fiercely loving abortion providers, advocates, and fellow parents of young children, whom I admire and revere more fervently than *any* celebrity or politician—are celebrating.

Storytellers are sharing their joy, their gratitude, their memories of abortion care they've received at all-trimester clinics like Partners, and the beautiful lives that such care has made possible for them and their families.

Elsewhere on the social media site, abortion funds are posting that they've helped 100, 150, 250 patients this month. They're tweeting about the small donations that make this possible—the monthly recurring $5 and $10 that broke people like me keep kicking in, making whatever small sacrifices we have to in order to keep from overdrafting when that automatic deduction hits our accounts.

If, as Kaba says, *hope is a discipline*—something we practice, something we *do*—then hope is everywhere I look tonight.

The care workers who tell me they have no optimism, see no light on the horizon, but who stay late at the clinic to make phone calls and find external ultrasound records and figure out ways to squeeze in just one more abortion patient tomorrow? Hopeful. The abortion seekers who move mountains to get to their appointments and the providers who move mountains to meet them there? The repro lawyer who pulls all-nighters to file briefs and emergency injunctions against proliferating bans, rolling the boulder up the hill again and again toward hostile judges and pernicious, persistent opponents, so that one more week, one more day, one more hour of abortion care may be legally sought and provided in a state far from her own?

These are the patterns, the rituals, the habits of hope. This is what it looks like to be hopeful.

I get off my phone, get my ass out of bed, and start to assemble a little post-abortion care package for a Mimi, a friend of a friend who lives across the country and is recovering from her in-clinic abortion procedure. I pack a journal, and a book, and some sea-salt caramels wrapped in wax paper and twine. I write her a letter telling her of my gratitude for her trust and for the privilege of witnessing and supporting her in this moment. I tell her what a gift she is. I seal the bubble-lined envelope and write her address carefully, the zip code so foreign to me. I try to imagine what it would feel like to bleed and cramp while riding her city's various forms of public transit, on the block where her apartment building sits, in such different weather and amid such different flowers and trees and birds. What it feels like to have just ended a pregnancy in the unfamiliar, faraway scenery—and life—through which she moves.

Hope is not the thing I'm feeling. Hope is the thing I just keep doing.

* * *

"I think, long-term-wise, there's a little bit more space for hope. But in the very close future, I don't know," says Rosie's voice in my ear. Rosie is an abortion doula in the Midwest, and they're telling me about their practice, their emotional state, their day-to-day relationship to their mental health. It's three weeks after my abortion. I'm walking my dog on the bike trail that runs through the woods near my home, the small brook babbling away under the cloudy windowpane of its frozen surface, the naked tree limbs stark and scrawny against the sky. Birds are trying, half-heartedly, to sing some life and color into the gray of the early February day.

"I'm a little bit of a pessimist, I guess. I don't feel super optimistic. It feels a little bit sometimes like this work is—okay." They stop and laugh, prefacing their next words with: "This is super cheesy, it's probably on every boomer mom's Instagram and Facebook, but! Okay."

Rosie begins, again: "Imagine: a person on the beach. And there are a million starfish washed up, and they're all drying up and dying. And the person starts walking down the beach and just throwing them back, one by one. And whoever is with them and watching them do this is like, 'What are you doing? This is so pointless.'

"But they pick up one starfish, and throw it back into the ocean, and say, 'Well, it wasn't pointless for that one.'

"And they pick up another one, and throw it back, and say, 'It wasn't pointless for that one.'

"And they pick up another one. . . ."

Now, thanks to Rosie, I can wake up on the bleakest days—when the sun has risen on another state's passage of a total abortion ban, or when a patient at the clinic will need more than I can give them, or knowing that a doula client is in distress or the Twitter timeline is a bonfire of rage, or all of these combined—and envision one starfish. Twenty dollars to an abortion fund, or a thank-you note to a provider, or someone who needs a ride and a hand to hold.

One little starfish.

Just take a step onto that beach. Just start with the first starfish you see.

Abortion Is Transformation

There is one perfectly ordinary moment, in all her years of doula work, that Gina Martínez Valentín will remember forever. She watched, through a series of otherwise mundane and unremarkable text messages—confirmations, scheduling details, and emojis—someone's life change, in real time.

"A client came to us who was a young college student," says Martínez Valentín, the executive director of the Colorado Doula Project. "And she had a pretty traumatic situation. But all of our interactions, over text, started out very one-word. *Okay. Thank you, ma'am. Yes, ma'am*, that kind of thing." The client was emotionally shut down, numb, just trying to survive her ongoing trauma from one unbearable moment to the next. She was in shock, far from home, terrified, and unable to communicate or express herself beyond the basics. Her pregnancy, the result of a sexual assault, was a weight she carried against her will. It flattened her spirit and made it unsafe to inhabit her own body.

"And then, after our doulas got her to her appointment, and to her hotel?" Martínez Valentín wraps her arms around herself in a hug and grins. "Suddenly, it was exclamation points, and hearts on my texts, and things like that. Because she no longer had to carry this pregnancy to term." The doula witnessed the shift, immediate, stark, and profound: the young woman was free.

". . . you know, her sadness and her fear came through. And then after she got her first pill, and knew she was going to be on her way home the next day, the whole communication changed," the doula says. "That's one that is really going to stick with me."

I've seen this transformation unfold many times, in someone's body and affect and mood, and I've felt it happen within myself. The churning brew of hormones and brain chemistry, bubbling over or upon the deliberate crossing of that strange threshold, from *pregnant* to *not pregnant*.

We recognize the period of time after someone has given birth as a unique hormonal and emotional season of transition: *postpartum*. There is a common understanding of those hazy first hours, days, weeks, and months as a singular space of strangeness, in which you might experience shifting and crashing hormones—combined with any number of circumstantial vectors of stress and exertion— as anxiety, depression, mania, confusion. A time in which you may not feel like yourself, you may feel out of control, or unfamiliar to yourself—both body and mind. Your own thoughts and actions can be foreign, surprising, and distressing.

When Zachi Brewster founded Dopo, the abortion-support co-op that has trained legions of abortion doulas and companions from around the world, she was naming that space. The Italian word, meaning "after" was the perfect thing to call her project, which would shepherd a whole new generation of doulas, care workers, and abortion companions into the work of that *after*— the post-abortion time of processing, healing, recovering, a time of overlooked or invisible need for support and care—while grounding their learning in reproductive justice and supporting them in a community that would love them, challenge them, and hold them accountable *and* accounted for.

Pregnancy itself is a transformation. And the longer a pregnancy continues, no matter its outcome, the more upheaval and change it will bring to a body, a mind, a family, a life. So as abortion bans and restrictions delay care, pregnancy will become a larger and larger part of an abortion experience: more symptoms, more hormonal shifts, more health risks, more emotional distress. Logistically, abortion care becomes more expensive and harder to obtain. Physically, a body takes on more stress.

It's okay for a pregnancy or an abortion to be *no big deal*. Some thing you don't think about much, something that doesn't change the rhythms of your life.

And it's also okay if it *is* a big deal. If, as you experience pregnancy and/or abortion, or even proximity to these things, you find yourself feeling the things that people have described to me, over the years: *out of control, wild, feral, not myself, like a stranger, night and day, a brand-new person*.

Transformed.

Abortion Is a Holy Blessing

I conceive of God, in fact, as a means of liberation
and not a means to control others.
—James Baldwin

I believe in God, and I'm not just saying that so my Lutheran grandparents hear me from the afterlife (though, obviously, I hope they do. I love you, Grandma Irene, and I *did* brush my hair this morning, even though it still looks tangled—I swear).

My relationship with God is deeply personal, attached to no one particular building or ritual or symbol or name. And I try, always—as I attend all the various religious ceremonies that are sacred to the people I love, and as I continue to explore the words and worlds of other people's gods—to avoid appropriating or claiming any faith traditions that are not mine.

The time I have spent with people through and after their abortions—in their homes, in their hospital rooms, in the snack-

and-comfy-chair mecca of the clinic's recovery room—has been, for me, the richest with epiphanic moments. Never are more frequent and intense feelings of connection to the divine generated than when I am present for a birth, a death, or an abortion.

So really, what I'm trying to tell you here is that I am that white-woman-with-a-nose-ring cliché you probably dread encountering at a party: *spiritual but not religious*. It's me. I'm sorry.

Over the course of my first year in the clinic, it quickly became apparent that virtually every person who harassed us, our providers, and our patients—the sidewalk protesters, the writers of the creepy letters and cards we received on a regular basis, the callers leaving threatening voice mails on our after-hours line—cited Jesus Christ (and/or his dad) as their primary source of intel on the evils and immorality of our work. There were, of course, the 40 Days for Life folks—a contingent of mostly-elderly white Catholics who would (illegally) lean their giant PRAY TO END ABORTION posters against the building. There was the suburban Evangelical church group, a crew of younger families who would shuffle their armies of children into the city and down our sidewalk once a week, to shout repetitive sermons at patients and escorts.

While I don't often see any particularly Christlike behavior from these folks, I *do* regularly encounter the presence of Jesus at work—on necklaces and prayer cards, and sometimes called by name in the voices of our patients. Many other gods join us there, too. Some patients bring with them tangible talismans of their faith, and many of those who don't, I came to realize, are still holding their god—Christian or otherwise—close to them before, during, and after their appointments. As a doula, I often ask if my client would like to read or hear any prayers or pieces of spiritual writing. I reflect and mirror whatever religious language my client uses—if they say "God," I say "God." If their god's pronoun is "she," I say "she." If someone says "the universe" or "Allah" or "the Virgin Mary" or "the baby's spirit" or "my mom in heaven," then I trust and believe that they are naming the source of strength who is with us in the room at that moment. Whatever is real for them is real for me, in that shared time and in that shared space.

Catessa, of the Alabama Cohosh Collective, identifies as a Christian (but also tells me that she doesn't like to subscribe to religious labels in general). "I'm aware that I am human and I do make mistakes, and I don't want to be nailed to a cross—much like the clients themselves," she tells me. "With their beliefs, you know . . . they don't want to be judged."

And what does judgment look like, in care work? Sometimes it is simply a failure to mind one's own business—asking questions that aren't relevant to someone's need for care, assigning a gender identity, sexuality, or social history to someone based on the information they've shared with you about their pregnancy or on their appearance and presentation, mining for details that aren't immediately pertinent to this moment in their life and the role you've been invited to fill. Sometimes it's a reaction of surprise or disbelief, rather than a neutral acceptance of fact, when they tell you a piece of their story. Sometimes judgment can take the form of skepticism, half listening, or assuming that your own knowledge and prior experience outweighs that of the person telling you about their own needs, their own life, their own body.

Catessa has no expectations of the patients she's supporting at the Alabama Women's Center, tailoring her offerings of spiritual companionship or support to each person: "If *they* believe in God, then I will pray with them. If they believe in affirmations, then I have affirmations for them."

Lindsey, another ACC doula, is cautious about bringing any religious elements to the support she provides—as an Alabama native, she is intimately acquainted with religious trauma and the way it can ripple outward through communities and families in the form of secrecy, abuse, oppression, and shame. She tells me, "I don't bring any explicit spirituality, because I'm so aware of how people have been potentially manipulated by religious spaces. It's like . . . you could be picking up something that you think is a plowshare, but someone else has been hit with it, so as soon as you pick it up and it's in your hands, you're harming them. There's always potential for that."

As I mirror someone's language around their pregnancy, I also take care to mirror the names they give to whatever forms of religion or spirituality are present in the room with us.

As a spiritually confused adult living and working within a decidedly more secular regional culture than that of Alabama's, I've found that accompanying someone through an abortion—if they *are* religious, or choose to bring faith into their experience—can be pleasurably reminiscent of my childhood weekends spent tagging along to the churches and synagogues and Unitarian summer camp gatherings of my friends. I show up when and where I'm asked to, I observe and listen, I show quiet respect, and—*if invited to*—I happily participate in carrying out the rituals or speaking the words that are holy and sacred to my hosts. Whatever they'd like to do together, we do together. Whatever they'd like to do alone, I witness, without intrusion or interruption. I follow their lead. I welcome *their* welcoming of me, however they express it, and remain open to whatever forces or ideas they choose to conjure or call upon, no matter how new or foreign to me.

Ava, a full-spectrum doula in the Midwest, practices in a similar fashion: "I really appreciate it when the folks that I'm working with are bringing a spiritual practice to their experience. I'm super supportive and open to that. Not something I'm gonna push, obviously, but always happy to connect this experience to spirituality."

Like me, she identifies as a spiritual—if not necessarily *religious*—person. "I grew up in a Christian church and was really disinterested in that for a long time. I've sort of started circling back—there are some things about it that I find really fascinating and beautiful, and then other things feel really harmful and not worth it."

Ava's own abortion, in 2017, felt charged and infused—joyfully so—with a feeling of liminality, of reverence, of the sacred and divine. "I really felt that I was in communication with whoever or whatever this being, spirit, creature was," she tells me, "and that the release was consensual. We were all on the same page. Everybody felt good about it."

To this day, Ava remains connected to that spirit and continues to encounter it, in different forms: "I think that whatever energy, spirit, connection that was . . . it has manifested in other ways that I was open to saying yes to, that I *wasn't* open to saying yes to as a human baby."

Others have told me, over the years, that they see the spirits of their pregnancies in all kinds of places: in stars and planets and constellations, unexpected visits from butterflies, the blooming of certain flowers, in animals they've adopted as pets, and tattoos they've commissioned in order to memorialize their pregnancies on their bodies forever. There are so many ways to honor and remain connected to the spirit, life-form, or energy you have released from your body back into the world—if you conceive of your abortion in that way.

Though my clinic is located in a state with a much smaller religious cultural presence than many others, we did have one explicitly religious resource for our patients in place, before COVID-19 protocols pushed companions and support people out of medical settings everywhere: a chaplaincy program. The program, through which a rotation of volunteer clergy members would be stationed in our recovery room on any given abortion day, was developed in the heady pre-pandemic days of the 2010s, when the health center could be packed to its fire-code-dictated gills with unmasked people, and when the act of holding hands with a stranger to pray didn't involve an awkward, frightening, complicated calculus of contagion and risk. As they recovered from their in-clinic procedures, patients could seek solace or conversation or prayer from these reverends and priests, each of whom emanated a warmth, a calm, and a stillness that touched staff and providers as well. The chaplains were a quietly radiant presence, a glowing core of love at the center of the bustling and often crowded health center.

Three of these wonderful folks, one autumn, decided to hold a clinic blessing—a ceremony and celebration to anoint both the physical space of the building and all the people within. They invited all employees, management, and clinicians and health care workers alike, to gather in a large conference room on the administrative floor above the health center. We were instructed to bring any festive refreshments we'd like, our family members or partners or friends, and our open hearts and minds. It really, *really*, felt like going to church. Many of my coworkers, who had distanced them-selves from the faith traditions that had brought them so much harm and manipulation and abuse, were skeptical. As we all filed into the room and congregated around the table piled high with potluck cookies and chips and wine, the vibe was hesitant, nervous, wobbly. The air in the room was a collectively held breath. Every-one's snark-and-sarcasm-as-defense-mechanisms kicked in, our fear sprouting spiky, sharp-edged jokes to be its armor. We were asked to sit, in rows of office chairs reminiscent of pews, replete with an aisle down the middle and the conference room's bright fluorescent lights buzzing away above our heads. A nurse rolled her eyes at me from across the room, as the prayers and speeches began; another made a wide-eyed face of discomfort when we spotted one another across the makeshift aisle.

But by the time one of the chaplains, a white-haired Episcopal reverend beloved by our patients and staff alike, was saying, "This place is holy, and beloved by God. Your work is holy, and beloved by God. *You* are holy, and beloved by God." I found myself blink-ing back tears, and I wasn't alone. A midwife sitting directly be-hind me reached forward to gently squeeze my shoulder, her own eyes welling up. God's love had been so weaponized against us— against everyone who provides and receives abortion care—and we had been told so frequently and with such conviction, for months or years or decades, that we were not deserving or worthy of this love, that many of us had numbed ourselves. We had cultivated a forced indifference, a defensive *Fuck you, too* stance in response to any overtures made by people we assumed (or had learned from past experience) would reject, condemn, and ostracize us. We had never heard words like this—not just tolerance, not just hollow

"God loves everyone," aphorisms, not a manipulative guilt trip urging us to repent or repair or reconsider. The reverend chose words that were affirming, deliberate, intentional, and glorifying: God loves *us*, specifically, for the abortion care (and all the other kinds of health care) that we seek, receive, provide, and advocate for, every day.

For many folks who access abortion care, faith and spirituality play a central role in their processing of the many complex emotions that can arise before, during, and after the end of a pregnancy. Humans love ritual, and we love belonging—the sense of a divine purpose, of being a part of something larger than ourselves. For some, prayer is a natural part of the abortion experience, a no-big-deal recitation or a habit they reflexively turn to when in need of comfort, peace, forgiveness, regulation of their nervous system, and/or reassurance of their goodness and humanity. They often don't need external acknowledgment or praise from anyone else in the room—they're having a private conversation with someone who knows better than any of us. For some other folks, emphatic and explicit reassurances from a human companion that their chosen God loves them and approves of their choice, and that they will continue to be embraced by their faith community, *is* needed and embraced.

People who've been raised in devoutly religious households have often been taught some pretty extreme things about sex, gender, medicine, and their bodies. There is a stark difference between the kind of generalized shame that any of us may have absorbed from the ether of our puritanical and stigmatizing culture, and the emotional anguish of undergoing a medical procedure that one's most beloved and trusted authority figures have explicitly taught them is murder, leading only to earthly misery followed by eternal damnation.

Hard to forget are patients like M., who believed that abortion *was* a grave and terrible sin . . . but so, too, was the use of contraception, in any form. On top of this, she had also been taught that she had a mandate to submit to her husband sexually. So she was trapped. Every day, she was forced to choose between three separate crimes against God, if she wanted to avoid a pregnancy that would threaten her life due to complications from a previous birth. Rather than leave her young children without a mother, M. broke her own heart, again and again. She was already in a kind of hell, grieving and racked with guilt, and—on top of the pain of her present circumstances—believing that an eternity of torment and suffering awaited her when she died.

Countering, shaking off, or breathing through some of the deeply traumatic messaging that a client may have absorbed and internalized over a childhood or a lifetime spent within a faith that condemns abortion can require a very specific kind of support. How can a doula or companion hold space for *all* the emotions that may arise, including those emotions that are negative toward our work, our existence? How can we view the moment through a lens that might feel foreign and ugly and alienating to them? How can we honor a person's attachment to traditions or communities that may appear to be causing them grave harm? That attachment, after all, belongs to them. It is part of them and what they bring to us in that moment and that space.

This is yet another way in which abortion care work has taught me how to be in the world, how to hold space for *anyone* with a quiet, open heart. We can never presume to understand the tangles of trauma and belief in someone's heart, the knot of influences and memories and religious experiences that often sits at the center of someone's view of the world and their own place in it. If someone lets me know that they are in search of some spiritual solace around their abortion, a connection with or a permission slip from their god(s), I turn to the faith leaders and care workers who have changed my own life with their writing and speaking on abortion.

ABORTION IS JUDAISM

The day of my Zoom call with Rabbi Danya Ruttenberg is a tough one; my baby is teething and cranky, my workday has been long, my type 1 diabetes is wreaking havoc on my sleep cycles and my body, and I've been wading through some grief with a post-abortion client who is struggling to find a rhythm of emotional healing. It feels as if a stone is settled deep within the center of my chest. But the minute that the rabbi appears on the screen of my laptop—which is balanced precariously on a stack of books atop the piano in my mother's living room, where I'm hiding while the baby yells his tiny head off down the hall—I feel the stone begin to crumble to dust and lift away on a breeze. As soon as I see her, bathed in sunlight and smiling warmly at me—the stranger who has barged into her extremely busy schedule to bother her for a private lesson—I find that my shoulders relax, and I can breathe a little deeper.

Hair tie around her wrist, she gathers her curls into a bun on top of her head (in the *Let's get down to business* move universally familiar to most long-haired people), and we start talking abortion.

Rabbi Ruttenberg, a scholar in residence at the National Council of Jewish Women and one of the founders of Rabbis for Repro, a network of nearly fifteen hundred Jewish clergy who preach, teach, and advocate for reproductive freedom, says—with no hesitation—that not only is abortion *allowed* by Jewish law but in fact: if the life or health—and that includes the *mental* health—of the pregnant person is at stake, abortion is *required*.

* * *

"The 'Old Testament' as Christians would say, the Hebrew bible, the Talmud . . . it's very clear on this," she tells me. For the first forty days of a pregnancy, she explains, the product of conception is "like water," and after that point, it is simply a part of the pregnant person's body. It is not until birth—until its head emerges from the pregnant person's body into the world—that a fetus takes on the status of personhood under Jewish law.

"Life and health are the most important things in Judaism, and whose health we're concerned about? Is the pregnant person's," the rabbi says emphatically.

When someone comes to her in search of spiritual guidance or solace regarding their own abortion experience, she is prepared to meet them with an incredibly rich and diverse variety of affirming and loving responses—as many different responses, in fact, as there are people and circumstances.

"It's a conversation that depends so much on context. If someone has had an abortion and is feeling unsettled, I would remind them again and again what Judaism teaches about personhood." Ruttenberg is drawing from her own complex lived experiences as well as her vast body of liturgical and spiritual knowledge.

"I understand, emotionally," she tells me. "I have been pregnant a bunch of times. I would make space for the grief. It's not just an intellectual conversation." She emphasizes the need for open, capacious, and expansive silence and listening.

"Honor what needs to be honored," she tells me, "make space for all of the feelings, including grief, including guilt, including relief, including guilt *about* feeling relief. Whatever is going on there, it all is worthy of being named." Here, imagining these conversations, she closes her eyes, and says emphatically to the hypothetical person in front of her:

"You are holy and created in the divine image. Your autonomy and your right to make decisions about your body is real."

* * *

Rabbi Ruttenberg knows very well the complex knots of identity, marginalization, circumstance, and emotion that shape each individual experience. "Abortion may be the correct answer for somebody, and they *still* may feel grief and wistfulness, and longing and relief. And, *and*: it's an extremely privileged thing to talk about abortion in the context of individual choice. If somebody has gotten an abortion because they can't afford more children, if somebody has gotten an abortion because they are undocumented and they cannot conceive of a way to have this child in a way that is safe, in a world where ICE is potentially coming to their door . . . that's a *very* different range of emotions that the person is going to be having.

"Potentially, we would talk about creating a ritual. Is there a letting-go ritual that needs to happen, is there a closure ritual that needs to happen?"

Ruttenberg goes on to teach me about the mikveh—a ritual cleansing bath. "One of the ways it's used is that after menses or after a miscarriage, it's used as a sort of spiritual reset button. And it's also used right before shabbat and right before Yom Kippur; it's really understood to be the thing that resets your energy. It's an energetic reset, it's powerful. There is a connection to reproductive spirituality. Healing after sexual assault, for example, or at the beginning and end of chemotherapy." And, she says, a mikveh makes a beautiful post-abortion ceremony.

"There is a lot of logic to it as a place to mourn, to let go, to release. You immerse in the ritual bath, you're totally naked, scrubbed clean. There is always natural water, rainwater or you go in a lake. And you design a series of intentions that can help somebody through a journey and a process, immersions that can help somebody have the emotional and spiritual release, and then come out in a different place."

* * *

There's no question that abortion bans and legal restrictions on abortion care in the United States violate the religious freedoms not only of Jewish Americans, but also of the many millions of *other* Americans who do not subscribe to the tiny religious subsets of faith tradition that explicitly teach that life begins at conception. Even folks who worship in all the same ways as those Christians and Catholics who subscribe to that one teaching, those of us who read the same texts and wear the same symbols but who have come to a different conclusion regarding our holy sovereignty over our own bodies, are experiencing a violation of our religious rights—and that's to say nothing of all the rest of us, the many Americans who may be reading different texts and worshipping different gods altogether. The Quran, for example, does not explicitly address intentional abortion, leaving Muslims to form their own views.

ABORTION IS ISLAM

The Ad'iyah Muslim Abortion Collective, a faith-based support network, operates from an immovable bedrock of belief that "Allah (swt) loves us all in abundance, and that we should be able to draw on Islam before, during and after our abortions, as we draw on Islam in all aspects of our life."[1] The community-based group, which holds monthly support circles for Muslims who have abortions and who support abortions, infuses its organizing and its gatherings with prayer and worship. Religion is central, rather than incidental, to its care work.

As Ad'iyah's founder, Ammaarah, wrote about this intersection in a piece for *gal-dem* magazine: "Islam compels me to fight for justice, but I cannot fight for anything unless I have full ownership and autonomy of my body."[2]

HEART, a national reproductive justice organization serving Muslims across the United States, now operates a fund specifically to provide financial assistance to those in need of pregnancy, miscarriage, and abortion care. And in a statement released with the American Muslim Bar Association in April 2022, HEART calls on us to meet any member of our community seeking abortion care and support with Rahma—the Arabic word for "compassion"—rather than judgment, persecution, control, or rejection.

Muslims are not a monolith, according to HEART, and do not hold a uniform religious view on when life begins. "Since Muslim pregnant persons, like others, are the only expert on their own lived reality, this complex, layered, and nuanced decision should be left to them and their individual conscience. And if they so choose, it's a decision that can be made with others, including their faith leader."[3]

* * *

Muslim community around spiritually supported abortion experiences is abundant: HEART has compiled a free downloadable guide of abortion resources on their website, Queer Crescent, a healing justice group of and for LGBTQIA Muslims, has launched both a reproductive justice storytelling program and a Bodily Autonomy fund, and social justice organizations like Muslim Women For, based in North Carolina, serve as a spiritual and political home and a wellness hub for those impacted by matters of reproductive justice.

Devout Muslims who have and support abortions are everywhere, and are engaging in abortion care prayerfully, thoughtfully, in conversation with God. The Religious Coalition for Reproductive Choice counts an Islamic prayer by the late imam Dr. Khaleel Mohammed among its many different blessings and meditations. "What is the first verse of the Quran?" Dr. Mohammed asks, before answering: "In the name of God, the Beneficent, and Merciful. It is not about judgment or forgiveness, even . . . but that beneficence and mercy and love that are part of God's essence.

"And for whom is the beneficence, this mercy, if not for you?"[4]

ABORTION IS CATHOLICISM

Much of our cultural messaging around abortion—namely the impressions of it as murderous, sinful, immoral, or evil—has roots in the Catholic Church. But a Catholic organizer and abortion doula named Lauren Morrissey tells me: "The truth is, in our faith, the Catholic Church has no official position on when life begins. Certain popes have staked out whether they think fetuses are human in encyclicals, but at no point does it say, in the Catechism, that life begins at x period of time." Morrissey explains, "It's in the Catechism that life begins at conception, but . . . what constitutes 'life'? When does the fetus have a soul? Why do fertilized eggs not implant sometimes? . . . These questions have been hotly debated over thousands of years of Church history. Still doesn't change the fact that this debate is used to distract people from the living, breathing, *definitely alive* pregnant person."

Catholics make up a sizable portion of Americans having abortions—and of the people I've supported in and out of clinics. According to the Guttmacher Institute: The majority of abortion patients indicated a religious affiliation: Seventeen percent identified as mainline Protestant, 13% as evangelical Protestant and 24% as Roman Catholic, while 8% identified with some other religion.[5] And many Catholics find themselves in need of abortion care after being discouraged—or outright prevented—from using birth control by their churches and communities.

One clinic staff member tells me of a patient who, at her seventh or eighth abortion appointment, reported: "I know that abortion is a sin, but so is using birth control. So I would rather sin ten times than wake up and sin every single day of my life."

I began collecting resources specifically for Catholic patients, clients, and community members, and for those who no longer identified as Catholic themselves but still wrestled with the stigma and shame they'd internalized through being raised in the Church. Catholics for Choice, an advocacy organization, became a frequent referral, as did Faith Aloud, a spiritual counseling organization with a toll-free clergy hotline[6] and an online library of religious abortion support resources for folks of any faith. Another essential resource for patients who wish to connect their experience with their faith is the Religious Coalition for Reproductive Choice, an organization that declares themselves to be "pro-faith, pro-family, pro-choice." Their online library of educational resources, the Religion and Repro Learning Center,[7] has taught me more about providing abortion care and support in different religious and spiritual contexts.

After a new doula client expressed that they were wrestling with shame and self-hatred because of their religious upbringing and the family members they knew would condemn them, I turned to my own Good Book: Instagram. I scrolled and scrolled through the hundreds of photos that had been posted under hashtags like #abortionisholy and #abortionisablessing. That's how I found Thank God for Abortion (TGFA), a radiantly positive, honest, and joyful multiplatform art project that celebrates and affirms abortion, queerness, sex, community, and humanity. TGFA uses Catholic iconography to change the narrative. It shouts and sings its glittery message of God's love through a bedazzled megaphone. It's miraculous.

Viva Ruiz, TGFA's luminous creator, self-describes as such: "The queer fluid descendent of Ecuadorian immigrants, and a community- and nightlife-educated advocate and artist, from and based in New York City." They tell me, "I come from people that believe in God and music and dance, and that's me, too." And those beliefs shine through in all of TGFA's effervescent pieces of public performance art, from the collective's fizzy eponymous anthem to its T-shirts and prayer candles, to its hit-and-run-style protest outside St. Peter's Square in the Vatican.

Ruiz, who prayed the rosary every night as a child, tells me, "I grew up in an extremely first-gen-in-America, Ecuadorian Roman Catholic way, meaning there were ancestral witchy practices, like herbal cures for evil eye, that somehow were a part of it, but they were against brujeria [witchcraft]. And we went to church every week."

From the very beginning, Ruiz strained against the rigid boundaries of their family's Catholicism, even as they aspired to rise within its ranks: "Gender roles were very binary, and very strictly enforced, at church and at home. I was devout, and was a lector—that was my first stage experience in life. I remember wanting to do the boys' parts but wasn't allowed, and I remember resenting that. I believed truly in Jesus Christ for a long time, I thought I would grow up to be a nun. I believed in and loved and needed the idea of sanctuary and unconditional love, I loved those aspects of the teachings: of justice, of caring for the sick and poor, of sibling-hood with everyone.

"My disillusionment with most of the clergy I actually knew— and with the Church, taking a genocidal stance while AIDS ravaged (our communities)—coincided with my discovery of punk rock music and alcohol. All that marked a big divorce with God and church. It seemed inevitable that I would, pretty soon after high school, be a sex worker, dancing in clubs all over the boroughs. Sex work was an important part of my sexual liberation: a kind of exorcism from stifling machismo control I had grown up under, and there was an inevitability to it, too, like it was where I knew I could find power and I needed to find that. I did consider myself priestess-ing in that work for that time, it was both holy and hell, because sex work with cis men can so quickly be dangerous. It's not something to idealize or demonize, it just was, and will be just another book I write someday, but sex work directly correlates to the way Christianity was imposed on me. Eventually I crashed and burned through substance use and found my way back to life through spirit. I had a reconciliation with the Church, or at least with the understanding of why people need church, remembering that original need for sanctuary that any kind of spirituality can provide.

"I never really had stopped being a believer or a seeker," Ruiz says, "and have since come full circle and beyond, in new spaces of communion with and about God/Spirit/Creator."

* * *

Lauren Morrissey is also a believer. Their undergraduate activism on the campus of their Catholic university—where they went to mass twice a week and navigated hostility from their fellow "diehard" religious students—is what led to the creation of the Student Coalition for Reproductive Justice, and they have been an outspoken religious and pro-abortion advocate at Catholics for Choice ever since. They have also trained to be an abortion doula, a role in which they live out their spiritual purpose gorgeously, authentically, sacredly. And, as they've grown and learned in these movements, they have made a spiritual home of direct abortion care work.

"It's extraordinarily difficult for me to think 'bigger picture' when the suffering is right in front of me," says Morrissey. "That's a very Catholic thing for me to say, too. Pope Francis and the Jesuits I learned from growing up were always calling us to encounter, to be in proximity to the suffering and injustice that exists from our sinful structures and systems. I think that's ultimately what led me to take the leap and become a doula and abortion companion. I want to support and hold space for the very real, very normal people seeking abortion right now."

It was only once Morrissey had started their doula training that they realized: "Abortion support work is literally ministry. *It's my ministry*. Ministry at its core is offering yourself up to another. Ministry is the work you do that is guided, driven, and fueled by your faith." Like many of the lay Catholic "saints," Morrissey says, they know now that they are ready and willing to dedicate themselves, heart, body, and soul to this ministry of abortion support. They are called by their faith, they tell me, "to give over my life to this work."

Morrissey asks, of the one in four US abortion patients who identify as Catholic: "Who is ministering to them? Who is ministering to the Catholics that want to pray before their abortions? Who is ministering to the former Catholics that still feel the guilt and shame about their bodies and their support of abortion that has been so deeply ingrained into their psyche? I need to step up.

"I do this all *because* of my faith," Morrissey says, "not in spite of it."

ABORTION IS CHRISTIANITY

Other denominations run the gamut on abortion—many devout and passionate Christians identify, publicly and wholeheartedly, as pro-choice and/or pro-abortion. The doulas of the Alabama Cohosh Collective, many of whom are deeply embedded in Christian families, communities, and traditions, shared with me the ways they incorporate prayers, rituals, and theologies from their various denominations and backgrounds into their abortion care— undeterred by the antiabortion messaging propagated by the politically conservative Evangelical churches who wield so much power over their state's laws and culture.

Eve, a doula client who was raised Methodist and still attends church most Sundays, told me about enfleshed, a religious nonprofit that provides liturgy and resources in what it calls "spiritual nourishment for collective liberation." Eve prayed before, during, and after her abortion—in fact, she told me, she prayed "harder than I ever have before in my life."

The day after my own abortion was complete, I remembered Eve's recommendation, and spent a quiet late night outside the baby's nursery reading through the organization's website. One piece of writing on the site, by cofounder and director Reverend M Jade Kaiser, had me weeping into my confused, but ever-tolerant dog's soft neck rolls, by the light of my laptop screen in my darkened bedroom, the baby snoring softly on the other side of the wall and cramps still rolling through my abdomen and lower back. It was the first time I'd cried since learning I was pregnant, a great gushing letdown of water and pain and guilt and relief and love, and the catharsis was coming not from the places I'd expected—my beloved friends and family, my books and music and theory—but from a stranger on the internet. It was coming from the words of a queer and nonbinary Christian reverend whose name I'd never heard before, whose work, church, and life were brand-new and wholly unfamiliar to me.

It was coming from God.

On Choosing Abortion

God is not a judge who sits at a distance
shaking "His" finger at us
about divine rules and regulations.

❦

God is within.
Like a whisper.
Like a question.
Like a knowing and a rising.

❦

God lures us towards each other. Towards collective flourishing.
Towards power growing from the margins. Towards our roots deep in
the earth.

℃

God pulls us in every direction that serves love and life.

℃

Sometimes that direction is abortion.

℃

(Excerpted from www.enfleshed.com.
Reprinted here with permission of its author,
Reverend M Jade Kaiser.)

Many doulas have created their own prayers, mantras, and in-cantations, in the contexts of their own cultures and communities. We've prayed with folks, listened silently as a client speaks directly to God, written letters to spirits both lost and found, burned hos-pital bracelets in a cleansing fire. We've thrown painted stones into the sea and buried memorial seeds and floated single flowers quietly out onto the still, dark waters of an alpine lake, in remembrance. We've helped to bless and sanctify too many abortions to count.

And I carry with me, offering it to anyone who needs it (a category which frequently includes myself) these shimmering and sacred words of wisdom from a fellow doula. They sit in my palms, on my tongue, in my pockets, at the ready, a delicate gift. They were first spoken to me by Catessa, holder of hands, wiper of tears, and soul-nourishing spiritual guide and companion, in Alabama, and I will repeat versions of it to myself and others for as long as I can speak. As Catessa says to anyone who is having, has had, or will have an abortion:

"I believe that God knew that you would be here, in this situation, and God knew that this would be the decision that you would make, long before you did.

"You don't need to explain anything to God."

Abortion Is Ceremony

I always remember the people who tell me of their ceremonies,
the letter they wrote to their spirit baby, or the dreams
they had that night. Abortions, like birth, can open a time
of deep reflection, a possibility to step into a new identity,
and an opening to connect with those around us,
the ancestors before us, and the ones
to whom we will become their ancestors.
—daena horner of Holistic Abortions

Six months from the day my abortion was complete, and a few
miles from the room where it happened, I stand at the edge of the
water, the stones under the soles of my soaked and frozen-numb
feet worn smooth by that gray-green Atlantic churn. I hold the yellow flower by its scrawny stem. After a minute, without thinking,
I bring its calyx to my face, the strange urge to kiss it on one of its
buttery petals overpowering my baseline of self-consciousness in
public places. A sudden rock in the motor of shame and embarrass-

ment that is always, quietly, humming along inside of me. *No one is watching you but the seagulls*, I tell myself, as one of the enormous and filthy birds dives screaming into the waves on the harbor, *and they don't give a fuck about anything*.

I kiss the flower once, twice, and then toss it outward onto the waves. It lands with a tiny slap, a shock of emerald stem and gold blooming across the dark surface of the water. The delicate petals, some ripped from their pistil by the impact, begin to detach and drift out with the tide. The little flower falls apart; it floats away; it is pulled and consumed and absorbed by the vast and freezing sea. I stand there for a long time, watching it leave.

I'm sorry, I whisper eventually.

And:

Thank you for coming to me.

And:

I love you.

And finally:

Goodbye.

* * *

Annie Finch, the witch and poet, was given a pebble to hold during her abortion. She chose it from the basket of pebbles on offer at the clinic, at the suggestion of the workers tending to her. She closed her fingers around its smoothness in her palm, clutching it tightly throughout her in-clinic procedure. The idea, she tells me, was that the little stone might receive and contain the soul she was releasing as her pregnancy ended. She kept the pebble for a while afterward. Then, when she was ready, she dug a little hole and buried it deep in the earth.

Molly, who identifies as a spiritual person, told me that after her abortion she felt a vivid and intense connection to the spirit of her baby—a little soul whom she felt *would* come to earth, but through another body, in a physical form other than that of the fetus she had grown so carefully and intentionally in her womb, had loved and bonded with so deeply, and then, distraught, had been forced to release back into the universe through the process of an abortion at twenty-five weeks. The pregnancy was not only long-desired but long-worked-for, at great financial, physical, and emotional cost. Its termination was for medical reasons only. Reasons that were, for Molly, heart-shattering. Utterly devastating. As a single mother by choice, she had spent years planning for this pregnancy and for parenting the child she hoped would result. She had endured fertility treatments, miscarriage, and the endless exhaustion of searching for sperm donors and health insurance and affordable prenatal care. And she'd undertaken *all* of this in a country, and a culture, as unsupportive of her desire to parent as it was disdainful of her eventual need for compassionate abortion care. Her post-loss rituals involved burial, memorial candles, stars, and flowers—and her daughter lives on in these.

Choice Words, an anthology edited by Annie Finch, gathers novel and memoir excerpts, poems, short stories, and essays on abortion by some of our all-time greatest thinkers—Audre Lorde, Ursula K. Le Guin, Langston Hughes, Amy Tan, Gwendolyn Brooks, Sharon Olds, and so many more. But after reading it, and after hearing of her work in other contexts, I became interested in Finch herself—specifically her work as a poet and a witch, in particular her epic-poem-meets-piece-of-radical-theater about abortion, *Among the Goddesses: An Epic Libretto in Seven Dreams*. The experimental writing includes a powerful healing ritual that Finch created for herself and her family after her own abortion. I have since shared it—along with her Ritual for Healing from Sexual Abuse—with many doula clients and friends in need of some closure, some ceremony to mark their loss or their transition.

A note: Finch does refer to the "baby" throughout; if this language doesn't resonate with you, feel free to replace that word with pregnancy, tissue, embryo, fetus, spirit, *or any other name that feels right for you.*

Finch writes, of the ceremony: "I developed it for myself and my family when I felt depressed after an abortion. For me the healing effects were immediate, complete, and lasting: in the twenty years since the ritual, I have felt only peaceful, calm, and grateful about my abortion. The ritual can be done any time after your abortion, even years later."

AFTER-ABORTION RITUAL
FOR RECOVERY AND HEALING

PREPARATION
This ritual can be done alone or with any or all members of the family or community affected by the abortion.

Prepare for the ritual ahead of time by taking quiet time to write a letter to the baby. Young children, or those who prefer not to write, may draw a picture for the baby, or create a piece of music or a dance. Bring along some grain such as millet, rice, oats, or flour. Also think about how you will give the four elements to the baby, and which chant or song you would like to sing.

THE RITUAL

*Build a small circular altar of sticks piled as high as you like.
Put anything you like on top: a shell, grass, special objects.*

*Arrange yourselves around the altar. If a family does the
ritual together, the parents might want to stand in the north
and south.*

*Create a sacred space around the altar. This can be done by
calling in the directions to cast a circle, or in any way you
like. To call in the directions, simply face each compass direction and ask "Spirits of the east (north, west, south, center),
please be with us."*

*Speak an invitation to any ancestors, spiritual guides, divine
beings, or presences whom you would like to support you in
the ritual.*

*Say hello to the spirit of the baby. Each person should use a
name that feels right to them; the names can be all the same
or different.*

*Convey your messages to the baby aloud. Read letters, talk
about pictures, and perform any music or dance messages.*

*Add the four elements to the altar: earth (perhaps a special
rock or stone), air (your letters or pictures, or a feather),
water (a little can be poured on the altar or left in a recepta-
cle), and fire (a crystal is good for this).*

Choose a simple song, such as "The earth, the air, the fire, the water, return, return, return, return." If you are in a group, sing it together standing still, then in a round (perhaps with female/male parts or however you want to break it up), then together again while holding hands and circling the altar (circle counterclockwise for releasing).

Scatter grain around the area to symbolize the life-force (or goddess/god) who gave the baby life, gave each of us to our parents, and is the source of life. You can sing another song together while doing this (A child in our family chose "Happy Birthday.").

Tell the baby goodbye, thank you, and that it will always be a part of your family.

Open (disband) the circle by reversing whatever you did to cast it. Say thank you and goodbye to any ancestors or spirits you invoked.

Be sure to allow some quiet time together afterwards to absorb the experience.

(Reprinted with the permission of Annie Finch.)

"It was very hard-won," says Finch of this ritual's creation, and of her subsequent post-abortion spiritual and emotional healing. "It didn't come easily. It had that feeling where you're kind of scraping by your fingernails up out of something really bad, and building it as you go."

* * *

If, as you read these words, you're thinking, *Well, I'm doing okay. I'm fine. My abortion was fine. Other people's situations are so much worse than mine*, I'm here to tell you that your own post-abortion ritual(s) can arise from anywhere. They can be made from anything, they can look and feel like anything, and you don't need to have endured deep trauma, grief, or hardship to need or want them in the hours, days, weeks, months, or years following your own abortions.

"The beauty of it," Finch says of her own ritual, which is meant to be adapted, played with, and fit to the lives and needs of any and all readers who find themselves drawn to it in any way, "is that *anyone* can do it on their own."

We're speaking to each other, the poet and I, after weeks of phone tag, our days piling up and overloaded with commitments—mine spent in the clinic and on doula shifts and futilely rocking and singing to my nap-striking toddler; Finch's fully booked with her schedule of readings and performances and her family's move to a new apartment.

"[My] abortion itself could not have been better," Finch says. "Ritual was the one thing that was lacking."

Like me, Finch was lent multiple layers of insulation from reproductive violence, emotional and physical safety, and legal autonomy by her social location when she found herself in need of abortion care. She was protected from criminalization and oppression by her material resources, class privilege, and the unearned benefits of moving through the world and the health care system in a white, cisgender body. She had support, comprehensive and compassionate care, and extensive community. She did not struggle with her decision to have an abortion, nor did she experience abuse or trauma in pursuit of it. And she describes the abortion itself, a straightforward in-clinic procedure at her local Planned Parenthood health center, as overwhelmingly positive and tender.

* * *

"But if you need ritual," Finch says, "you're going to need ritual. No matter what."

After her abortion, despite its relative ease and simplicity, Finch found herself plunged into an unfamiliar well of emotional darkness. She describes feeling "this incredible weight. Every morning when I woke up, it was just this something . . . *hard*. And it lasted months and months and months . . . almost a year of waking up with this heavy, depressed, bitter, hopeless feeling." She felt spikes of anger rise from a constant low hum of bitterness and resentment toward her husband, which was "kind of free-floating, and kind of related to the fact that I had done this thing and he didn't have to," she says. "He didn't understand."

Her voice falters as she calls forth the name that she's since been able to give that void, that state of static, hollow, darkness: "Aloneness. Alone. Everybody else was going on with their life, and I just felt stuck. And alone." She struggled to care for her children, one of whom was just four years old at the time, and to get through her days. Though she didn't regret her abortion, and though she thought only fondly and joyfully of the procedure itself and the care she had received throughout, that darkness—the weight pulling at her body, mind, and heart—never seemed to fade or shrink.

Nearly a year after her abortion, it hit her: what she needed was *closure*. A ceremony, a memorial, a formal goodbye to the pregnancy she'd ended. She couldn't open a new door, step into a new life and walk forward on a new path, because she hadn't yet closed the door of her abortion behind her. As she'd marinated in her grief for all these dark and heavy months, she had also been exploring spirituality, and ritual, and learning about her own spiritual power as she gradually came into her identity as a witch. Armed with new tools of transformation, and new depths of understanding her place in the world around her, she felt a light go on.

"One morning, I just woke up and put two and two together. Like, *Oh! We need a ritual.*"

Often, when I introduce the idea of a post-abortion ceremony, or memorial, or ritual, people ask me what they can expect to feel. "Will I cry?" one doula client asked me, looking hopeful. They'd been numb since their medication abortion three weeks earlier, their limbs heavy and their eyes dry as they went through the motions of their days and sent their emails and ran their errands, just as they'd always done. "Can we make it fun?" asked another, who'd been deeply unsettled since her own complicated procedure, unable to sleep and isolating from her partner and friends as she tried to process what had happened and why.

Just as with every other piece of your abortion experience, you may feel many things. You may even feel them all at once, or in rapid succession, or on a delayed release, emotions appearing much later than you expected and often out of the blue. Grief does what it wants inside of a body. As does trauma. As do joy, and love, and acceptance.

* * *

"I didn't know what would happen the next day, I just knew that it was this really, really beautiful, deep, wonderful experience that we all shared, and we were all humbled and moved by it. We were all so present in it. And then the next morning, I woke up with a light heart. I was so free of all of that shame and resentment. And it never came back. That was it.

"That was the only thing I needed."

While putting together *Choice Words*, Finch tells me, she noticed just how often an abortion experience was a powerful turning point. For self-empowerment, self-awareness, "for really coming into one's own as a woman," she says. "You know, that really was the moment when I fully came into my power as a witch, a priestess, a spiritual force. And claimed my spiritual sovereignty over my life." Which is one of the reasons Finch gives for her emphasis on reproductive autonomy as a spiritual right, and a religious freedom.

"The capacity to give life, and to not give life, is like the spiritual fulcrum of many of us who are childbearing people," the poet tells me. I run my hands across my abdomen as she speaks, envisioning little yellow flowers blooming inside my body as they bloomed on the ocean's surface. "And if we don't have full autonomy over that, it's taking away our spiritual core in a certain way . . . you don't just feel it in your mind and body. You feel it wholly."

"Abortion is a sacrament," says Finch.

"And I didn't understand that for a long time. But now I do."

Abortion Is Queer

I show up to the Dyke March after-party early, a truly impressive feat of uncoolness considering that the party's advertised start time is 6:30 p.m. and the sun is still high in the sky. The party is being held outdoors, in the parking lot of a kombucha fermentory. (We only live out our *favorite* lesbian stereotypes in this town, apparently.) I'm feeling unsure of myself, of my usefulness or desirability in this space, for many reasons: because of the still-unfamiliar shapes and angles of my postpartum body, because bisexual-girl-married-to-a-cis-dude can be a hard sell (or so I've been told, at great length and volume), and because COVID-19—and its attendant long stretches of isolation—have absolutely ravaged my social skills.

My social footing is still unstable, to say the least, as I park said husband's old pickup truck and hop down from its driver's seat, psyching myself up for the one and only Pride event I'll be attending this year—I'm in my thirties, after all, and there's a pandemic, and also my back hurts. As I cross the parking lot in my too-short baby-doll dress and my beat-up Birkenstocks, around the corner comes the glimmering spectacle of the chanting, dancing, sun-kissed Dyke March. I'd missed walking in it myself, due to some especially long hours at the clinic that day. I couldn't make it on time for the meet-up at the starting point, the procession of motorcycles known as the Dykes on Bikes out front, followed by a sweaty-but-joyful foot parade of truly gorgeous local queers, many I know and many more I don't, crossing the city to this kombucha-soaked outdoor after-party. I wave to my friends as they pass, cheer on the love and community and perspiration, and then I stand awkwardly, waiting. Waiting for the people I know to find me, waiting for the burlesque show or the poetry reading or the arm-wrestling match to start, waiting for attention and connection.

Then, I see them. Their face is unmistakable to me, because I met them long before the wearing-masks-in-the-clinic days of COVID-19, the days when I'd see whole faces, mouths and chins and nose rings like the one I recognize now. The owner of this jewelry has glitter splashed across their cheeks, their arm slung around the shoulders of some brawny and beautiful someone in overalls, grinning. When they catch sight of me, I watch their face move from neutral to surprise and then to excitement, as if their eyes and smile are bounding up a flight of stairs. They wink at me, give me a small wave. In a flash I'm transported to a day years earlier, holding their body up, rubbing circles on their back, feeling myself lose circulation as their strong hand clutched tight to my index and middle finger. After their abortion, I assumed, I'd never see them again. But here they are, sparkling away. I blow them a kiss, which they return, laughing. Then they disappear into the crowd, just another anonymous stranger at Pride.

Abortion care work is inherently queer. Intentionality; self-creation, self-determination, and self-possession; bodily autonomy; keeping one another safe and healthy despite the best efforts of the state; building our own selves and communities and families and futures and lives from scratch. Consent. Having sex for reasons other than procreation. Decoupling femininity from pregnancy or womb ownership, womanhood from motherhood, the expectations placed on our bodies at birth and our sovereignty in and over those bodies. That's queerness, baby.

Additionally, LGBTQIA youth are twice as likely to experience an unintended pregnancy than their counterparts, according to a study of high school students in the *American Journal of Public Health*.[1] And, as the CDC reports,[2] queer folks also experience higher rates of sexual assault and nonconsensual pregnancy. Many people find themselves in need of abortion care *because* of their queerness, not in spite of it.

Which is why, as of late, I've been especially distressed at the irony and the violence of all the TERF-y[3] rhetoric being launched at us, from all the usual hateful "conservative" sources and also the gray-haired cannons firing away from behind the money-lined fortress walls of "liberal" outlets like the *New York Times*, the *Atlantic*, etc., etc.—boom boom boom. Their outsize rage over seeing the term *pregnant people* supplant the (objectively less precise) *women*, for example, or their hand-wringing about being expected to use accurate pronouns and up-to-date trans-inclusive language in their reporting and editorializing.

Because I live in the icy darkness, at the northeasternmost tip of our country—where snow pelts us in our faces, and our gate freezes shut, and we are compelled by our bundled-up bodies and numb fingers to chop firewood (okay, fine, my husband chops all the wood) for approximately nine months out of the year—I own and wear a large collection of sweatshirts.

My very favorite sweatshirt, the one I find myself reaching into the chaotic depths of my drawer for first and frequently, is a soft and well-worn heathered gray crewneck, a variety of line-work-illustrated fungi screen-printed in black ink across its chest. The mushrooms are drawn in a variety of shapes and textures: long and conical, short and chubby, furry-looking. They grow in knobs and caps and tangles and stems of different sizes. Under them reads, in beautiful black script: *protect trans families*.

Moss Froom, the doula who designed this beautiful sweatshirt (and who, incidentally, is still selling it in a variety of sizes and colors[4] at the time of this writing—*all* the cool doulas and care workers have a minimum of one in their possession), is based in Baltimore, where they serve as a full-spectrum, queer-and-trans-centered birth worker.

"I actually started practicing when one of my close friends got pregnant," Froom tells me. "I was like, *Oh, I trained as a doula a long time ago, let me help you find your trans-affirming doula and your trans-affirming resources.*"

But their search—though Froom lived deeply and actively in the community and knew where to look and whom to ask—turned up a shocking and disheartening dearth of options. "I was like, *Oh shit, that's not a thing that exists, so I guess I'll just be that!*"

Now, Froom practices as a full-spectrum doula in private practice and also as a member of the Baltimore Doula Project. They offer their community a wide range of birth, postpartum, abortion, loss, and fertility support, and they also coach and train other folks in the practice of gender-affirming doula care. They have been especially sad to see the proliferation of misinformation and gaps in knowledge around fertility and conception when it comes to hormone replacement therapy, or HRT.

"There is definitely trans stuff around abortion that I think is worth keeping in mind," Froom tells me, "which comes up a lot in my workshops for other birth workers when I talk about trans-affirming practice." For example: "One big piece of misinformation about going on testosterone, where even doctors are telling people that taking testosterone as gender-confirming hormone therapy makes you infertile, which is just not true."

Froom is right, of course: testosterone is *not* a contraceptive, nor is its administration—even at high doses—in any way a reliable pregnancy prevention method. In fact, according to a 2018 study, rates of unplanned pregnancy in transgender men with a uterus are similar to those of cis women. This is true even when testosterone has caused amenorrhea, or the loss of a regular period.[5]

"So for a lot of people," Froom says, "after a certain amount of time taking testosterone, your ovulatory cycles may pause, but not for everybody. And some people—because of being told completely wrong information by their health care providers—*do* often get accidentally pregnant while they're taking testosterone. And not all of those times do people decide they don't want to (continue) those pregnancies, sometimes they do."

Maybe, I ask the doula hopefully, naively, this misinformation is simply a by-product of a form of transphobia that many providers are slowly (too slowly) unlearning and letting go of? And maybe they're dropping this advice from their counseling as they review the data, lose the antiquated research, and update their guidance for their patients? And the rates are going down, as these providers attend to correcting it?

But no. "There's a huge thing of trans people getting left out of the abortion conversation, while simultaneously, we often are needing to seek abortions because of this fucked-up, totally wrong information that spreads. Even now . . . it's not old information," Froom says, shaking their head sadly. "I have a friend who went on testosterone just last year and was told by their doctor that it was going to make them infertile. There's *no* clinical research [to indicate] that has happened. So because there's no research, providers have to assume worst cases, but they're assuming worst cases in this direction that is causing people to have unwanted pregnancies. I think they're worried about liability . . . being on the hook if somebody does experience infertility later. So it's a pretty common script for doctors to talk to their patients about fertility preservation."

Lauren Morrissey, the doula and organizer with Catholics for Choice, remembers: "I supported a college friend of mine in coordinating abortion care during the height of the pandemic. Not only did we both face barriers to access due to the impacts of COVID, but my friend is a trans man, so getting gender-affirming care was of utmost importance. We decided that a medication abortion was the best route, with time, access, and affirmation being the constraints.

"At the same time that I was supporting him through this process," Lauren tells me from their home in Washington, DC, "I was coming to terms with my own gender identity, and had begun asking friends to use they/them pronouns for me. While even before this change, I have always known that I would get an abortion if I was pregnant, listening to my friend process his feelings about the pregnancy was the most difficult part. Not only are we running the clock to terminate the pregnancy, but at every turn he had the added layer of seeing *women's health* in Google search results; pink, purple, and gendered colors on websites; and the pregnancy tugging him back into a headspace where his true identity was not valid to those around him, and [instead] tied to the capability of reproduction. I began to witness and share the pangs of sadness, hurt, and anger any time it arose. And ultimately, medication abortion was the way forward to remove that layer of stress from his abortion experience."

The easiest part of his experience? The abortion itself—thanks in large part to the care and support of his queer and trauma-informed community of friends and loved ones. "Medication abortion allowed my friend to take full control and be in the driver's seat," Lauren says. "He was safe, affirmed by his community, and grateful not to be pregnant. And that is all I could ever ask for."

"This issue is not merely philosophical for our community," Imara Jones, the founder and CEO of TransLash Media, told *Teen Vogue* in a 2022 interview. "Trans people have babies, need general access to reproductive medical services, and have abortions. However, we do so within a health care system that is often hostile to our very existence. By not including trans people in this fight, the overall reproductive justice is smaller and weaker."

Other essential voices at the intersections of trans liberation and reproductive justice include that of Cazembe Murphy Jackson, a Black trans man from the South who tells his abortion story through We Testify and writes for publications like *Esquire*. "In these moments," he wrote for the magazine in June 2022, responding with clarity and power to the Supreme Court's decision to overturn *Roe v. Wade*, "I often think about what my grandmother used to tell me: *If they come for you at night, they will come for me in the morning.* In other words: If you are not safe, then I am not safe, either. That is why this has to be all of our fight. Collectively. All of us."

Over the course of his appointment, for example, Max will be confronted more than once with his deadname—the name he was assigned at birth (and which has become synonymous, for him, with the years of abuse and violence he's suffered while inhabiting the feminized and sexualized body that doesn't match his actual gender or self). He has to see it on his paperwork, his real name relegated to a *Nickname* box and given quotation marks on his intake forms, and even to overhear it spoken in error, at one point, by one medical assistant to another. This is because the clinic can only bill his health insurance company if his name in their medical software system matches the legal name attached to his insurance policy. Because he has not yet finished with the arduous (and often dehumanizing) process of a legal name change, his insurance card and all associated documents bear this name, which is not his.

While it's obvious that trans, nonbinary, and gender-expansive people who were assigned female or intersex at birth experience pregnancy and have abortions, the data that has been published on their care preferences and outcomes is, at the time of this book's publication, scarce and woefully insufficient. The cited statistics that inform our concepts of abortion often refer only to women, and so often abortion is discussed in euphemistic terms like *women's health* and phrases like *a woman's right to choose*. Many independent abortion clinics and advocacy organizations still bear names that include the word *women*, and—not having the budget for a rebrand or the household name recognition to keep their communities aware of their continued operations if they *did* change their branding—are unwilling to make a shift to more inclusive or accurate language (though most *have* made that shift in their day-to-day patient interactions, and in all discussions of the health care they provide and the populations they serve).

Abortion care and gender-affirming care (such as hormone replacement therapy) are deeply connected—many abortion clinics also provide transcare, using an informed consent model to ensure that someone is able to make the medical choices that belong to *them*, and trusting that *they* are the expert on their own body and what is "medically necessary" for their own health, safety, survival, and happiness. It is no coincidence that those lawmakers who seek to ban abortion care also attack gender-affirming care (for trans people, that is—cis women's breast implants and BBLs, and cis men's usage of testosterone, are notably *not* subject to transphobe's insistence that gender cannot be changed, enhanced, performed, or played with). A citizen maintaining and exercising control of their own body—and especially of its sexual and reproductive organs and functions—is a frightening prospect to a white supremacist state which seeks to keep us poor, tired, busy, working in order to spend money and spending money in order to work, and always producing more laborers (our children) to replenish the workforce, to be chewed up and spit out by racial capitalism.

But for the trans, intersex, and gender-nonconforming members of our communities, sexual and reproductive health care settings are often not the safe spaces they should be—and this can be especially true of clinics and organizations managed and staffed by cisgender care workers and providers. The doulas and companions

You or Someone You Love

who operate outside of these institutions can be instrumental in partnering with trans people to figure out where and how to get their abortion options counseling or their care, and in helping to ensure that they are not only tolerated or respected, but honored, seen, and heard for exactly who they are while doing so.

An example: often cis care workers revert to gender-*neutral* language when we need to be using gender-*appropriate* or gender-*affirming* language. If the person in front of you tells you that he is a man who identifies with the concept of fatherhood, refer to him as a "pregnant person." He's a dude, who might think of himself as a future dad, and might want you to use the language that applies to *him* and *his* care specifically.

Being Ezra's doula meant using the words *dad* and *father*. Being J.'s doula meant asking, "What words do you like to use to describe (body part)? What language do you want me to use when we talk about the things that may happen in your body?" Being Ruthie's doula meant fighting for her right to bypass an internal ultrasound that she knew would trigger gender dysphoria and intense physical and emotional distress. Being Nico's doula meant never touching their body. (Being *anyone*'s doula, of course, means asking, always: "Can I touch you here?" And then "Is this okay?")

Sometimes they'll shrug, or say it doesn't matter to them, or they'd really rather not even get into it—often they are trying to maintain a level of dissociation, a distance from their body and surroundings that allows them to make it through the next ten minutes, next hour, next two days. Capitalism doesn't give us breaks for our breakdowns, after all, and they can't afford the interruption of a bad day, let alone a full-blown mental health crisis. People often understand that they have neither the time nor the capacity to fully engage with the trauma of their lived realities. So, as I move forward with any conversation of their body and its processes, I defer to the most gender-neutral terms possible. As simple as substituting *chest* for *breast*, or *internal pelvic area* for *vagina*, there are many resources for gender-neutral or trans-inclusive terms and concepts—I lean on the compiled knowledge and tool kits of programs like Rainbow Health, the Transgender Law Center, UC Davis's LGBTQIA Resource Center, and the expertise of the queer and trans abortion storytellers who share their experiences and their preferences. The terms don't always feel graceful in my mouth, at first. And that's okay.

"Using language like chestfeeding, front hole, etc. is a stumbling block for some people," says A. J. Lowik, a postdoctoral fellow and instructor at the University of British Columbia and the creator of the Trans-Inclusive Abortion Care Manual. And Lowik knows better than most, from their years of research and teaching and from their work consulting on issues of trans inclusion in reproductive health care spaces, what most often trips cis care workers up. Pronouns and terms and concepts that are new to you may elicit anxiety or discomfort if you're worried about messing up and causing harm. But, they say, as with every other aspect of providing abortion care or support, we must remember: it's not about us. If we stay busy cringing at the sound of our own clumsy voice, or analyzing our own performance for gaps in our confidence and competence, we've forgotten to hold the person we are supporting in the center of the frame.

Centering that person, and deferring to their authority on the subject of their own body and care needs—that is the first step toward the light for anyone, whether you hold a medical school or a middle school degree, whether you've read volumes of research and theory or just a few basic online articles. "Trans-inclusion is just trauma-informed,[6] patient-centered care delivered in a way that is non-assumptive about gender," says Lowik. "If you are already committed to asking for consent prior to touching someone, fostering agency and autonomy in decision-making among your clients/patients, mirroring your clients/patients' language . . . working to build trust with your clients/patients . . . then you are *already* doing the work!

"I use the adage: 'Nothing about us, without us,'" says Lowik. "Let's face it, trans people are everywhere, and there is no reproductive health or justice issue that isn't also a trans issue."

Abortion Is for Every Body

Kiki was turned away from the abortion clinic where she'd made her appointment. She was turned away, even though she'd scraped together enough money to pay for her abortion, and even though the gestational age of her pregnancy was well within the clinic's scope of practice. She was turned away, even though she'd already completed the intake process and signed the forms documenting her full and informed consent to the procedure. She was turned away because, as a type 1 diabetic, her blood sugar was ruled to be "too high." It *was* high—fluctuating between the high two hundreds and low three hundreds.[1] Kiki was unhoused at the time, rationing her insulin, and didn't have a primary care provider (let alone the ability to see the type of specialist that would typically be overseeing the resource-draining and labor-intensive management of her extraordinarily complex chronic illness).

She was stunned, as was I, when the clinic offered her no solutions other than to ask to reschedule her abortion procedure; the staff asked, instead, about what she had eaten that morning, and what she was doing to "control" her illness in general. The illusion that we, as humans, have control over our bodies and our health, is a primary contributor to the ableist and moralizing rhetoric harming disabled folks even in the most progressive and "inclusive" movements and spaces. There is a reason that, in many disability justice circles, we hold that a person can only be *temporarily* abled. That there exists *no* perfectly abled human being, no body capable of meeting every one of our society's "health" performance metrics for the entirety of its life span.

As someone who works for a clinic myself, I understand the squeeze of a packed patient schedule. I understand the rigid boundaries put in place to keep patients and providers safe—especially patients and providers who are already under siege, in legal and political arenas and in the all-important megaplex of public perception that contains them. But as a doula and a disabled person, here is what I understand: Kiki needed an abortion and did not get one, because she was disabled.

The very people who should know better than anyone how to listen to a patient about the realities of their own body and life and circumstances—that is to say, abortion providers—did far too little listening to the person inside the body producing too much glucose for their liking. Had they done more of it, Kiki could have explained that she was in a post-meal spike and that—given water and time, and a correctional dose of insulin, once she figured out how much of the $300-a-vial drug she could afford to spare—she'd be back in her typical glucose range within an hour. Or that she had previously been sedated for medical procedures while maintaining a similar blood sugar reading, and it had not posed a problem.

Diabetics wouldn't last a week, were it not for an extraordinarily detailed level of self-knowledge, and a constant engagement with the complexities of our bodies. We simply would not survive if we needed doctors and nurses to manage our illness for us. *No-body* could have understood the unique and specific risks and benefits of undergoing this procedure in this moment better than Kiki. But rather than being consulted and respected as the expert and the authority on her own disability—and thus, her own body—she was denied this safe and straightforward health care. She was made to feel broken, unwelcome, *other*. On the day she was scheduled to return, she didn't eat much all morning—though she was hungry and though there was no medical guidance to avoid food or drink leading up to her specific procedure. She sat shakily in the clinic's colorful waiting room, her empty belly growling, flooded with nausea and hormones and now also with fear, of what her blood sugar levels would be and what might be said to her about it.

My blood sugar level, at this particular moment, is hovering around 241 mg/dL. *Your* blood sugar level, if you are not diabetic, is almost certainly resting somewhere between 90 and 120 mg/dL, the range that keeps your body safe and healthy and functioning. A reading of 241 is high, potentially dangerously so, but better than the levels in the 300s and 400s that my continuous glucose monitor was reading last night, the *BEEP BEEP BEEP* of its alarm piercing my dreams and driving me, dehydrated and nauseous and frantic in my half-waking state, to inject myself with insulin again and again—insulin that wasn't working in my bloodstream anyway, because ketones had already spilled into my urine and I was dehydrated and confused.

Like Kiki, I have type 1 diabetes, meaning that my pancreas fails to produce the insulin necessary to keep my blood moving through my body at the levels of glucose that would keep me alive. So, in order to keep *myself* alive, I use a small robotic device, an insulin pump, as a substitute for the loser-ass organ who didn't even give me two weeks' notice before it up and quit on me. The long plastic tubing of my pump is nearly always visible under my clothing, and if you spend any time around me you will likely also notice me pricking my finger and measuring the glucose in my blood, filling my pump with more insulin, or inserting new cannulas into my skin with tiny spring-release needles. While I don't face the same barriers to access as does someone who uses mobility aids like a wheelchair, for example, or who requires ASL interpretation, my disability shapes and colors my every minute on this earth— my work, my relationships, my choices, and my bodily autonomy.

To survive a day on earth, I rely on machinery, on flimsy plastic cannulas and needles, on wildly unaffordable health insurance, and on what meager subsidies and miserly insulin assistance programs have cropped up among the health insurance companies and pharmaceutical giants holding our heads underwater. I relied on abortion funds for my own procedures in large part because my savings had long been depleted by the thousands of dollars in co-pays, co-insurance charges, and deductibles that I owe to various medical providers at any given moment.

Disabled and chronically ill folks face a different set of rules entirely when it comes to accessing reproductive care that is safe, affirming, nonjudgmental, and loving—or any other such health care, for that matter. The world does not intend to allow us much beyond survival, on the days it grants us even that. As Kiki's story tells us, ableism is so rampant and so normalized in every facet of our society that it is baked into the business models and the structures of even the most progressive and "inclusive" abortion clinics and reproductive justice organizations.

Leaders like K (Toyin) Agbebiyi are bringing disability justice to the forefront of abortion care. Agbebiyi, a Black nonbinary
femme lesbian and a disabled organizer, writer, and macro social
worker based in Atlanta, has been working and dreaming at the
intersections of reproductive justice and disability justice for years.
Agbebiyi has written extensively about the imagination required to
build new structures of care. Who can access not just the event, but
the *meetings* about the event? Who is being asked to do the labor
of making special requests, sharing personal information, engaging
in needless debate or discussion? Who is being told, implicitly or
explicitly by a care worker or organization, that their presence and
their contributions—that their bodies and comfort and health and
safety and *existence*—don't matter?

"For me, it's been really meaningful to be an out and proudly
disabled person in repro," they say, when I ask about how their
work is feeling these days. "I like knowing that I can push us (I'm
including myself here) to think about access in more radical ways,
and to make sure that disability justice isn't just a talking point."

Disabled, mad, and chronically ill folks are often denied care,
or harmed by the care they *do* manage to access. And—as holds
true in all forms of oppression—ableism baked into our systems of
abortion care and support hurt *every* person in need of an abortion.
It's not just those of us with official diagnoses, or who bear the label
of "disabled," who suffer. As the COVID-19 pandemic sickens and
disables more and more of us, often without official diagnoses or accommodations in place, we will need to consider what "accessibility"
means in our work. We've seen repro-related events, conferences,
parties, social gatherings, and even—in perhaps the most distressing example of our abandonment—workplaces go mask-optional

or entirely mask-free. We've seen testing and quarantining precautions fall completely by the wayside in favor of more productivity and profit, more fun, more inaccessibility to those most vulnerable in our movement. This despite the reality that the virus and its ripple effects—just like the abortion bans, the violence of the medical industrial complex, and the reproductive injustices against which we spend our days, our lifetimes, fighting—disproportionately kills and impacts Black and other people of color, poor people, sick and disabled people, marginalized people. *We* are the "patients" to whom our bosses and donors and even some respected movement leaders refer, in their justifications for inaccessible spaces, inaccessible care, inaccessible employment practices, and social expectations.

Moss Froom, the full-spectrum doula in Baltimore, recounts to me an experience they'll never forget, of a person's own body being used against them as they sought care. Froom watched in dismay as their client's legal clocks ran down and then, heartbreakingly, as they were ultimately denied the procedure. The stated reason? Low iron levels. The patient, who did not identify as disabled at the time, was shuffled from clinic to hospital, where they endured invasive tests and painful blood draws.

"This person got the appointment, found childcare for the day, and then they got there and because their iron was too low, they were sent to the hospital for a blood transfusion to try to get their iron up," Froom tells me. "And they were in the last days where they could qualify for this abortion, even at this clinic.

"I had not realized what a specific set of circumstances you have to maintain in order to qualify to get an abortion, especially later in a pregnancy. I had never heard of someone getting turned away because of something like low iron before. I was just like, yeah, I'm going to just hang out with you and try to help you advocate for yourself in this Adventist hospital.

"It was like running out a clock on so many levels. The clock for the day to try to get back to the clinic before it closed so they could get the appointment for the day they had and then that clock ran out so it was just trying to get out of there, and figure out childcare back home, and then one by one, all these clocks were running out." Unable to stop time, Froom felt powerless. They sat beside their doula client, listening, talking, witnessing their distress, their anxiety, and their pain as each of these artificial deadlines approached and then passed.

To engage with this person—their suffering and their loss—was all that Froom could do. It was long, and ugly, and exhausting. But they were there, from the beginning of the experience to the painful end. Listening, accompanying, advocating. They never left the person's side.

There are more than one billion disabled or sick people on this planet, a number that grows every second. And you can never assume that you know who these people are. My disability is relatively invisible, but it affects every decision, every expectation, every moment of my life.

Agbebiyi described the core of this intersection beautifully when she tweeted, "Repro justice without a commitment to disability justice just gets us back to square one. Like if you want to talk about groups of people who routinely have their reproductive autonomy violated . . . and we're just expected to take it."[2]

"Disability justice means realizing that disability intersects with all other forms of oppression to shape the way that we all navigate our lives," Agbebiyi tells me later, via email. "Therefore, a commitment to disability justice to me means that we are consistently fighting for, centering, and remembering and caring for the disabled people in our communities because we view ours and their freedom from oppression as intrinsically tied together.

"I'm seeing a lot of people discuss disability justice now, especially with COVID," Agbebiyi continues, "but as things are shifting around, I still don't see DJ actually being used as a framework for organizing. People frequently only think about one type of disabled person (usually white) when they discuss disability justice, and that shapes the ways that they organize. For me, it's been really meaningful to be an out and proudly disabled person in repro. I like knowing that I can push us (I'm including myself here) to think about access in more radical ways, and to make sure that disability justice isn't just a talking point."

For a space or organization to be acting in accordance with the values of reproductive justice, it must be safe and accessible for everyone—that means masks and COVID-19 precautions so that immunocompromised and disabled people can be safe, wheelchair and other mobility accommodations, considerations of language justice and of light and volume and ASL interpreters, closed captions, service animal access. Not only do I have the right, as a disabled person, to exist safely and comfortably in a space, but also to be admitted into the conversations which concern the accommodations necessary to honor that right. Nothing about us, without us.

The same principles can be applied to providing abortion care or support to people who use drugs. More vulnerable to criminalization at nearly every stage of their pregnancies, people who use drugs deserve not only to be allowed into our spaces of abortion care but to be allowed into the rooms where decisions are being made about the ways they experience those spaces, and the ways in which we are (or are not) protecting their autonomy and their sovereignty over their bodies and medical decisions in those spaces. And we can start with ensuring their survival of them.

The National Harm Reduction Coalition (NHRC) is a good access point for doulas and community care workers—and really, for anyone at all—into the work of unlearning our shit around (certain) drugs and (some of) the people who use them. Because we all use drugs, all of us. The NHRC's website also has a useful tool for finding Narcan—or naloxone—a synthetic drug that blocks opiate receptors in the nervous system, thereby reversing an overdose.

At the clinic—because we are a medical facility—we have Narcan on hand at all times. As a doula—because I am a person moving through a world in which people (including my ex-husband, a beloved son and brother and a young father of two) are dying tragic and preventable deaths by overdose every day—I keep it on hand, too.

Every body on earth belongs to someone, and only mine belongs to me. Keeping my abortion care and support practices accessible to everyone ensures that I am never making decisions for someone else's body—that they don't need or deserve the abortion care they want, when and how they want it—when I should not be.

As the disability and transformative justice movement worker and educator Leah Lakshmi Piepzna-Samarasinha expresses in the essay "Care as Pleasure," (a piece of writing that set off fireworks

230 YouYou or Someone You Love

of understanding in my brain when I first read it, in the pages of adrienne maree brown's effervescent and radiant book, *Pleasure Activism*): "I want there to be a diversity of care tactics. And I want everyone to create wildly intimate, healing relationships where your care needs are present in the room, not crammed in the garbage. I want everyone to have access to this joyful, dangerous, wide-open pleasure, because it's the vulnerable strength we all deserve."

* * *

Many of the people who don't identify as disabled—those who are, however temporarily, considered to be able-bodied—who are fueled by illusions of self-reliance, "health" and wellness, control, and individualism, have so much to learn from these communities of disabled people. The ways in which our health depends on the health of others, our immunities and vulnerabilities inextricably tangled up in one another's. And how we must work together, if we are to survive and thrive.

Abortion Is Consent

For many people, their abortion is the first truly consensual experience of their lives. It is the first time they are empowered to do only what their body consents to, and the first time that claiming that power does not have a price of conflict. It's the first time they are asked, start-to-finish, at every step of a process they've initiated:

What does your body need? What do you?
Where do you want to be, and when?
Is this okay? Is this?
What would you like me to avoid?
How can I make this part feel safe?
Is it okay if I touch you? Would you like me to tell you before
*   I do?*
Would you like to know what's happening?
How does that feel?
How does this?
What do you need as you recover?
How else can I care for you?

Of course, nonconsensual abortion care happens—people do experience threats, persuasion, controlling behavior, intimate partner violence, and reproductive coercion by a partner or family member. And sometimes, abortion providers or care workers violate consent, in all the ways endemic to the medical-industrial complex, through which capitalism and white supremacy are wielded against the individual human bodies, needs, and desires of the people it labels "patients"—especially patients who are Black, Indigenous, or other people of color, those who are trans and queer, those who are poor, and those who are disabled.

Screening for the signs of reproductive coercion, asking explicitly for someone's consent and checking in frequently on its status, and always, always *believing* someone when they tell you about what they've experienced—in their homes and relationships, during sex and pregnancy, while seeking or receiving abortion or other health care—are the first steps to partnering with someone in protecting their dominion over their body, their life, their choices, their consent.

* * *

Two years before Tessa's first abortion, she was a fresh-faced first-year undergraduate student, eagerly searching her state university's campus bulletin boards for fliers about the club she already knew she wanted to join: Students for Life of America.

You may know Students for Life of America—also known as SFLA, SFL, or just by the concise (and kind of hilarious) misnomer Students for Life—by their branding. WE ARE THE PRO-LIFE GENERATION, their bold, jewel-toned posters and shirts proclaim at their marches and demonstrations (belying the fact that nearly 70 percent of Americans under thirty believe that abortion should be legal in all or most cases, according to the Pew Research Center).

Tessa's childhood and adolescence had taught her *very* well in the matters of belonging, believing, and behaving. As I click through the sections of its website to read about Students for Life's various programs for youth, one of which is represented by a child-like icon of a yellow school bus, I imagine little Tessa among the groups crowded into the classrooms and summer camps of the organization's stated methods therein. I see her big brown eyes and monogrammed backpack in every sentence of SFLA's official strategy for, in their words, targeting "young people during their crucial developmental years." That formative education is why—before the abortions that would save, and also create, her life—she was wandering her college campus, looking for the inaugural meeting of the student club whose self-proclaimed mission was—and still is—to "abolish abortion."

She can recall in vivid detail, all these years later as we sit together in her living room, the moment she finally, triumphantly, became a member of her college's SFLA chapter. It was one of her first priorities as a freshly arrived student, both because she wanted to make friends and because she was deeply passionate about the organization's cause—she felt deeply that abortion was killing a baby, and that it was incumbent upon her and all good people to stand up against it.

"I was like, *Dead babies are bad, full stop*," she tells me with a wistful laugh. She describes the T-shirts they wore, which bore tiny footprints—the very same footprints printed in pink and blue on my son's hospital-issued receiving blanket when he was born. Baby footprints.

The group met frequently, and made themselves a vocal presence on campus. Some were the kind of politically conservative young people one might see crowding the front row of a service at a suburban megachurch, eyes closed and hands raised in worship, tears streaming down their faces. Some were the kind who might mix American flag iconography with Bible verses, silhouettes of guns, and abstract crucifix designs on the throw pillows and fleece blankets that decorated their dorm room bunk beds. And some, like Tessa, were less politically expressive, certainly less overtly religious, and concerned themselves more frequently with humanity and concepts like "kindness" and "peace" than with hell and who might be going there.

When they caught wind of the fact that their university's rival club, called Students for Choice, was planning to host a talk that would be given by a local Planned Parenthood representative, SFLA decided that they would "crash" the event. Tessa naively assumed that this would entail some sort of peaceful protest outside the lecture hall where the talk was to be held. But when she arrived, wearing her SFL baby footprint T-shirt and ready to take a (silent, nonconfrontational) stand against abortion, the president of the group led them all through the doors into the SFC event, which was already in progress. She led them up the aisle to the hall's back row of seats, holding their brightly colored poster boards bearing Sharpie-drawn slogans like PRO-WOMAN, PRO-BABY, PRO-LIFE / WOMEN DESERVE BETTER THAN ABORTION. They sat. The SFC members, stunned, looked at one another, unsure how to proceed. There were whispers, heads turning back to steal quick glances at the SFL crew in their matching shirts and their stony expressions. Tessa quickly realized, watching these students—even though *they* were the bad guys, the baby murderers, they were afraid.

The tension in that lecture hall, she tells me, was unbearable.

If the speaker from Planned Parenthood noticed the seismic shift in the mood of the room, she took care to stay focused on the task at hand—she blinked once, confused, but smiled as she continued her talk. She was a petite woman, who looked to be not much older than the undergraduates in front of her, and her face is burned into Tessa's memory. She had dark and curly hair, wore a yellow sweater, and had a warmth and a brightness to her that Tessa says she won't ever forget watching darken and dim, as the Students for Life took their stand, in that too warm and too-quiet auditorium.

At first, their interruptions were sporadic—a hand raised here, a question shouted there. But then the SFL escalated, employing more aggressive tactics in an attempt to provoke an emotional response.

"Can you explain why you think killing babies is okay?" one of the leaders called out. The Planned Parenthood speaker wavered, momentarily, before continuing. She was immediately interrupted by another voice from the back row: "How does it feel, when you kill the babies?"

The speaker faltered and fell silent. Tessa noticed that her hands were shaking. She was quiet for a moment, then continued her lecture, but her voice dropped out of her words. Her chin quivered. She started her sentence again, her eyes wide and her arms hugging herself in the universal body language of self-protection. Her posture was shrinking.

Tessa's heart pounded in her ears. Was she doing the wrong thing? The students who had been quietly sitting in this lecture hall hadn't been bothering her. They were the enemy, sure, the baby killers. But they were also young and idealistic, like Tessa and her friends, and wanted to help people. They thought they were doing the right thing, just like her. A sudden, powerful urge to smooth out the unbearable tension, to bridge the gap in the room, to somehow connect the two groups of impassioned student activists, overtook her body. Before she even realized it was happening, she was raising her hand. The speaker ignored her, expecting more harassment, so she rose to her feet. She called out, hopefully:

"Maybe Students for Life and Students for Choice could unite to educate people about birth control, so there will be fewer abortions!"

The speaker sighed, resigned, and gave a nod. "Planned Parenthood absolutely provides and supports access to methods of birth control."

Tessa was pleased, feeling that she had found some common ground. But as she lowered herself back into her seat, she saw two of the Students for Choice exchange an exasperated eye roll. She was confused—hadn't they just been excited about promoting birth control on campus? She looked to her left and was shocked to find her own group's leader glaring at her.

"We consider birth control to be an *abortifacient*, Tessa," the leader hissed, in a rage-filled whisper. Her eyes narrow, she turned back to the front of the hall, and shouted, "Murderer!"

At that moment, it hit Tessa square in the chest—the full weight and velocity of the realization that had been brewing to a boil from the moment she took her seat, uninvited, in that lecture hall. Her friends didn't care about saving babies—at least not nearly as fervently as they cared about controlling and policing the bodies of other adults. Suddenly, she didn't want to be here.

Or did she?

She was interested in what the speaker from Planned Parenthood had to say. She was interested in what the Students for Choice had to say. She wasn't sure she supported abortion, or what it would look like if she did, but she knew she wasn't a Student for Life. She knew she didn't feel whatever it was her friends were preaching. She put her poster board quietly on the ground, picked up her backpack, and stood. She exited the row, ignoring the anger radiating off of her fellow club members as she brushed by their knees. When the echoey lecture hall door closed behind her, she steadied herself, feeling dizzy and sick. She wandered the building's dimly lit basement hallway until she found a restroom. Tessa studied her reflection in the warped and streaky mirror above the sinks. She ripped off her club T-shirt, with its baby footprints and its antiabortion slogan, and dropped it, disgusted, into the large metal trash can overflowing with tampon wrappers and used paper towels.

From that day forward, Tessa avoided both her former Students for Life friends *and* the Students for Choice members she recognized around campus. She went to class, studied, tried to keep her head down. She became an RA and then an orientation leader. It was through these new extracurriculars that she met a new crew: a pack of women she didn't yet know to call queer, short haircuts and masculine clothing; cargo shorts, carabiners hanging from their belt loops, baggy T-shirts, backward baseball caps, and men's suits on any occasion that called for formal dress. She was drawn like a magnet to these students' swagger, and relished the feelings she had in their presence. Over a decade later, she closes her eyes and smiles as she describes falling in love with her new friends: their boisterous presence, their unshaven legs and armpits, the space they allowed themselves to take up in any given room, the bottomless self-love and confidence and the ease with which they carried themselves. Her butch friends introduced her to a new student organization, the Women's Union.

"They *really* radicalized me." Tessa laughs. The moment she joined the Women's Union, her trajectory changed forever. She started taking gender and political science classes, discussing feminist theory with fellow students in her downtime, and even attending local feminist actions and demonstrations—including protests for abortion rights. Still, she continued to avoid any social interaction with the Students for Choice and any official participation in the activities they organized, the painful memories of that confrontation and the shame and alienation she had felt that day still fresh in her mind.

Growing up in a rural community, Tessa remembers the intense social conservatism and the "angry" anti-feminist sentiments of her military family. "There was a lot of talk of 'sluts,' single mothers, and babies born out of wedlock—sex and pregnancy were always a woman's responsibility, and always her fault." When she started to have sexual encounters of her own, at the age of twelve, she had been given no education and no language or tools when it came to advocating for herself. The sex was sometimes unwanted, and almost always unprotected, and Tessa didn't know that there was any other way her life could be, as a girl. She remembers hearing about birth control pills, and briefly considering trying them— until she learned that in order to obtain a prescription, she would first have to be examined by a doctor. The thought of undressing in a brightly lit room, an adult inspecting her body and her genitals, and being asked frank and explicit questions about her sexuality and menstruation: it was not a possibility. So sex continued to be shameful, secret, something that happened to her in the dark, a mundane and regular event in which she had no agency and asked for no joy or pleasure or fulfillment for herself.

Throughout high school, Tessa continued to live what she now describes as a double life. In one of these lives, she was a dutiful scholar. She made excellent grades and engaged in wholesome extracurricular activities, always seeking the approval of adults for her achievements and her good-girl compliance. The focus of her other life was compliance as well, but to different authority figures altogether. In the context of the older peers she had met while working in restaurants and called her "friends," compliance meant coolness, "dangerous men" and partying. Alcohol, drugs, and unprotected sex with much older guys were all functions of this compliance.

Casual and unprotected sex continued to be a mainstay of Tessa's life through high school and college—even throughout her Students for Life tenure. She rarely said no, regardless of her own attraction to, or feelings for, the guys who initiated sex with her. And she never voiced desires of her own, set boundaries around how and when those guys could touch her, or insisted that they use a condom. Having sex, she felt, was being "useful"—doing what was expected of her. In retrospect, Tessa says, it's a miracle that she never got pregnant. Until the day she did.

"I totally dissociated," she tells me, before she takes a long and quiet pause. We are sitting in the living room of her apartment, her rescue dog snoozing beneath our feet. Tessa is a person who loves to laugh, and who—like so many of us—often runs her trauma and pain through a powerful filter of sharp, acerbic humor, both for her own ease and for the unburdening of those around her. But it's clear to me now, in this room, that there's a point at which the laughter ends, and something else begins. That she has carried with her from her childhood a feeling that some things are, literally, unspeakable. No one has ever asked Tessa for her life story before, a story which includes three abortions. Now that we've arrived at the first, she finds herself reeling from the memory.

"I was already numb going in, and then I numbed myself further afterward," she finally says.

More quiet. Rather than pushing her to speak with a follow-up question, I reach down to pet the dog. I smooth the silky little triangles of her ears flat against her head, then scratch her chest as she straightens her legs and paws at the air in pleasure. The second hand of the clock on the wall ticks upward. The words hang quietly in the air. Finally, Tessa speaks again.

She says, "Let's fast-forward."

She graduated, found a new city and a new job. New loves, new sexual relationships, new distraction and addiction and connection. Another unintended pregnancy, three years later. Following this next abortion, Tessa felt a new kind of grief, a sharp and jagged sense of loss. She remembers asking herself, again and again, not only how she had allowed this pregnancy to happen, but how she had sunk to these depths in her life as a whole. She also found herself, unexpectedly, at the bottom of a deep well of sadness.

"As ardently pro-choice as I am, I still felt that there was something of a soul when I got the abortion," Tessa tells me. She is describing a complicated grief that is felt by many but rarely expressed.

Any feelings of sadness or loss experienced after an abortion have been so weaponized by the antiabortion movement that we have come to feel as if they are unacceptable emotions for anyone who identifies as pro-choice. But abortion is transition, it can be loss, it can be trauma—physical, financial, spiritual, emotional—and as such, it can be enormously painful, even for those who know that it was the right decision for them, those who would choose it again without a second thought. Tessa felt this grief deeply, and then—because of her politics, her communities, and her fluency in the language and the messaging of pro-choice activism—she felt ashamed of it.

We are not moving through a black-and-white world of binaries, in which the presence of one feeling negates or invalidates another. Tessa doesn't regret her abortions, not a single one of them. But her lack of regret does not negate her pain. She is entitled, also, to her grief, her belief that there *was* a soul other than hers involved in each of her pregnancies. Just as every pregnancy is as unique and unrepeatable as a snowflake, so is every birth, every miscarriage or infant loss, every journey through infertility, and yes, every abortion. Because abortion is a normal and ordinary part of the reproductive life cycle of so many of us, we must honor it in every form it takes. For some people, abortion is mundane, routine, a no-big-deal stop at their doctor or a health clinic on their way to work or whenever they can find a few hours of childcare. For others, it is deeply transformative and significant. It is hugely meaningful and memorable, and will be carried forward in their minds and bodies and hearts for the rest of their lives.

Tessa is thirty-five now. She has done years of healing and growing, and has worked to put addiction, self-destructive sexual relationships, and the trauma-responsive patterns of her youth behind her. She is not a parent, though she thinks she may someday like to be, preferably through adoption rather than pregnancy and birth. It has taken her some years to find and make peace with her abortions, tangled up as they were in the traumas and wounds of her childhood, her adolescence, and her twenties.

For her, and for so many of my antiabortion (or *formerly* antiabortion) patients and clients and friends, abortion was the first truly consensual experience that Tessa had. Abortion was her choice, sought and asked for. Her need, met. An act of receiving only what her body consented to, between the violations and abuse it endured.

About a year after her last abortion, she enrolled in the volunteer clinic escort program at the same Planned Parenthood where she was shown such concern and kindness as a patient. Part of her volunteer training found her inadvertently left alone for a moment in a room of paper medical charts; without thinking, she searched for her last name and grabbed her own chart, with its descriptions of abuse and injury and psychological state, of previous pregnancies and sexual history. She still has the chart to this day, several pages of typed and handwritten clinical notes in a nondescript manila folder, and she keeps it with other important records and documents.

I ask Tessa what it feels like to look at that medical chart now, and what she felt in that moment, when she spontaneously stole it from the clinic's files. She shrugs her shoulders, smiles big, releases a musical laugh.

"My only thought was, and still is: *This is private information*," she says. "*It belongs to me.*

"*This is mine.*"

Abortion Is Grief

The tears we cry from a place of emotion—tears of sorrow, fear, anger, joy, love, despair—are made up of their own unique chemical composition, distinct from that of the tears we cry when chopping onions or standing near a smoky fire. They have a higher concentration of protein-based hormones like prolactin, making them stickier and more viscous.[1] They fall more slowly, linger on our cheeks, stay on our faces longer than do the tears triggered by environmental or physical irritants. This is by design, in pursuit of one goal: *that emotional tears have a higher chance of being visible to those around us.* Tears of grief and loss are made to elicit a reaction of community, of connection, of care.

Our bodies are designed to be comforted and soothed. Our bodies are built to be cared for. Our grief is made to be seen.

I grieve my abortion. Every day.

Many of the folks I've supported or spoken to have described simultaneous, tangled-up struggles: one with their post-abortion grief (or with any and all of their other post-abortion emotions—anger, joy, shame), and another as they decide if and how to express or even acknowledge it. There is a sense that this grief is not allowed, not acceptable in someone of their situation or their politics. That it should be kept quiet out of fear that their pain will be weaponized by antiabortion ideologues. *See? She regrets her abortion! Abortion hurts women!!* (These people only ever say "women.") *Abortion brings only pain and sadness and guilt! You'll miss your baby!!* (These people only ever say "baby.")

Out of fear that it will further stigmatize the care they are receiving or self-managing, they don't express this grief, articulate it, or seek to heal it. They often feel shame and secrecy around their sadness or loss, which then breeds isolation and loneliness—even and sometimes *especially*, among the folks who move through solidly pro-abortion communities.

But abortion is a transition, a crossing from one side of your life to another. And any transition can bring a wistfulness, an awkward parting, a difficult end. The reasons for an abortion can be as delicately multilayered as the reasons for any life transition: an intentional pregnancy carried to term and ending in a choice to parent, a career change, a divorce, an adoption, a marriage, a suicide. *All* transitions can bring a significant volume of world shaking, vision blurring, heavy, heavy grief. I know that all of *my* transitions have.

My own grief has, at times, felt literally unspeakable. I have felt the uncharacteristic shyness, have been squeezed by those common and familiar fears and pressures felt by so many in our movement. *Can I safely say that my emotions about my abortion experience include sadness? Will that be weaponized against me by the antiabortion (and the "pro-choice") folks who use stigmatizing rhetoric about a grief like this, and who seek to use emotion as a tool to police and moralize about the bodies and the choices of others? Will saying this out loud, or writing about it, harm other folks who've had abortions? Will they feel that their abortion experiences are being disrespected or misrepresented, by the language I use to describe my own?*

But neither these particular stress nightmares, nor the monsters who star in them, are the tellers of my story. I'm fucking sad about my abortion sometimes. There are nights my body is filled and aching with it, days when I feel crushed under the weight of it, and that sadness is real and worthy of my attention and my love and my honesty, too.

I often remind the people I support that watering down our stories will not serve anyone in the ways that our truth and vulnerability could. I honor my grief. It's real, and it's in my body, and I won't pretend otherwise. The two abortion processes my body went through were absolutely necessary, and they were healthy and safe, and they were made possible and even joyful by my communities, and they were acts of love for myself and my family. I'm so grateful for them. They were beautiful and positive experiences. And also? I grieve them. I have felt deep sadness, physical ache, and the deep hollowing of loss. And that's okay for me to share. That's an okay thing to say out loud—hell, a beautiful and true and important thing—to write down, here or anywhere else. All of it.

Grief is normal. Grief is important. Grief is sacred. You have the right to experience your own unique and evolving blend of emotions about your abortion(s), including grief in whatever forms it may take. Your grief belongs to you. You have the right to embrace it and express it. It is part of your story like any other.

In her compelling and beautiful book *Like a Mother*, the brilliant Angela Garbes writes not only of the pregnancy that resulted in the birth of her daughter but also about the others she's knowingly experienced—the pregnancies that ended in miscarriage or abortion:

"I picture pregnancy loss as a primordial river rushing through me; it carries forces so big, they eclipse my imagination. It runs through my femoral artery and vena cava, through my spleen, my brain, and the chambers of my heart. At first, this force is so strong like rapids, flooding everything. With time it slows, but it never goes away. It rearranges my cells like stones in a riverbed. It never stops running, even after I can no longer see or feel it."

Have I properly mourned my own abortion(s), as I've helped to facilitate the mourning of, the grief baths and healing practices and memorials and closure rituals for, other people's? No. In part because I'm still not sure what that grieving will look like, for me, over time. And also, in part because my abortion is a loss sustained by my body; its memory lives in my body still. It is still in me, with me, walking around the world, going to work, helping other people have (and process and think about and talk about) *their* abortions. My abortion is with me when I'm alone and when I'm in a crowd and when I'm having sex and when I'm holding a friend's new baby. It's in me as I'm changing diapers and washing little spoons and kissing toes and wiping boogers and engaging in all the other verbs of motherhood. We've created this parent-of-one-child, full-time-working, unpregnant life that I have today, together, my abortion and I. So while the pregnancy it helped me to end is a past state of being, the abortion itself is still here in my present tense.

Much of the language we do have around abortion care is politically charged, and has been so thoroughly weaponized by one side or the other in our nation's debate over its citizens' right to reproductive health care as to be rendered virtually meaningless.

"Women regret their abortions!!!" antiabortion pamphlets and billboards will crow, with no regard for nuance.

"No they don't!!!" pro-choice advocates and organizations will reply, with a similar disregard for the realities of emotional complexity, an equal and opposite reaction that makes the people actually *having* the abortions feel alienated, isolated, and ashamed of their feelings and reactions to what can be an incredibly complicated, murky, gray-area experience.

Referring to the product of conception as a "clump of cells," asserting that abortion is always wholly positive, easy, fun, no big deal; this type of sloganeering has only alienated the people whose own abortions have been sources of deep and lasting trauma, or have been followed by periods of mourning or depression. We cannot abandon the people who really did connect on an emotional or spiritual level with the pregnancy they ended, or the people who feel conflicted about their choices and experiences.

Antiabortion narratives are also—unsurprisingly—generally devoid of nuance and emotional honesty: these oversimplified stories tell us that people grieve after their abortions, because abortions are, necessarily and without exception, tragedies. They also insist that most people deeply regret their abortions, an idea which can be traced to "crisis pregnancy centers" (just like their wholesale creation and promotion of "post-abortion stress syndrome," an imaginary psychological condition that is not recognized by either the American Psychological Association or the American Psychiatric Association) and which has been widely debunked. In fact, the most common emotion people report experiencing after an abortion, by far, is relief.[2]

In real life, through transitions or changes of all shapes and sizes, we humans are constantly grieving what could have been. Parenthood involves a near-constant landslide of grief—as does birth, miscarriage, infertility, or a pregnancy that looks different from the one we'd planned or hoped for. Abortions of all types, and borne from all circumstances, can involve grief—even when they are also colored with joy, relief, or the exhilarating feelings of freedom that can accompany acts of exercising our power over our bodies, movements of self-determination and self-creation. Building a future for oneself always necessitates a constant reckoning with the loss of other possible futures, and so there are natural processes of mourning and closure built into the act of living. All we have to do is notice them, name them, and sometimes create a structure around them, in the form of a ritual or ceremony.

* * *

In the summer of 2020, Naomi learns that she is pregnant, again. The emotion that arrives first, settling into her body to sound its earsplitting 24/7 car alarms, is fear. Her only experience of a known pregnancy thus far has been a miscarriage, a loss that she felt deeply, only a few months ago. *Don't get excited*, the fear shrieks from its little burrow, the space in which it's buried itself deep under Naomi's skin and in her bones. *You do not get to have a baby*, it calls.

But once she gets through her nine-week prenatal checkup and sees her growing embryo on the ultrasound machine's screen, she finally begins to believe that she will, in the end, have a baby to hold in her arms. She and her husband, Ryan, both believe it, enough that they finally feel confident enough to share the news with their families. They plan creative pregnancy announcements for their parents and siblings, "filled with giddiness and blissful ignorance about what was to come," as Naomi will describe it to me that fall.

Ten weeks into her pregnancy, Naomi undergoes a standard NIPT (noninvasive prenatal testing), as offered—but not required— by her doctor. At eleven weeks, she opens an email that seems to contain the results of this test, expecting to receive confirmation of a healthy baby growing and thriving inside her body. Instead, she finds a referral to a genetic counselor. The next day, she speaks with the counselor, who tells her that the fetus's results have come back with a high risk of a genetic abnormality. However, the counselor says, the chances of this particular screening returning a false positive result are around 50 percent—a number that feels staggering when I write it here now, considering the financial and logistical inability of most Americans to access multiple health care providers and undergo multiple rounds of testing over the course of a pregnancy. The counselor tells Naomi that if she wants more accuracy, a more solid confirmation, or even just more information about her pregnancy at all, she will need another test.

Naomi spends the next week waiting for an amniocentesis she dreads. The screening feels invasive, and her anxiety sails on a new headwind. A shipwreck feels imminent, even before the fog clears and she can see the rocks ahead.

When the genetic counselor finally calls, she confirms that the fetus inside of Naomi is indeed carrying the suspected genetic abnormality and that she and her husband must now decide how to proceed.

Naomi and Ryan spend the next several days agonizing over the decision. It is not a clear-cut diagnosis—if she carries to term and gives birth, her baby could be only moderately impacted by the condition. Or, the child could be severely impaired, and in a great deal of pain from the very beginning of its life. There would be no

' way to know which of these paths their child's life would follow until after their birth. The overwhelmed couple consults whatever research they can find, googling and Redditing furiously, obsessively, torturously. They speak with their genetic counselor again, ruminate with their families, and ultimately decide to terminate the pregnancy.

This is the start of Thanksgiving week, and Naomi's fourteenth week of pregnancy. She calls the genetic counselor on Monday morning and is told that because of the holiday, the earliest they can schedule her abortion procedure is the following week. Naomi is, at this point, experiencing daily nausea and vomiting (symptoms that she now suspects were exacerbated or even generated by the force of her grief, stress, fear, and anxiety). The thought of carrying this fetus, which she knows to be male and which she has already begun to conceive of as her baby, of continuing to grow him in her body and deal with all the symptoms of a pregnancy while knowing she is going to end it, is excruciating. At this moment, she begins to understand the desperation of a person who has agonized over and finally come to the decision to have an abortion, to end a wanted pregnancy, and is then faced with roadblocks and delays. Naomi's are relatively small, compared to those for so many people in other states, other communities, other socioeconomic realities. But she can feel it pulsing under her skin at every moment of the wait—how the urge to resort to "any means necessary," she says, is never far from her mind.

Naomi follows up, she circles back, she calls and calls and leaves long-winded voice mails. She begs to be seen sooner, and eventually the counselor concedes that there is one slot available, Friday morning in San Francisco. She needs time to obtain a negative COVID-19 test result anyway, she is told, a requirement for any "elective" surgical procedure. At the use of that term, *elective*, Naomi wants to scream.

She takes the week off from work, and her younger sister comes to stay with the couple as they process and prepare for the end of their pregnancy. Naomi cries in the shower (and everywhere else), paints with watercolors, writes in her journal, watches a collection of *Real Housewives* get drunk and fight. She vomits, listens to meditations, hugs her husband and her sister, and cries some more. She and I speak throughout this waiting period, and I pour every affirmation and expression of love into her ears that I can, desperate to somehow make her feel held by my words, across thousands of miles and through the barrier of our phones.

Naomi's sister, with the help of an abortion counselor she's consulted, encourages her to write a letter to herself about how she's arrived at the decision. The letter includes statements of self-forgiveness and some final, loving, words to the potential child who might have existed, in a different future from the one laid out before her now.

On Wednesday, she takes a phone call with the doctor who will be performing her abortion. On Thursday, she and Ryan go to the pharmacy to pick up the medication she is prescribed—misoprostol.

She's been told to arrive at the hospital at 6:00 a.m. on Friday. Because she is in her second trimester, she is asked to take the miso four hours prior to her procedure, to start the long process of dilating her cervix. She sets her phone's alarm for 2:00 a.m. and places the bottle of pills on her bedside table. In large capital letters, the FDA warning on its label reads: *DO NOT TAKE IF PREGNANT*.

The image of those words, of reading them and of opening the bottle and placing the pills between her bottom teeth and gums as directed, is one that she says will stay with her as long as she lives. She weeps as she holds the pills in her mouth, buccally, waiting for them to dissolve. Ryan holds her, her mouth closed tightly and her body wracked with sobs.

About a half hour later, Naomi begins to experience what she describes as the most painful cramps she's ever felt. She tries to breathe through them, but her anxiety is already shortening her breath, and she feels panic rising in her chest. After thirty minutes of this, Ryan calls the hospital to ask if his wife can take any kind of medication to help with the intense pain. The nurse said that she could take Advil, something she's become used to regarding as prenatal poison. *That's right*, Naomi almost laughs. Pregnancy-safe drugs are no longer needed. Naomi takes the Advil and starts to feel some relief. At nearly 4:00 a.m., she sleeps another hour.

She wakes with her alarm at 5:00 a.m. and vomits into the bin at her bedside. The sky above her squat apartment building is still dark, the lemon trees and bougainvillea outside her bedroom windows just beginning to take on a glow. She gets up, dresses in silence, and is driven by her husband into the city, her sister riding along for support. When they arrive at the hospital entrance, she hugs them both goodbye and goes inside, alone. The hospital's COVID precautions, at the time, include a provision that only patients are allowed inside—no guests, no family members, no familiar hands to grip or shoulders to bury her face into.

It isn't long before she's called from the waiting room. She is taken to a room, directed to a bed, and the nurses begin their work. They insert an IV cannula and administer a first dose of anti-nausea medication. She is asked—for the first of many, many times that morning—what procedure she is here to undergo today. Each time, she is forced to answer, like a windup doll who says only one phrase: a D&E—dilation and evacuation. *A D&E. A D&E.* Naomi is still unsure if it's the hospital's way of confirming her informed consent to her abortion procedure, or if it is just standard practice for any scheduled patient. But she floods with shame and distress each time she is forced to say it, and after several repetitions she finds herself gripped by a new fear: that a member of her medical team may disapprove of the decision she's made. Of course, none of them express disapproval, or even surprise. But each time she is forced to reveal what feels so intensely private, personal, sacred—*I'm here for a D&E*—the fear of judgment or stigma blooms.

At the clinic, we often say—so often, in fact, that I have scrawled it across the top page of more than one of my clinical training notebooks—"This is our *every* day, but it may be the patient's *only* day." No matter how routine and frequent and ordinary abortion care is for us—how many pregnancy tests we run, how many dilators and speculums and cannulas and surgical trays we handle, how many finger pricks to determine blood type and RhoGAM shots we give—each and every one of the human beings who come to us for care are singular and unique, and so are their lives, their experiences, the contexts from which they come.

* * *

The resident who will be assisting Naomi's doctor with the procedure approaches her bed and greets her with a small packet of paper, asking how she would like the hospital to handle the remains.

Our baby's remains, Naomi thinks. She hasn't prepared for this and can't bear the thought of engaging with or managing the remains herself. She signs a form giving the hospital permission to dispose of them. (She has since questioned that decision, as she now longs for "pieces of this baby we lost," she tells me, but it was all she could do at that moment, paralyzed by grief and shock and overwhelm.)

Naomi is wheeled into the bright white procedure room, where she is transferred from her bed onto the operating table. She begins to count backward, as directed by the anesthesiologist, and the next thing she remembers is waking in another room. Someone is handing her a juice box. It's over. Everything has gone well, they tell her. Her nausea and all her other pregnancy symptoms have disappeared. Her limbs feel light and loose. Naomi is overcome by a wave of relief. But each moment of this deep relief is followed on its heels by a painful reminder that she is no longer pregnant.

Her physical recovery is quick—she is able to manage the pain with only the aid of ibuprofen and a heating pad. Her emotional recovery is ongoing and may not find its end in her lifetime. But she is managing, with the help of the most loving partner, the warmest therapist, and an incredible local support group of couples who have terminated pregnancies for medical reasons. That group has been instrumental in her healing.

She has since carried a third pregnancy to term and given birth to her first child. But her abortion experience, like her miscarriage, cannot be shoved into a box of toxic positivity and cheesy aphorisms (you know the ones—*everything happens for a reason* or *look on the bright side* or *find the silver lining* or *God works in mysterious ways*): for Naomi, it was simply a tragedy, a loss, and a death, and she grieves it still.

You have the right to feel how you feel about your abortion, as deeply and as intensely and for whatever length of time you feel it.

SOME POST-ABORTION COMFORTS

Ceremonies, such as the one designed by Annie Finch, can be instrumental in soothing or riding out emotional pain, in processing a loss, in closing a circle and finding peace. You can create new memories, and objects, and experiences. A comforting ceremony or ritual or practice will not erase or bury or sublimate the pain, but instead will live and breathe alongside it, keeping it (and you) company. You can create beautiful vessels for your grief, your anger, your loneliness, your guilt. You can carry them with you always, just as you do your love for the pregnancy or for what it taught you. Just as you carry your memories of your abortions and all that they were. Dark and light.

Writing a Letter

The letter that Naomi created is an object of her love for herself. Nearly two years later, when we brave the connectivity hiccups of FaceTime, and when we reminisce and reflect on one of our rare in-person visits—her beautiful son on her lap—Naomi expresses that she is so grateful she wrote that letter. She has returned to it many times since, unfolding and refolding its corners again and again to read and reflect on her own thoughts, and to seek out and receive her own forgiveness.

But the letter itself is not the only instrument of healing—so, too, in the days after her abortion, was the act of sitting down to write it. Pouring her focus, presence, and attention into the words she was writing—not only to the potential life that she was mourning, but also to her precious, living, whole, and worthy self—brought her some physical and emotional release. Giving herself permission to express *every* thought and emotion, no matter how ugly or complicated, turned out to be a powerful antidote to her shame and guilt.

Making Art

Grief can pry open new spaces of beauty in you. Fill them, if you want to, with color and sound and texture. Learn to make something new and make it over and over again—the practice of it meditative and the product of it chic or cute or funny or moving, or at least interesting. Write a song. Write ten songs. Knit hats and scarves for all of your loved ones, or to drop at a community shelter or hand out on the street. Compose poetry in different forms, read it aloud in bed to your lover or at the open mic night to a crowd or to yourself, secretly, in your bathroom mirror or your closet or wherever you may find yourself in privacy and solitude. Design a birdhouse or a feeder and build it and watch the birds come and gather and eat and grow and heal. Plant a garden for the bees and name each one that comes to drink from your flowers. Write *FUCK THIS SHIT* on the sidewalk in chalk, all over your city. Whatever feels like it might work.

Two of Naomi's richly rendered watercolors, the deep blues

and purples and greens she brush-soaked onto thick cream paper in the depths of her grief and rage, hang on my walls. I see them every morning as I take my Zoloft, drink my enormous black coffee, stumble over toy fire engines and helicopters as I rush around the house, gathering the things I need for clinic work and daycare and doula clients and writing. They are my favorite pieces of art that I have ever owned.

Holding a Funeral or a Memorial Service

This can look like so many things—Finch's ritual, adapted to your own family and life and needs, or a similar ceremony, performed with loved ones or alone. Standing, as I did, at the edge of the sea with some flowers. A full-on religious service at a supportive place of worship. Holding hands with your best friend and screaming at the top of your lungs. Writing down a name for the spirit you are releasing, if you want to give it one, on a surface that feels sacred to you. And then saying *goodbye*, or *see you later*, in any way that feels right: praying, loving, speaking, singing, burying, burning, floating, growing, tattooing, whispering it into being and out of it again.

Callie planned to hold a memorial gathering for the pregnancy she had ended, with a circle of friends and a piece of artwork she intended for them to make together. But on the morning of the gathering, she decided: *This isn't how I want to say goodbye.* So she sent a text to the group chat, canceling, turned off her phone, and walked into the woods near her house. There she spoke aloud to the pregnancy as she walked. She cried. When she emerged from the woods, she was finished.

* * *

When I say, *This abortion belongs to you,* I mean: These parts of it, too. From beginning to end—if there ever is an end for you. Every last little piece of it. It's yours.

Interlude:

Abortion Is a Gift (Some Things to Make and Buy and Share and Send)

If you or someone you love has had an abortion, or is waiting to have an abortion, well, that calls for a gift or two. People who have abortions—of any kind and for any reason—deserve gifts, full stop. And it is incumbent upon us, the people around them, to show up in this way. Ranging from free to expensive, tiny to big, I've made a little list (as you'll have noticed I like to do): a few of the things and experiences I give to the people I love or support after their abortions.

FOOD

I will never forget the homemade chicken noodle soup, or the brownies from scratch (with a separate little container of vanilla ice cream), that community members brought me after my abortion. Give people food. Food you know they'll like, food that is meaningful to you and your family and ancestors, food that is easy and comforting. Ask them what their favorite meal is, or find a recipe that speaks to you, and get your cute butt into that kitchen. And if you can't cook, well . . . as our queen Ina Garten says, barefoot and all: store-bought is fine. Pick up some takeout, send some delivery, email a gift card, take them out to their favorite spot. Food—once any nausea or vomiting or diarrhea is sorted, of course—is the very best post-abortion gift.

FLOWERS

An oft-cited-by-florists behavioral study, conducted by Rutgers University, found that the mere presence of flowers in someone's space or eyeline immediately triggers heightened feelings of happiness and satisfaction *and* has long-term impacts on their depth of joy and positive social behavior. Flowers are magic. They are a perfect gift, regardless of the details surrounding someone's abortion experience, emotions, and healing process. They are the perfect language in which to communicate *Fuck yes* or *I'm so proud of you*, just as clearly as they can say *I'm so sorry this happened* or *I see your grief, and I offer my love.* Have them delivered, if you can afford to do so. Pick them if you can't. Bring them. Give them. Share them.

HEAT

Did you know that you can make a homemade heating pad? You can, in many different ways. A sock filled with rice. A simple hand-sewn cloth bag or cotton pillowcase filled with dried corn, dried beans, all sorts of grain. (Of course, you can buy heating pads,

too—from basic to high-end—at any drugstores or big box stores.)
Bring extra blankets and sweaters and sweatshirts to someone. Tuck
them in. Candles are nice, too. Light whatever fires you can, and
keep them burning as long as you need or desire.

WORDS

Write a letter, honey. Or a card. Even if you're afraid of being
cheesy. Even if you don't know what to say—find a poem, an ex-
cerpt, a song lyric that speaks to your admiration and respect, your
fondness and trust, your love. Write it all down for them. Trust me.

Abortion Is Creation

When Molly felt her milk come in after her abortion, it was like an emotional riptide. She was pulled under the waves, unable to breathe, overwhelmed by panic and distress. The physical reminder that her body had been preparing for motherhood all this time, was hard at work, now, to feed a baby who would never be born, was unbearable. Like many people who have later abortions, she found the experience of post-abortion lactation to be one of agonizing stimulus, every physical sensation a weapon of her tragic loss. A tangible and intolerable reminder of all that had disappeared at the moment of her fetal diagnosis, all the plans and dreams she'd attached to a future that had crumbled like dust in her hands. Her first instinct was to interrupt the lactating. To tell her body firmly, "Not now," and dry up her milk supply as quickly and effectively as she could. In a photo taken shortly after her abortion, she is lying in bed, on her back, wearing a tight sports bra stuffed with cabbage leaves straight from the freezer. She is pale and drawn, skinny tears streaming from her exhausted eyes.

But then, something changed. She changed course, from urging the milk to dry up and disappear to wanting a supply as abundant as possible. "As if my boobs were a faucet!" she cackles. And so they became, as she worked around the clock to turn on the tap. She worked with a lactation consultant to induce the faucet-like flow. She used a breast pump, religiously, day and night. Her milk supply returned, with a vengeance. Molly pumped, collected, froze, and donated every ounce of it to local milk banks in her home state. They fed thousands of newborns who—like my son, when my own breast milk supply was delayed and then insufficient—were fed by anonymous donors through hospitals and milk banks.

Because of Molly's abortion, the loss that knocked her off her feet and into the depths of grief, babies grew and thrived. This is not a silver lining or a bright side of her pain. Abortion, miscarriage, birth; these things are not equations to be solved, or simple if/then, cause-and-effect riddles or puzzles.

But Molly does feel, deep in her bones, that the evidence of creation—the fountain of milk and the babies it has fed, the new and abundant life that blooms from the wreckage of the abortion she experienced as a kind of death—is real, mysterious but undeniable.

An abortion opens a door—not to a world of parenting the child that *this* particular pregnancy may have become, but perhaps to a future in which you parent a different child, one whose existence will bring you more joy than you can currently imagine from where you stand now. Or maybe your abortion opens another door, leading somewhere else entirely: a job, a dream, a healthy body, a degree, a life of freedom and peace, an escape from ongoing violence or trauma, an opportunity to heal. Or maybe it opens all of these doors. Maybe it gives you the long clear views down all of these hallways that you require in order to take a step in any given direction. An ending is a beginning. One thing makes another possible.

Abortion may not create everything, but it can create anything.

Abortion Is Joy

For once we begin to feel deeply all the aspects of our lives,
we begin to demand from ourselves and from our
life pursuits that they feel in accordance with that joy
which we know ourselves to be capable of.
—Audre Lorde

"You know," Colleen says, smiling sheepishly, "as soon as I decided that this was what I was going to do, I almost felt . . . happy?"

"You are *not* the first person to tell me that." I laughed. "And also, just so you know, you don't have to add an 'almost' to that 'happy' for me if it doesn't belong there. If you felt happy about having your abortion, you can say that you felt happy."

A wide smile broke her face in half, the golden New England late-afternoon light streaming in through the window behind her. Bathed in this glow, her head took on a luminous halo.

"Yeah . . ." she said, nodding slowly, her smile warm and brilliant. "Okay. I felt happy."

Colleen was twenty-nine when she had her abortion, and she was living in Washington, DC. It was just after Thanksgiving. When she discovered she was pregnant, after a casual encounter with a man she called her friend with benefits, she was flattened by the revelation, even as she felt the possibility in the soreness of her breasts, the fatigue like weights strapped to her limbs. It was nearing midnight when she first peed on the drugstore test in her apartment, a sickly hope turning to numbness and the full-body ice bath of shock. She was leaving early the next morning for an urgently important work trip to Arkansas. Absorbing the impact of seeing those two bleeding pink lines of dye, she packed. Just a few hours later, seeing no option but to keep moving through her life as she normally would, she headed for the airport to catch her flight.

Colleen stumbled through Chicago O'Hare, Christmas decorations everywhere, in a daze. Wandering through the fog of twinkling, sparkly, tinsel-wrapped surreality in a stunned panic.

"I just kept thinking, *What am I going to do? What am I going to do?*" She pushed through the next few days—the neon-lit conference tables, the continental hotel breakfasts of weak coffee, nauseatingly sugary yogurts, and pale, watery chunks of honeydew melon—on a numb autopilot, adrenaline powering her limbs and her small-talk smiles. The second she returned home from her trip and found herself alone again in the safety of her condo, she collapsed.

"I had a breakdown," she said. The anguish and panic she'd been holding in her body made its exit with the gale force of a hurricane that had only been picking up speed and power as she'd worked to ignore it.

She called her parents, terrified to tell them about the pregnancy. They met her news with love.

"Just come home for Christmas," her dad told her. "We'll all
be together, and we'll talk about it. We'll figure it out." So she did,
feeling a bone-deep relief as she stood in the doorway of her childhood home and was embraced by the tangle of familiar arms, arms
that looked like hers and bore the freckles and scars and jewelry
she knew as well as her own. After settling in, Colleen's dad sat her
down for a story she had never heard before: as a college student,
his then girlfriend had unexpectedly become pregnant. Together,
the couple had decided not to become parents, and the woman had
gotten the abortion that would free both of them. The abortion
that would enable *him* to graduate, to go on to marry Colleen's
mother, and to become the adoring and adored father at the center
of Colleen's and her sister's lives.

Abortion joy can take many different forms. It can be latent,
disconnected—the feelings of happiness or contentment or relief
that will arrive at some mysterious moment in time, over the course
of creating the future that the abortion has made possible. The joy
that slips in through the back door, before you even realize it's been
approaching your house. The perfectly individual and uniquely
wonderful child born years later, the only human being on earth just
like them, whose parents are able to bring them into the world *because* of the abortion. The freedom and capacity of the childless person's life, bending and stretching to accommodate so many forms of
love, building the rich, full, complicated structures of their dreams.

When I look at my son, an only child, whose mother is not
debilitated by nausea and the struggles of a high-risk diabetic pregnancy, a kid whose parents can afford to keep him safe and well-fed

and well-read with the hundreds of board books that teach him about the world—when I look at his perfect round baby cheeks and the eyes that look like my husband's and gummy (but newly tooth-dotted!) smile, I see the joy of my abortion.

When I look at his father, a man who channels his love for his family, his dog, his tiny house and vegetable garden and woodshed, through hours and hours of focused time spent laboring to tend to them; a man who is happily at capacity when it comes to beings who need his time and care—when we are alone together or I hear him humming in the next room, because our one and only child has gone to bed and he can wash the dishes while listening to music before we sit and read together, my legs draped over his lap, I see the joy of my abortion.

When I go for a long walk alone—only my *own* health and well-being at the mercy of my blood sugar, no embryo or fetus to be endangered by its fluctuations, my phone in my pocket full of its usual bleak and frightening news but not waiting to show me the grim results of the blood tests and kidney scans I can't afford, the lab results that speculate about a fetus's prognoses and likely survival rates? Well, I feel the joy of my abortion.

And when I start an eight-hour shift at work, knowing my child to be safe in the care of grandparents who can still—at least for now, as their knees and eyesight and balance will allow—chase one toddler around their home, bend and crawl and (mostly) contain him and prevent him from throwing himself down their front steps or running into traffic, and who can pour themselves into his safekeeping and his education and his thriving, *only* because there is no fragile newborn in tow? That's when the joy of my abortion arrives, with bells on.

When my toddler is sick or exhausted, and he nestles into the soft hollow my body made for him, the soft place where my belly folds over onto my hips and my thighs cushion his bum as he burrows into my chest and I have nowhere else to be, no one else to care for, no one crying for me across the room? The house is silent except for our slow tandem bicycle of breathing? My joy bursts through the door carrying a six-pack of my favorite beer in one hand and a jar of my favorite flowers (it picked them for me by the roadside) in the other, a book of my favorite poetry in its back pocket.

Viva Ruiz, the incomparably joyful creator of Thank God for Abortion, radiates encouragement and laughter. The TGFA anthem's music video is a glittering celebration of abortions and those who have them, anthemically asserting (complete with foghorn sound effects) that God is cool with us, and we are not just acceptable but blessed. Consider its overflowing joy.

* * *

Or, consider: the glistening tiny jewels of joy that can be found in the immediate *after*, the minutes and hours and days and weeks following even the most difficult abortion. The disappearance of nausea, and other pregnancy symptoms, the favorite dinner or flavor of ice cream, the love of your favorite people, the favorite movie or TV show. The cat curled against the small of your back. The hummingbird outside the window.

However small, or ordinary, or faint: joy is here with us at the table.

* * *

Imagine: you enter someone's home. It is a pretty little space, cozy but not crowded, natural light streaming in from large windows. Bookshelves and vases of fresh wildflowers and artfully arranged furniture that looks like you could sink into it comfortably for hours. Inviting colors and a candle that smells like a tropical beach or a Christmas tree farm or an acre of freshly mown grass on a dewy summer morning. Objects both deeply meaningful *and* aesthetically pleasing.

But. *But.* Though the house is meticulously designed and curated, and though every inch of it reeks of taste and intentionality, you do *not* feel nervous to sit down. You do not search frantically, in a silent, sweaty, diarrheal panic, for a coaster. You are not terrified of spilling, or moving something out of place. You do not tell yourself sternly to keep your hands in your pockets, *don't touch*, or apologize every thirty seconds for the space you take up inside this home. You are not a guest or an intruder but company. You're allowed to make a mess, eat seconds and thirds, kick your shoes off wherever. The house trusts you. The house knows you'll do your best to be mindful and to clean up after yourself if you can, and that sometimes neither of those is possible for you (or for anyone).

This is what I'm trying to build. This is the space I dream of holding for pregnant people, whether they need it for an hour or a year, whether they need abortion care today or a baby shower next month, or whether they will, a year or a decade from now, be looking for information about their options as they make the decision that belongs to them. *Make yourself a house.*

* * *

How would I defend other sick and disabled people, other diabetics, other queer folks, other sexual assault survivors, other struggling and exhausted parents of young children? How would I listen to them and speak to them? How would I defend other people's rights to tell their abortion stories, ask difficult, thorny, questions about their own experiences, to cry and laugh and be loud and build the futures and access the healing and keep the secrets that belong to them? Angrily, yes. But also joyfully.

That is how I will defend my own.

* * *

When I am at a bedside, or filling a bathtub, or fielding a call, I ask: *What would someone who deserves the honor of being this person's doula do? How can I behave as if I am the person who deserves to be afforded the unspeakable privilege of this person's trust?* And when I am in my own bed, my muscles aching and tears drying to salt on my cheeks and my brain running back its blooper reel, its loop of footage capturing only my errors and flaws, I can only change the channel once I ask myself: *What would you say to this person's doula? Would you tell* them *how miserably they'd failed, how short they'd fallen?*

And in the posing and the answering of this question, I find my way back to joy.

Abortion Is Love

When Camila Ochoa Mendoza first comes to me with her idea, the force of its beauty nearly knocks me over. I have to sit down. I've been reading my emails on my phone—its screen doomed to the nicks and cracks of my clumsiness and to the perpetual stickiness of baby oatmeal and spilled coffee—as I rush from room to room, brushing my teeth and tossing the dirty laundry that litters the floor in the general direction of the hamper. I'm, as always, bone-tired and manically distracted, my thoughts scattered. But my friend Camila's words stop me in my tracks. I feel a light suddenly go on, in some long-dark part of me. And Camila, from 3,500 icy miles away, has flipped the switch.

Camila lives across an ocean from me, in Sweden. She and I originally met in a virtual doula training and its adjacent community space, and I was immediately drawn to the quiet warmth that emanated from her voice, the curiosity in her beautiful brown eyes, clear and sharp even through the screen of my laptop. I became a fan of her podcast, *Abortion, with love.* Each episode is like a shimmering, multifaceted little jewel, light reflected and refracted at brand-new angles into some new, vibrant shade of a color you've never given much thought to before: an honest, challenging, surprising, heart-filling and mind-expanding conversation about abortion. Each hour spent listening to Camila laugh and cry and learn with a different guest about their own abortion experiences, or their work in the world of reproductive care/rights/justice, is an hour perfectly passed (even if the hypothetical listener is also, for example, changing diapers or washing speculums, while passing it). Camila is both an expert storyteller and an expert story *asker*, a master of questioning and listening, of sound and language.

* * *

And because I am the luckiest girl on earth, we are going to make something together.

The Abortion Love Letters project grows from the seed of an idea that comes to Camila one winter, as she's working in a restaurant (to make money) and for various abortion access organizations (to make community and care and love and safety and healing and humanity and justice and joy). She is busy this season, recording podcast episodes and pouring wine and supporting abortion seekers through Women Help Women, an international nonprofit that provides abortion pills, resources, and information across four continents. She's been working in sexual and reproductive health for six or seven years—getting her master's degree and researching and going to conferences—but she's hungriest, at this moment, for some Abortion Love. A wraparound hug, a kiss on the cheek, an affirmation and celebration of abortions and the people who have them.

So that's what we do. We publish love letters—to and from

folks who've had abortions, friends and partners and lovers, parents and children and midwives and doulas and anyone who loves anyone. Each week on the podcast, the writer of a letter reads it aloud. And each week, I publish the letter, replete with a gorgeous collage illustration by the artist Idalina Lehtonen, on my email.

After each letter goes out, the responses pour in, from listeners and readers alike.

I wept in my car.
I am happier than I have been in months.
I felt so loved. I felt so much love.
I don't feel alone anymore.
Thank you. Thank you. Thank you.

Many people experience their abortion as an act of love. For those who don't, there are ways for *you* to love them through it. Providers are loving their patients. Funds are loving their communities. Friends and family members are loving one another. Abortion experiences can be soaked in love from beginning to end—regardless of what other sensations and emotions are swirling around in the mixture. A body carries everything. Love is never the only guest at the table.

Abortion can be a powerful act of self-love. But, as I tell every single person whose abortion I witness or support: it's okay if you don't feel that love in the wake of yours. No feeling is unacceptable, and no feeling is required. I'll hold space for your anger at yourself, your guilt, your spiky and uneven waves of shame, even your self-hatred, if it's here in the room with us. It all belongs to you. It's all okay to name, and sit with, and observe as it ebbs and flows and rolls through the vast, deep, ever-changing (and often stormy) sea of your healing.

I love the person who wept, and wept, and brought their ultrasound images home to treasure and to grieve just the same as I love the person who said, "I just want to see what it looks like, I'm so curious!" and laughed at their ultrasound images, before handing them back to me to be shredded and recycled. I love them the same. And I love you, even and especially if you don't love yourself at this moment.

I love you even if you can't meet me there.

Abortion Is the Beginning

I walk Essie to the elevator and push the button, her bag slung over my shoulder. Her ride home is stuck in traffic, and I'll wait on the corner with her until he arrives. I won't take my eyes off her until she's safely in his passenger seat. She leans on my shoulder, woozy and tired. "What do you feel like you might want for dinner tonight?" I ask, adding: "After my abortion, all I wanted was sushi and wine."

Her eyes widen. "Whoa," she says, the first time I've heard her speak more than a *thank you* or *okay* in more than an hour.

"That actually sounds so good," she says. "Like, really good."

We both laugh, nod, *hell yeah*, the best. We have the same favorite sushi spot, they deliver in thirty minutes, and she tells me there's a bottle of chardonnay already chilling in her fridge at home. She deserves a damn treat.

Essie's going to watch her favorite movie tonight. Her girlfriend will sleep over; her mom will watch her kids. The physician who performed Essie's abortion procedure is going straight to watch her son's Little League game, the sun setting over the cold metal bleachers where other team parents have brought her an extra folding chair, an extra blanket, an extra beer. The executive director of the fund that paid for Essie's abortion is going to stay up late, looking at spreadsheets and worrying. Eventually her partner will come to rub her shoulders, offer a snack, encourage her to take deep breaths, say, "Let's take a break, let's go for a walk." Essie's doula is going straight home, exhausted, to the borderless garden of vegetables grown with seeds our community has given us, where my son is reaching his chubby arm in the air to grab at a tiny green peach on our neighbors' young tree, where there is an unexpected package waiting on my porch—surprise! With a dog-eared copy of a poetry chapbook I've asked to borrow and a card of loving words, a salve I'll apply to the scrapes and bruises inflicted by my own experiences.

The elevator carries us down to the street. It dings; its doors gently separate. Essie and I step out of its hands. We step into the world together.

* * *

I can feel myself bleeding as I step out of the elevator, after my in-clinic abortion. The pregnancy is gone; the blood that flows now is just pieces of my unpregnant body, as it's always been before. I push open the lobby's heavy glass door and the liquid gold sunlight covers my body, the body which is good and whole and mine, pregnant or not, same as it always has been and always will be. I step out into the cold air, the noises of the city, the new afternoon. I head toward home, the snowy backyard and the unmade bed and the bird feeders alight with sparrows and squirrels alike. I move forward.

I, I, I.

But that's not quite right. That's not the whole story, is it, that *I*?

I is sharp and true and beautiful, and it has its place at the center of a life and a body that are mine. But *I* is not nearly a big enough word here, after everything that's happened in all the pages before this one. *I* is not the hero here. *I* alone did not make my abortion happen.

Will is here with me, too, after all, heavy steps beside mine in his work boots, his hand a calloused but gentle guide on the small of my back. Our child waits for us at home.

But even the three of us are just drops in the deep blue ocean of this day.

The protesters are here, too, of course, and all the others eager to condemn and degrade us—the people who will frown at this book's cover on a shelf, those who will sneer at me on Twitter or send me hateful, violent emails, and those who will never read *any* of these words as a matter of principle.

But everyone else is here, too.

Someone donated $5, and another someone $50, and someone else $500, to the abortion fund that would go on to pay for my abortion. Someone at the clinic called that fund's request line. Someone made my appointment for me, typed in my name and birthday and noted my disability and my anxiety. Someone thought about my blood type and my medical history and my schedule and my child waiting at home for me, and consulted someone else about the specifics of my previous pregnancy and my postpartum body and all the quirks and questions of my birth. Someone explained *every* little piece of the whole. Someone trained me as an escort; someone trained me as a clinic worker; someone trained me as a doula. So many someones wrote the books and made the websites and created the knowledge-shares and hosted the gatherings and brought the conversations to me which have made my care work what it is. Someone told me about all the small stories playing out inside my body, the bodies around me. Someone told me the stories that had played out in the bodies before mine.

Someone held one of my hands through my abortion, and someone else held the other. Someone texted me affirmations, laced with vulgarity and dirty jokes, and someone silently recited the prayers that reached me, somehow, like so many bright singing little birds flying in through the cracked-open dusty old windows of my grief and despair to perch in my rafters and watch over me. Someone took care of my baby for me; someone read his favorite books to him and gave him a bath and taught him how the chickadees and bluebirds are calling to each other from the trees in our backyard, *See them? Hear them?*, telling one another, and thus reminding themselves:

Here I am. Here I am. Here I am. (Where are you?) Here I am.

Someone will call me later to ask if I need anything. Someone else will bring me chicken noodle soup. Someone will bake brownies and leave a few on my doorstep. Someone will braid my hair and someone else will rub my emptied belly.

Someone will listen to me; from the breath I take in before speaking, to the rise and fall of all my hesitations and mistakes, to the very end of every sentence, no interruptions, no shocked or judgmental faces or reactions. Someone will hold space for everything I bring to them, ugly and beautiful alike. Someone will go out into the world, and remember the sight of my tears and my smile and the sound of all my clumsy, broken words about them.

Someone will tell someone else, *I'm here for your abortion, for all of it, whatever happens. I'm here with a container for your joy, your relief, your pain, your fear, your grief, every last drop of it. Here. Pour it in here, if you want. Here I am. Here I am. Here I am.*

Someone will feel safe enough to say, *I'm having an abortion, and I need a ride home.* Or, *I had an abortion, and here's how I feel.*

Someone will ask me to write it all down, the stories and questions and memories that will become this book.

Someone will publish it.

Someone will read it.

And someone, someday, will put it in your hands.

Resources

For Finding Abortion Care, Funding, Support, and Information Online

INeedAnA: a simple, localized, and up-to-date directory of clinical and telemedicine abortion care, www.ineedana.com.

Apiary: resources for, and directories of, practical support organizations, www.apiaryps.org.

National Network of Abortion Funds: the GOAT, abortionfunds .org.

All-Options: free hotlines, tool kits, resources, information, care. www.all-options.org.

2+ Abortions Worldwide: a stigma-fighting project with a library of stories and a wealth of resources and information, www.2plusabortions.com.

We Testify: An organization supporting the leadership of abortion storytellers and gorgeously busting stigmas and shifting the conversation with facts, art, comics, and of course, stories. www.wetestify.org.

For Abortion Doula / Companion / Support Worker Trainings

Consider first connecting with (and investing in; pay them, if you can!) any doula collectives or abortion support networks near you, as they will be the experts in the reproductive justice needs of your local communities and may offer workshops, knowledge-shares, and trainings. Beyond that, there are some truly transformative national and international trainings and communities to be found online, facilitated by some truly luminous leaders in our movements. Some of these include:

Dopo: www.wearedopo.com.

Birthing Advocacy Doula Trainings: https://www.badoulatrainings .org/abortion-doula.

Colorado Doula Project: www.coloradodoulaproject.org/abortion -doula-training.

Radical Doula Volunteer Programs Directory: where state-specific US doula programs and trainings are gathered, www.radical doula.com/becoming-a-doula.

Some of the organizations, leaders, and resources I look to for all things RJ 101 and beyond include:

SisterSong Women of Color Reproductive Justice Collective
New Voices Women of Color for Reproductive Justice
Indigenous Women Rising
National Latina Institute for Reproductive Justice
URGE: Unite for Reproductive & Gender Equity
In Our Own Voice: National Black Women's Reproductive Justice
     Agenda
Black Women's Health Imperative
National Asian Pacific American Women's Forum
Black Mamas Matter Alliance

The many local and regional reproductive justice organizations you can seek out, invest in, learn from, and support when living or working in a particular city or area—or from afar, if you are privileged enough to inhabit a higher-access space—such as **the Afiya Center in Houston** or **SPARK Reproductive Justice NOW in Atlanta**. Look for the reproductive justice organizations in your own communities, and show up for them and their specific needs in whatever ways you can.

Some Essential Reading: Books, Ebooks, and Zines

The Radical Doula Guide: A Political Primer
By Miriam Zoila Pérez

The Doulas: Radical Care for Pregnant People
By Mary Mahoney and Lauren Mitchell

Reproductive Justice: An Introduction
By Loretta Ross and Rickie Solinger

Handbook for a Post-Roe America
By Robin Marty

"Racism, Birth Control and Reproductive Rights" (in *Women, Race and Class*)
By Angela Y. Davis

Killing the Black Body: Race, Reproduction, and the Meaning of Liberty
By Dorothy Roberts

Policing the Womb: Invisible Women and the Criminalization of Motherhood
By Michele Goodwin

Choice Words: Writers on Abortion
Edited by Annie Finch

I Deserve Good Things: An Introductory Guide to Abortion Support
By Ashley Hartman Annis

We Organize to Change Everything: Fighting for Abortion Access and Reproductive Justice
A free downloadable ebook from Verso Books, edited by Natalie Adler, Marian Jones, et al.

Acknowledgments

This book was made—like everything I could ever make, or do, or learn, or be—in community. Each and every single person who has held me afloat through these pages deserves an entire book devoted just to their grace, kindness, and power. *YOSYL* would not exist without the knowledge, support, partnership, and generosity of the following people. If you see your name here, it's because you've changed my life (and if you don't, it is due only to sleep deprivation and high blood sugar and the limitations of a word count, and not to any lack of appreciation and love. You are my beloved *anonymous* book doulas, and you know exactly who you are).

Jade Wong-Baxter, the first person who saw and understood what this book could be before I even wrote it, and who was the ultimate doula from its very inception. Thank you to Stephanie Hitchcock, my superhuman (and superhumanly patient) editor, wading through my tears (and my soggy drafts) as I processed what was happening and tried to put it to the page, and fighting for this book's many possible futures. Thank you to Erica Siudzinski, for your sharp editorial eye, your kindness, your hard work, and the grace you extended to this first-time baby author. Thank you to

Zakiya Jamal, Karlyn Hixson, Joanna Pinsker, Debbie Norflus, and everyone else at Atria, for making my wildest (and least realistic or practical) dreams come true.

Thank you to Emily Wunderlich and Emily Hartley, for your knowledge and your friendship and your time, Rupali Sharma for wine and work dates and the countless evening hours spent being bullied by our toddlers as we tried, desperately, to type one (1) single sentence or finish one (1) single thought, for mothering and fighting through the ongoing storms with me, and for being an abortion champion for so many of us, in and out of the courtroom. Thank you to Amanda, Lana, Girl-Mike, and Django.

Bottomless thanks are owed to Loretta J. Ross, to the providers and doulas who told me the stories of their work, to Poonam Dreyfus-Pai and Parker Dockray of All-Options, to Gina Martínez Valentín and the Colorado Doula Project, to Morgan Nuzzo and Diane Horvath and the Partners in Abortion Care team, to Makayla Montoya-Frazier and the Buckle Bunnies Fund. Thank you to Erika Christensen, and to Hayley McMahon. Thank you to the PPNNE providers and staff who spoke with me. Thank you to the storytellers, with all my heart.

Thank you endlessly to Cait Vaughan, Doran Lovell, Molly Hawkey, Jay Thibodeau, Camila Ochoa Mendoza, Viva Ruiz, Kamyon Conner and the TEA Fund, Tannis Fuller and the Blue Ridge Abortion Fund, Zachi Brewster, Carly Manes, the Dopo community. Thank you to Rabbi Danya Ruttenberg, the Rev. M Jade Kaiser, Josie Pinto, and the Reproductive Freedom Fund of New Hampshire, Catessa and Kirsten and the doulas of the Alabama Cohosh Collaborative, the Exhale Pro-Voice community, daena, Kimya, Moss Froom, Sasha, Chrysanthemum, K, to Angi

Connell, Hannah Lord, and the Exhale team, the SAFE Fund, Becca Starr, Sarah La Monaca, Meghan Gilliss, and Christine Vines.

To all the staff and patients of my beloved local clinics: Mabel Wadsworth Center, Maine Family Planning, and Planned Parenthood of Northern New England.

Thank you to my midwife, my providers, my surgeons, my doulas. Thank you to everyone who cared for me through my pregnancies, my abortion, my labor and delivery, and beyond. Thank you to everyone still loving me through those things today.

Thank you to Will, without whom there would be none of this. Thank you for taking the baby out of the house. Thank you for loving what turns out to be the absolute worst version of me—the version who is trying to finish a book. Thank you for accepting all of that version's—and this one's—apologies, for the hours I've been away and the calls I've taken at dinner and the interviews I've conducted late at night. Thank you for telling me to write. Thank you for my life.

Thank you to my parents.

Thank you to the one who made me a parent: my son, my moon, my stars.

Thank you to my beautiful extended families, from New Zealand to Kansas—this book would not have happened without each and every single one of you.

Thank you, as always, to Juno.

Thank you to anyone who has ever trusted me with your abortion story or your care. It is the honor of my lifetime to have walked these paths with you or held space for your bodies, your emotions, your safety, and your truths.

And thanks to you, who have traveled all this way with me (I know I can be long-winded). Here we are, together. Thank you.

Notes

Introduction

1. Throughout this book many subjects' names and identifying characteristics have been changed to protect their privacy and safety.

2. The 2022 decision that overturned *Roe v. Wade* and *Planned Parenthood of Southeastern Pa. v. Casey*, eliminating the federal right to abortion and "placing it back into the hands of the states" (many of which were standing by, draconian trigger bans without exceptions for rape or incest waiting on their books for just such an opportunity to arrive). Of course, this stance was a hypocritical farce, as many of the same lawmakers who had lobbied the court for "states' rights" on the issue would soon begin trying to pass sweeping *federal* bans and restrictions, in their efforts to strip the entire nation of our reproductive rights.

Abortion Is Mine

1. Of twenty-four individuals charged with crimes after seeking urgent post-miscarriage or post-abortion care in 2020, seventeen were turned into law enforcement by the medical providers entrusted with that care.

2. An ectopic pregnancy is one that has taken root outside the uterus, where it cannot survive and will kill the pregnant person if left untreated. The only treatment is abortion, so an abortion ban with no provisions for ectopic pregnancies essentially serves as a death sentence for both the pregnant person and the pregnancy.

3. G. R. Bond and L. K. Hite, "Population-based Incidence and Outcome of Acetaminophen Poisoning by Type of Ingestion," *Academic Emergency Medicine* 6, no. 11 (November 1999): 1115–20.

4. SMA is a commonly used shorthand for *self-managed abortion*, meaning abortion care undertaken on one's own (but often with the support of doulas or loved ones), outside of a clinical setting and the supervision of a nurse, midwife, or doctor.

5. 1-844-868-2812 or reprolegalhelpline.org.

6. According to SASS's website, "How to Use Abortion Pills," https://abortionpillinfo.org/en/using-abortion-pills-for-safe-abortion-usa.

7. Ibid.

8. To take a medication buccally is to place it between your gums and your inner cheek—your buccal pouch—and let it dissolve.

9. Ilana Löwy and Marilena Cordeiro Dias Villela Corrêa, "The 'Abortion Pill' Misoprostol in Brazil: Women's Empowerment in a Conservative and Repressive Political Environment," *American Journal of Public Health* 110, no. 5 (May 2020): 677–84.

Interlude: Abortion Is a Story

1. Anonymous and secure abortion support hotlines include All-Options (1-888-493-0092), which also provides resources and support around parenting and adoption, and the Exhale After-Abortion Textline (1-617-749-2948). INeedAnA, or INeedAnAbortion.com, the clinic map that helps

folks find the care that is easiest for them geographically, also operates a textline of its own.

2. Monica Simpson, "To Be Pro-Choice, You Must Have the Privilege of Having Choices," *New York Times*, April 11, 2022, https://www.nytimes.com/2022/04/11/opinion/abortion-black-brown-women.html.

Abortion Is Yours

1. Maeve Wallace, Veronica Gillispie-Bell, Kiara Cruz, Kelly Davis, and Dovile Vilda, "Homicide During Pregnancy and the Postpartum Period in the United States, 2018–2019," *Obstetrics & Gynecology* 138, no. 5 (November 2021): 762–69.

2. Ursula K. Le Guin, *The Lathe of Heaven*, Narrated by George Guidall. (Recorded Books, 2016. Audiobook.), Chapter 10.

3. Welcomes and openings, to help with full presence in a space and the emotional and physical regulation of our bodies, often featuring breathing exercises and visualizations.

4. Long-acting reversible contraceptives, such as IUDs or implants.

5. Katherine Kortsmit, et al., "Abortion Surveillance—United States, 2019," CDC *Morbidity and Mortality Weekly Report* 70, no. 9 (November 16, 2021): 1–29, https://www.cdc.gov/mmwr/volumes/70/ss/ss7009a1.htm.

6. www.all-options.org

7. Randy Beck, "Self-Conscious 'Dicta': The Origins of Roe v. 'Wade's' Trimester Framework," *American Journal of Legal History* 51, no. 3 (July 2011): 505–29, http://www.jstor.org/stable/41345374.

Abortion Is Justice

1. The twelve Black women who were involved in coining the term *reproductive justice* and laying its original framework were Toni M. Bond Leonard,

Reverend Alma Crawford, Evelyn S. Field, Terri James, Bisola Marignay, Cassandra McConnell, Cynthia Newbille, Loretta Ross, Elizabeth Terry, "Able" Mable Thomas, Winnette P. Willis, and Kim Youngblood.

2. Combahee River Collective, "The Combahee River Collective Statement" (Primary Document, 1977), https://www.blackpast.org/african-american -history/combahee-river-collective-statement-1977/.

3. "Reproductive Justice," SisterSong, accessed June 2022, sistersong.net/re productive-justice.

4. All clinics have different policies and protocols, but most do *not* require a follow-up appointment for the majority of their abortion patients.

5. Dorothy Roberts, *Killing the Black Body: Race, Reproduction, and the Meaning of Liberty* (New York: Vintage Books, 1997, 2017), 4.

6. "Culture Shift," National Latina Institute for Reproductive Justice: What We Do, accessed September 2022, https://www.latinainstitute.org/en/cul ture-shift.

7. "NYC Asian American Organizing Blueprint for Reproductive Justice," NAPAWF, November 22, 2017, https://www.napawf.org/our-work/content /organizingforreproductivejusticeinnyc.

8. Always pay the Black people and the Black-led orgs you learn from on the internet. Always.

9. M. Antonia Biggs, Heather Gould, Diana Greene Foster, "Understand- ing Why Women Seek Abortions in the US," *BMC Women's Health* 13 (July 2013), https://bmcwomenshealth.biomedcentral.com/articles /10.1186/1472-6874-13-29.

10. "Advocacy: Federal Issues," National Diaper Bank Network, accessed Au- gust 2022, https://nationaldiaperbanknetwork.org/federal-issues.

11. Kimberly Knisley, "How Many Diapers Do I Need? A Guide to Stocking Up," *Healthline*, May 2020, https://www.healthline.com/health/baby/how -many-newborn-diapers-do-i-need.

12. Jennifer Randles, "'Why Don't They Just Use Cloth?' Gender Policy Vacuums and the Inequalities of Diapering," *Gender & Society* 36, no. 2 (April 2022): 214–38, https://doi.org/10.1177/08912432211067966.

13. More information can be found at the All-Options Pregnancy Resource Center's website, www.alloptionsprc.org.

14. "United States Abortion Demographics," Guttmacher Institute, accessed September 2022, https://www.guttmacher.org/united-states/abortion/demographics.

15. "Federal Poverty Level (FPL)," HealthCare.gov, accessed August 2022, https://www.healthcare.gov/glossary/federal-poverty-level-fpl/.

16. "United States Abortion," Guttmacher Institute, accessed September 2022, https://www.guttmacher.org/united-states/abortion.

17. Loretta J. Ross and Rickie Solinger, *Reproductive Justice: An Introduction* (Oakland: University of California Press, 2017), 30.

18. The term *intersectionality* was coined by law scholar Dr. Kimberlé Crenshaw in 1989 to explain how the dominant single-axis understanding of identity and discrimination distorted and erased the experiences of Black women who were subject to both racial- *and* gender-based oppression. Intersections are where one piece of a person's identity meets another, where they experience multiple axes of discrimination, rendering their experience of marginalization unique and distinct.

Abortion Is Indigenous

1. Native Land, accessed December 2021, https://native-land.ca/.

2. The Indigenous Women Rising fund can be reached for requests or donations at iwrising.org/abortion-fund or 1-505-398-1990.

Abortion Is Nature

1. Feminist activists Carol Downer and Lorraine Rothman (who went on to invent the Del-Em menstrual extraction kit) developed this technique in the pre–*Roe v. Wade* 1970s. The underground or "self-help" abortion, in which a thin, flexible plastic Karman cannula (about the size of a soda straw), a 50 or 60 mL syringe, and a one-way bypass valve. The device could be operated by more than one person, which made for easier training and greater accessibility to those outside of the medical field to more safely and comfortably perform early abortion procedures on one another in nonclinical settings. Menstrual extraction would only be performed at the time that a person's period was due, and they would not confirm a pregnancy beforehand with a test, to ensure plausible deniability for everyone involved.

Abortion Is Care

1. Donna L. Hoyert, "Maternal Mortality Rates in the United States, 2020," NCHS Health E-Stats, Centers for Disease Control and Prevention, February 23, 2022, https://dx.doi.org/10.15620/cdc:113967.

2. Reproaction Education Fund: Anti-Abortion Fake Clinic Database, accessed October 2022, https://reproaction.org/fakeclinicdatabase.

3. Julius Lester, "James Baldwin—Reflections of a Maverick," *The New York Times*, May 27, 1984, https://archive.nytimes.com/www.nytimes.com /books/98/03/29/specials/baldwin-reflections.html.

Abortion Is Survival

1. This increase, a fourteen-fold jump in distance as reported by the Guttmacher Institute, rendered the *Roe v. Wade* concept of "accessibility" effec-

tively meaningless for one in ten United States women, as well as the men, nonbinary, two-spirit, and gender-nonconforming Americans in need of abortion care.

2. The Abortion Support Network of the United Kingdom, Fondo MARIA of Mexico, and Women Help Women, an international online fund.

3. Apiary, accessed February 2022, https://apiaryps.org/pso-list.

Abortion Is Parenthood

1. "United States Abortion Demographics," Guttmacher Institute, accessed December 2021, https://www.guttmacher.org/united-states/abortion/demo graphics.

2. Carly Manes (author) and Emulsify (illustrator), *What's an Abortion Anyway?* (Self-Published, 2022), https://www.whatsanabortionbook.com/shop.

Abortion Is a Holy Blessing

1. "About," Ad'iyah—Muslim Abortion Collective, accessed September 2022, https://adiyah.community/about.

2. Ammaarah, "Why I Founded an Abortion Support Network for Muslims," *gal-dem*, August 3, 2022, https://gal-dem.com/abortion-support-network-muslims/.

3. "The Islamic Principle of Rahma: A Call for Reproductive Justice," Statement by the American Muslim Bar Association and HEART, April 15, 2022, https://www.ambalegal.org/ambainthenews/the-islamic-principle-of -rahma-a-call-for-reproductive-justice.

4. "An Islamic Prayer," Religious Resources, Religious Coalition for Reproductive Choice, https://rcrc.org/prayers/.

5. Jenna Jerman, Rachel K. Jones, and Tsuyoshi Onda, "Characteristics of U.S. Abortion Patients in 2014 and Changes Since 2008," Guttmacher Institute,

May 2016, https://www.guttmacher.org/report/characteristics-us-abortion
-patients-2014.

6. The Faith-Aloud Hotline: 1-888-717-5010.

7. Religion and Repro Learning Center, accessed September 2022, https://
rrlc.thinkific.com.

Abortion Is Queer

1. Lisa L. Lindley and Katrina M. Walsemann, "Sexual Orientation and Risk
of Pregnancy Among New York City High-School Students," *American
Journal of Public Health* 105, no. 7 (July 1, 2015): 1379–86.

2. "NISVS: An Overview of 2010 Findings on Victimization by Sexual Orientation," National Intimate Partner and Sexual Violence Survey, accessed
March 2022, https://www.cdc.gov/violenceprevention/pdf/cdc_nisvs_vic
timization_final-a.pdf.

3. If you're not familiar, TERF stands for "trans-exclusionary radical feminist,"
and is the moniker borne by a loud and very sad little club, whose hateful mem-
bership is comprised largely of miserable, bathroom-obsessed people. TERFs
use Twitter, the *New York Times* Opinion page, and their platforms of academic
and political power to complain that they are being censored and oppressed.

4. Bonfire, accessed June 2022, https://www.bonfire.com/protect-trans-fami
lies-black-print160/.

5. Alexis Light, Lin-Fan Wang, Alexander Zeymo, and Veronica Gomez-Lobo,
"Family Planning and Contraception Use in Transgender Men," *Contraception* 98, no. 4 (October 2018): 266–69, https://pubmed.ncbi.nlm.nih
.gov/29944875/.

6. *Trauma-informed* is the term for health care that recognizes and responds to
the signs, symptoms, and risk factors of physical, sexual, emotional, or other
trauma. It involves taking steps to ensure that patients feel safe, empower-

ing them to set boundaries and make health care decisions for themselves, and taking a more collaborative approach to providing someone with care, rather than assuming a position of authority or expertise in what a patient is telling you about their own lived experiences. It also involves incorporating racial, gender, and class analysis into your practice.

Abortion Is for Every Body

1. Average blood glucose levels, for a nondiabetic adult, fall between a range of 90 mm/dL and 120 mm/dL. A blood sugar reading below 70 is generally considered to be "low," or an indicator of hypoglycemia, and a reading above 150 is generally considered to be "high," or hyperglycemic, according to my endocrinologist

2. "Public Opinion on Abortion," Pew Research Center, May 17, 2022, https://www.pewforum.org/fact-sheet/public-opinion-on-abortion/.

Abortion Is Grief

1. Lauren M. Bulsma, Asmir Gračanin, and J. J. M. Vingerhoets, "The Neurobiology of Human Crying," *Clinical Autonomic Research* 29, no. 1. (February 2019): 63–73.

2. Zawn Villines, "Post-abortion Syndrome: Is it real?," *Medical News Today*, June 26, 2022, https://www.medicalnewstoday.com/articles/post-abortion-syndrome.

3. www.abortionwithlove.com.

Index

About the Author

Hannah Matthews is an abortion doula and funder, clinic worker, hotline counselor, and writer. Her writing has appeared in the *New York Times*, *ELLE*, *Esquire*, *Teen Vogue*, *McSweeney's*, *Catapult*, and other publications. She lives in Maine with her family. More information can be found at www.HannahMatthews.me.